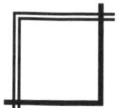

The social psychology of drug abuse

Applying social psychology
Series editor: Stephen Sutton

Published and forthcoming titles

Richard P. Bagozzi, Zeynep Gurhan-Canli and Joseph R. Priester: *The Social Psychology of Consumer Behaviour*

Mark Conner and Christopher J. Armitage: *The Social Psychology of Food*

Steve Sussman and Susan L. Ames: *The Social Psychology of Drug Abuse*

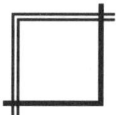

The social psychology of drug abuse

Steve Sussman and Susan L. Ames

Open University Press
Buckingham · Philadelphia

Open University Press
Celtic Court
22 Ballmoor
Buckingham
MK18 1XW

email: enquiries@openup.co.uk
world wide web: www.openup.co.uk

and
325 Chestnut Street
Philadelphia, PA 19106, USA

First Published 2001

A catalogue record of this book is available from the British Library

ISBN   0 335 20618 2 (pb)   0 335 20619 0 (hb)

Library of Congress Cataloging-in-Publication Data
Sussman, Steven Yale.
  The social psychology of drug abuse / Steve Sussman and Susan L. Ames.
    p. cm. – (Applying social psychology)
  Includes bibliographical references and index.
  ISBN 0-335-20619-0 – ISBN 0-335-20618-2 (pbk.)
    1. Drug abuse. 2. Drug abuse – Prevention. I. Ames, Susan L., 1956–
  II. Title.   III. Series.
HV5801 .D953 2001
362.29–dc21
                                                                2001021948

Typeset by Graphicraft Limited, Hong Kong
Printed in Great Britain by Biddles Limited, Guildford and King's Lynn

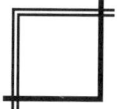

Contents

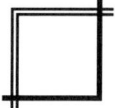

Series editor's foreword

Social psychology is sometimes criticized for not being sufficiently 'relevant' to everyday life. The Applying Social Psychology series challenges this criticism. It is organized around applied topics rather than theoretical issues, and is designed to complement the highly successful Mapping Social Psychology series edited by Tony Manstead. Social psychologists, and others who take a social-psychological perspective, have conducted research on a wide range of interesting and important applied topics such as consumer behaviour, work, politics, the media, crime and environmental issues. Each book in the new series takes a different applied topic and reviews relevant social-psychological ideas and research. The books are texts rather than research monographs. They are pitched at final year undergraduate level, but will also be suitable for students on Masters level courses as well as researchers and practitioners working in the relevant fields. Although the series has an applied emphasis, theoretical issues are not neglected. Indeed, the series aims to demonstrate that theory-based applications of social psychology can contribute to our understanding of important applied topics.

This book, by Sussman and Ames, is the first in the series and, in its scholarship and clarity, it sets the standard for the others. In it, the authors tackle the complex problem of drug abuse, which has significant costs to individuals and to society. Starting with the question 'What is drug abuse?', they discuss definitions of abuse, dependence and disease, and consider drug abuse in the context of other problem behaviours. Predictors of drug abuse are examined, including intra- and extra-personal factors, and this leads to a discussion of integrative theories. The authors draw on a wide range of ideas and theories from social psychology and other fields and disciplines. They go on to argue that drug abuse arises from numerous factors interacting in complex ways, and tease out some of the multiple pathways involved. Attention then turns towards current approaches to prevention and treatment, and an examination of the evidence for their effectiveness. The book ends with a discussion of future directions, which raises a number of challenging questions for future research. Although there are few easy answers in this field, Sussman and Ames have succeeded in clarifying what we know and what we need to know about the causes, prevention, and treatment of drug abuse.

Stephen Sutton

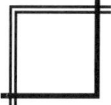

Preface

Drug abuse continues to present a significant public health problem. Drug abuse and dependence are associated with disproportionate costs to society in terms of criminal activity, spread of HIV infection and other **diseases**, medical expense, deaths on and off the road, and disruption of local communities and families. The sequelae of drug abuse may begin as a picture of prolonged personal risk. However, drug abuse inevitably becomes a societal problem when criminal activity is the only means of obtaining moneys to support the **addiction**, when innocent bystanders suffer the effects of drug-related crime or accidents, and when health insurance and medical costs rise for everyone because of drug abuse. Before the 1960s, the general public was aware that many individuals were abusing **alcohol** but the perception was that only some individuals were abusing illicit drugs. Then, something happened. In the 1960s, use of alcohol and illicit drugs appeared to increase radically, peaked in the 1970s, lowered in the 1980s, and began to increase again in the 1990s. Drug use may or may not be levelling off in the 2000s, but its cumulative negative impact on our world community cannot be ignored.

What is drug abuse? When trying to answer this question, other questions may come to mind. Has a favourite celebrity been seen hanging out of the window of some posh detoxification facility, somewhere between jobs? Did you hear this person just died? Is someone in your family the life or death of the party? What's going on? Why are these seemingly normal human beings killing themselves? Are these people diseased, conditioned, injured, engaging in shoddy cultural practices, immoral, socially alienated, genetically challenged, coping poorly or just making poor life decisions? The purpose of this book is to provide a resource for discussion of these and many other questions.

This book can provide the basis for a course in the issues pertaining to the **aetiology**, **prevention** and cessation of drug abuse. It is tailored to the upper level undergraduate student. It is assumed that some courses in the social sciences have been completed and that this book can build on that knowledge. Basic definitions of the field are taught. Predictors of drug abuse are presented. Types of drug abuse prevention and cessation **programmes** are presented. There are many issues and perspectives regarding drug abuse. After reading this book, the student should have a good understanding of major issues in the drug abuse prevention and cessation fields, and should be able to 'straddle' the perspectives of drug abuse practitioners and researchers from varying orientations.

While this book is developed for students, drug dependency counsellors, researchers, educated lay persons or others interested in issues inherent in the drug abuse field may find this resource useful. We focus on core issues; we also take a social psychological slant. We look at people's perceptions of others, interactions between persons, and **social influences**. In doing this, we draw on some of the social psychological literature on the addictions. We also draw on work in public health, clinical psychology, sociology and **recovery movements**, as well as on our own experiences as observers of human behaviour.

There are many complexities in the drug abuse arena. All drugs used recreationally can be abused, but some drugs have minimum addiction potential. The aetiology of drug abuse is related to genetics, **self-medication** and other intrapersonal factors. It is also related to social influence processes. Media portrayals of drug use (for example glamorization), social thermometers of perceived acceptability and danger of drug use, and accessibility of drugs may influence fluctuations in use. Understanding such numerous aetiologic factors is essential in containing drug abuse, and may help to produce a more functional society. Effective drug abuse prevention includes **comprehensive social influences programming**; however, this programming may not be effective with older, higher risk youth populations. Perhaps an increased focus needs to be placed on intrapersonal factors, as people become more involved in use. Drug **treatment** may lower social costs; however, a majority of persons in treatment **relapse**, and 90 per cent of drug abusers appear to stop on their own. Are you confused? If you are, good – we all are. On the other hand, we do hope that this book will help clarify some of these issues. Possibly, some reasonably valid answers will come to you as you read this text.

Overview of the book

The book is divided into three parts. The first part presents general issues pertaining to drug abuse, and consists of four chapters. We begin the book in Chapter 1 by introducing classes of drugs of abuse, distinguishing use from abuse, providing definitions associated with abuse and dependence, and describing some of the **negative consequences** of drug abuse. Chapter 2 addresses the issue of whether or not drug abuse should be considered a disease.

Chapter 3 addresses drug-related and other compulsive **problem behaviours,** and the overlap and non-overlap of drug abuse with other addictive behaviours. In Chapter 4, we provide an overview of some current methods of assessing alcohol and other drug abuse and the utility of these methods.

The second part of the book presents an account of the many predictors or **correlates** of drug use and abuse, and consists of three chapters. Chapter 5 addresses extrapersonal predictors of initiation, experimental use and abuse; this chapter looks at environmental and social influences affecting someone's decision to use drugs (for example **media influences**). Next we address individual difference variables or factors that may account for why some individuals who use drugs become drug abusers and others do not. We refer to these factors as intrapersonal **predictors of drug use** and abuse. Intrapersonal factors may become increasingly more influential as an individual 'transitions' from drug use to problematic use or abuse (for example self-medication). Chapter 7 examines integrative theories of drug use and abuse. These theories consider concurrently a variety of environmental, social or individual factors.

The third and final part of the book presents the issues and contents of current drug abuse prevention and treatment approaches, and consists of three chapters. Chapter 8 discusses effective universal (general population), selective (high-risk indicators) and indicated (high-risk behaviour) drug abuse **prevention programming**. Chapter 9 discusses a myriad of different treatment options, including spiritual and secular approaches, and cessation and **relapse prevention** strategies. The book concludes with a discussion of future directions in the prevention and cessation of drug abuse. Potential avenues for development of promising novel aetiologic, prevention and cessation ideas are mentioned. The first mention of new terms are emboldened to assist the reader in drug abuse-related vocabulary development.

We hope that this text will help to contribute to a quest to control the prevalence, and minimize the harm, of drug abuse in the near future. We wish you a good adventure as you begin to tackle the issues presented herein.

Repetition is easy, it's improvement that's frightening.

(the authors)

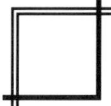

About the authors

Steve Sussman, PhD, received his doctorate in psychology from the University of Illinois at Chicago in 1984. He served on a clinical psychology residency at Jackson Veterans Administration and University of Mississippi Medical Centers and is now a Professor in the Departments of Preventive Medicine and Psychology and Institute for Health Promotion and Disease Prevention Research at the University of Southern California. He has published over 160 articles or books in the area of drug abuse prevention and cessation. Sub-areas of particular focus are psychosocial prediction of tobacco and other drug use, drug abuse prevention and cessation, and other research with high-risk populations including placing an emphasis on the use of programme development methods. Recent projects include Project Towards No Tobacco Use (TNT), a tobacco use prevention programme which is a Centers for Disease Control and Prevention 'Program that Works'. Also included are Project Towards No Drug Abuse (TND) which, along with Project TNT, is considered a model programme by the Centers for Substance Abuse Prevention, and Project EX, which is among the largest and most successful teen tobacco use cessation trials to date.

Susan L. Ames received BAs in clinical psychology and social work from the University of Wisconsin, Madison, in 1978. She received an MA in psychology from California State University, Los Angeles, in 1994. She expects to receive her PhD in health behaviour research from the University of Southern California in June 2001. She has been a research assistant and doctoral student at the Institute for Health Promotion and Disease Prevention Research, Department of Preventive Medicine, University of Southern California since 1994. She has had a National Cancer Institute pre-doctoral training fellowship since 1997. She is currently a part-time staff research associate at the Department of Psychology, Substance Abuse Research Center, University of California, Los Angeles. Her research interests include implicit cognition and substance use in high-risk populations, the impact of memory on addictive behaviours, developing prediction models of substance use, prevention and harm reduction of addictive behaviours, and psychosocial correlates of drug use.

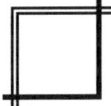

Acknowledgements

We would like to thank the University of Southern California, the National Institute on Drug Abuse and the National Cancer Institute for giving us the flexibility to write this text. We also would like to thank Open University Press and Stephen Sutton for their interest in working with us. We have tried to provide an international relevance to the book. We also would like to thank our previous Health Promotion 410 students who helped us to clarify concepts during classroom instruction of drug abuse issues. Also, we would like to thank Beth Howard and Jennifer Zoff for their editorial assistance and Alan Stacy for providing a flexible and supportive research environment. Finally, we would like to thank our families (Rotchana, Guang, Evan, Max, Woody, Mikey, Terry, Bill, Karen and Pam) for providing the balance in our lives that makes a text like this one a treat.

Part  1

General issues pertaining to drug abuse

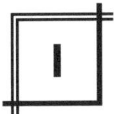

Definitions of drug abuse and drug abuse consequences

Sometimes it is difficult to draw the line between drug use and abuse. For example, some of us know people who smoke **marijuana** every day. These individuals appear to be 'stoned' all the time, but they also seem to avoid detection by unsuspecting others and always get their jobs done. They may never have been arrested, report no obvious physical problems and seem to be satisfied with their social lives. Are these individuals drug abusers? Their circumstances are very different from those of skid-row drunks who have lost everything, and are near death. We would most likely classify skid-row drunks as drug abusers, but we might debate the case of daily marijuana users. These marijuana users do not appear to have suffered any consequences of their use. Or have they? One may wonder from whom they have been purchasing marijuana. Are they interacting with potentially dangerous people? What has been the effect of use on their lungs, memory and emotional development? Do they use marijuana to cope with life stresses? Do they spend a lot of time searching for marijuana? Do they feel that they cannot live without it? Do their clothes or breath smell of marijuana? Do others tend to avoid these individuals because they are 'stoned' much of the time? As the number of potential problems associated with use of a drug is considered, the 'gate' of inclusion into the concept of 'drug abuse' widens.

Given this introductory caveat of scepticism, experts do provide consensual identification of problem drug users. Individuals become labelled as 'problem drug users' by experts through contact with treatment, service and law enforcement agencies. Around the world, approximately 15 per cent of the population over 18 years of age is considered to have serious drug use difficulties (other than **nicotine** addiction, which itself may involve up to 25 per cent of the world's population) and this percentage has remained fairly constant since the mid-1970s. Of these drug abusers, about two-thirds abuse alcohol and one-third abuse other drugs. Across the continents, the other major drugs of abuse are marijuana, **amphetamines**, **cocaine** and **heroin**. Approximately 2.5 per cent of the world's population abuse marijuana, 0.5

per cent abuse stimulants, 0.3 per cent abuse cocaine or opioids, and up to 0.8 per cent abuse other drugs (for example, **inhalants, depressants, hallucinogens**: White 1999). Many individuals who try illicit drugs do not go on to abuse them. As examples, approximately 33 per cent of the populations of the United States and Australia, and 10 to 20 per cent of the population of different European countries, report lifetime use of marijuana (US Department of Health and Human Services (DHHS) 1998). Yet, only 2.5 per cent of the world's population use marijuana so regularly as to incur recognizable consequences.

Drug abuse incurs great financial losses to the world's legitimate economy. Costs to society may be more than $600 billion per year ($200 billion dollars per year in the United States alone). For example, many people know the statistic that 50 per cent of vehicle fatalities involve a drunk driver. Many such accidents also involve chronic marijuana or amphetamine users. These costs-to-society statistics do not include nicotine addiction, which is the Number One behavioural killer of people worldwide because of its influence on heart disease, lung cancer, chronic obstructive lung disease and numerous other diseases (US DHHS 1982; Sussman *et al.* 1995a). Drug abuse appears to be a serious international calamity. To achieve a better understanding of this problem, we briefly review **drug processing** and a variety of specific drugs of abuse. Next, we attempt to define drug abuse and dependence.

A brief review of drugs of abuse

Drug processing

Entire books have been written about the different drugs of abuse, their pharmacology, effects, mechanisms of action, and consequences (for example see Winger *et al.* 1992; Julien 1998). A complete discussion is beyond the scope of this book, but we do provide a brief summary of these drugs of abuse. Each drug class is involved in four steps of drug processing, and these drugs also may have various effects on each other when used together.

First, *administration* refers to how the drug enters the body (for example ingestion, inhalation, injection or absorption). Most classes of drugs are used through several alternative methods. For example, marijuana may be smoked or swallowed. **Methamphetamine** may be swallowed or injected. Heroin may be sniffed, smoked or injected.

Second, *distribution* refers to how efficiently the drug moves throughout the body (which is influenced by the size of drug molecules and solubility – protein, water, fat-bound – among other factors). As a general rule, the rate of entry of a drug into the brain is determined by the fat solubility of the drug (Julien 1998). The rate of entry is faster if the fat solubility is greater. Conversely, highly ionized drugs, such as penicillin, penetrate the blood–brain barrier poorly. Most drugs of abuse exert their effects within an hour of intake, although some exert their effects within minutes of intake.

Third, *action* refers to the means of effects. All drugs of abuse 'feel good' in different ways (for example the user may feel more alert or relaxed or expanded). Most or all drugs of abuse act directly or indirectly on brain reward systems (that is dopaminergic and probably serotonergic systems), although each drug may have specific receptor sites in the brain. For example, there is a rich concentration of **opioid receptors** in the nucleus accumbens, whereas there appears to be functionally important nicotinic receptors in the medial habenula, the superior colliculus, and the anteroventral thalamic and interpeduncular nuclei. **Benzodiazapines** (for example Valium) are less likely to be abused as a sole drug of abuse, perhaps because they act primarily on the Gamma-aminobutyric acid (GABA) **neurotransmitter** system, not the dopaminergic system.

Fourth, *elimination* refers to breakdown and excretion of drugs from the body. Drugs are excreted in time through sweating, trips to the lavatory and sometimes by vomiting. Drugs have measurable and differential distribution and elimination half-lives (that is the amount of time it takes for half of the drug to reach sites of action and be eliminated from the body). For example, nicotine, when smoked in a cigarette, has a nine-minute distribution half-life (very fast) and a two-hour elimination half-life. Marijuana, when smoked, has a similar distribution half-life, but it also has a 28–56 hour elimination half-life, which involves complex metabolic processes. Nicotine is metabolized mostly through the liver, whereas THC (the active ingredient of marijuana) may be stored and released slowly from various bodily organs.

Finally, drugs can have four different types of **interaction effects** when used together. First, these effects may be additive ('1 + 1 = 2': the effects of the drugs simply add together). Second, these effects may be synergic ('1 × 1 = 5': the effects become much, much stronger when the drugs are used together). Third, these effects may be potentiating ('0 + 1 = 2': a drug may exert its effects only in conjunction with use of another drug). Finally, these effects may be antagonistic ('1 – 1 = 0': the effects of two or more drugs may cancel each other out).

What are the main classes of drugs of abuse?

Various classifications of drugs have been compiled. There are at least five noteworthy classification perspectives. These classifications are:

1 the *Diagnostic and Statistical Manual of Mental Disorders* (**DSM-IV**) (American Psychiatric Association (APA) 1994)
2 the **International Classification of Diseases** (for example Ninth Revision: ICD-9 or ICD-9-CM, **World Health Organization (WHO)** 1998)
3 the US Drug Enforcement Administration (DEA) and National Guard scheme
4 the **Julien biomedical-type scheme**
5 the **Sussman/Ames scheme** (a health promotion-behavioural scheme).

The DSM-IV (APA 1994) divides drugs of abuse into twelve classes: (1) alcohol, (2) sedative-like drugs, (3) amphetamine-type drugs, (4) cocaine, (5) **caffeine**, (6) **cannabis**, (7) hallucinogens, (8) inhalants, (9) nicotine, (10) opioids, (11) **phencyclidine (PCP)** and (12) 'other'. It is useful to distinguish these classes for the purpose of medical and psychological treatment recommendations (clinical diagnostic utility). For example, the DSM-IV discusses differences in drugs potential for dependence, abuse, **intoxication, withdrawal**, psychotic and mood effects (see APA 1994: 177).

The ICD-9 (for example see WHO 1998) divides drugs of abuse or dependence into nine categories: (1) alcohol, (2) opioids, (3) **barbiturates** and similarly acting sedatives or **hypnotics**, (4) cocaine, (5) cannabis, (6) amphetamines and other **psychostimulants**, (7) hallucinogens, (8) **tobacco** and (9) 'other' (for example glue, laxatives). These drugs are divided up to discern abuse, dependence and psychological (for example psychosis) and medical consequences, quite similar to the DSM-IV formulation.

The US Drug Enforcement Administration and the National Guard (1996) divide drugs up by effects into six categories: (1) narcotics (for example **opium**, heroin, **meperdine**: twelve types listed), (2) depressants (for example chloral hydrate, barbiturates: five types listed), (3) stimulants (for example cocaine, amphetamines, ritalin: six types listed), (4) hallucinogens (for example peyote, LSD (lysergic acid diethylamide): six types listed), (5) cannabis and (6) steroids. These categories are considered in terms of their abuse potential, safety or dependence liability, and degree of therapeutic benefit (US DEA and National Guard 1996).

Julien (1998), in his text *A Primer of Drug Action*, divides drugs of abuse by specific neuroanatomical effects and topical interest into nine types. These nine types are: (1) depressants-type 1 (which includes barbiturates, **sedative-hypnotics** and general **anaesthetics**), (2) depressants-type 2 (alcohol and inhalants), (3) benzodiazepines and 'second generation' **anxiolytics**, (4) psychostimulants (cocaine and amphetamines)-type 1, (5) psychostimulants-type 2 (caffeine and nicotine), (6) opioids (**analgesics**), (7) cannabis, (8) hallucinogens (anticholinergic, catecholinergic, **serotonin**-like and PCP types) and (9) steroids (steroids may help build muscles but they can also disrupt mood and may make one angry).

Finally, Sussman/Ames have developed their own system. We divide drugs of abuse by behavioural effects into eight classes: (1) depressants (alcohol, sedatives for relaxation, hypnotics to induce sleep, anxiolytic to reduce anxiety, and **anti-convulsants** such as barbiturates), (2) PCP, (3) inhalants, (4) stimulants, (5) **opiates**, (6) hallucinogens, (7) cannabis and (8) 'other'. All depressants are classified together because they slow down and relax the individual, or knock out an individual. PCP is placed in a separate category because its effects are both depressant and hallucinogen-like, and may precipitate violence. Inhalants generally exert sedative effects, but their administration (sniffed or huffed) is quite different from other depressants. All stimulants tend to 'speed up' the individual, make them nervous or more aware. All opiates relieve pain, and may relax or amotivate the user, whether or not they are derived from opium or are synthetic. All hallucinogens expand one's cognitive perceptions and may lead to perceptual distortions and easily agitated behaviour. Marijuana may cause one to 'mellow out' or alter one's perceptions. Finally, there are 'other' new drugs of abuse, which may or may not fit into one of the previous seven health behaviour-related categories. We mention them in the 'other' category because they have short abuse histories (less than 20 years' duration). Although there appears to be a fair amount of overlap among schemes, there is also some non-overlap. To reduce our shared confusion, please realize that there is no universal scheme. Given that, we provide the following brief review of drug categories based on the Sussman/Ames perspective.

Depressants

Depressants are generally taken orally and slow down the central nervous system (CNS). Intoxication may include slurred speech, deficient coordination, nystagmus (rapid eye movements), attention or memory impairment, sedation, anxiety reduction and euphoria, and generally lasts four to five hours on a single dose. Alcohol is the most commonly used depressant. Other depressants include alcohol-like barbiturates (for example Seconal, Nembutal), **methaqualone** (dopers, Quaaludes), sedative-hypnotics (for example Placydil, Doriden) and minor **tranquillizers** (for example Valium, Librium, Tranxene, Rohypnol). There are also sedative-hypnotic look-alike drugs, which generally contain 25–50 mg of the **antihistamine**, doxylamine succinate, which is found in Formula 44 and Nyquil.

PCP (phencyclidine)

PCP was originally developed as an animal anaesthetic and tranquillizer, but is no longer used as such. PCP can be smoked or taken orally, and intoxication involves intense analgesia, delirium, stimulant and depressant actions, staggering gait, slurred speech and vertical nystagmus, and it can produce catatonia and paranoia, flushing, coma, violent behaviour and memory loss effects. Some researchers label PCP as a hallucinogen rather than a depressant because of its mixed actions (Winger *et al.* 1992).

Inhalants

There are four main groups of inhalants: solvents (for example glue, typewriter correction fluid, petrol, antifreeze), aerosols (for example spray paint and cooking spray), **amyl nitrite** and **butyl nitrite** (for example Rush, Locker Room – room deodorizers) and anaesthetics (for example nitrous oxide, 'laughing gas' – used as a propellant/food additive). Glass vials of amyl nitrite make a distinctive noise when crushed – hence the term 'poppers'. There are about 23 chemicals involved in inhalant abuse. Inhalants are well-known causes of kidney, brain and liver damage. One of the most preferred inhalants is **toluene**, which is a solvent used in such adhesives as airplane glue, such aerosols as spray paint, and such commercial solvents as paint thinner. Its long-term use destroys functioning of the cerebellum. Inhalants are cheap, available, inconspicuous, fast and tend to involve few legal hassles. Use is through huffing, fluting or bagging (through mouth, nose or nose and mouth). Inhalant highs last 5–15 minutes. Inhalant intoxication includes euphoria, headaches, dizziness, nausea and fainting.

Stimulants
Stimulants generally are taken orally, though they may be smoked or injected. They include cocaine (such as freebase and 'crack'), amphetamines (for example Dexedrine, Benzedrine), methamphetamine (methedrine: 'speed', 'crystal', 'ice', 'crank'), MDMA (**ecstasy**), nicotine, caffeine and amphetamine-like products (preludin or ritalin). Stimulants speed up the central nervous system, for as long as two to four hours on a single dose. Intoxication generally includes euphoria, fatigue reduction, a 'sense' of mental acuity, energy, emotional lability, restlessness, decreased appetite, irritability, hyper-vigilance, and can include paranoia. Cocaine, despite its different chemical structure, operates in a similar way to other stimulants. For example, both amphetamines and cocaine increase the action of dopamine, although amphetamines stimulate its release whereas cocaine primarily blocks its reuptake. Amphetamines remain in the blood longer than cocaine, and most have more peripheral sympathomimetic ('electric') effects than cocaine. The only current primary clinical uses for stimulants are for hyperactivity and narcolepsy and, for a few people, as a means of weight control. This drug category is perhaps the fastest growing category internationally. Stimulants often enter a country through its 'club scene' and then become more widely used as a means of keeping people awake while working long hours.

Ecstasy (3,4-methylenedioxy-N-methylamphetamine; MDMA), synthesized in 1914 as an appetite suppressant, is also called 'XTC' and 'Adam'. There are numerous names for specific concoctions. It is a ring-substituted amphetamine congener of the methoxylated amphetamines; one structural congener is MDA (methylenedioxyamphetamine). It exerts an amphetamine-like reaction: the heart rate goes up, there may be an occurrence of tremor, tight jaws, grinding of teeth, back pain, numbness of extremities, feeling cold and – for some people – nausea, nystagmus, heart attacks, seizures and possibly death. Positive reactions include enhancement of communication or intimacy; it generally is not an aphrodisiac, as some folklore suggests. Some people might classify MDMA as a hallucinogen (it may produce perceptual changes such as increased sensitivity to light; it acts on serotonergic neurotransmission), but its effects primarily are stimulation (for example it increases heart rate and awareness). Chronic abuse of MDMA may produce long-term damage to serotonin containing neurons in the brain (National Institute on Drug Abuse (NIDA) 1999a).

There are several legal stimulants. Caffeine, of course, is contained in coffee. **Ephedrine** is a stimulant contained in Vicks Inhaler or Sudafed, and is five times weaker than amphetamine. Chemically, it is levo-methamphetamine, an isomeric form of the street drug, d-methamphetamine. Phenylpropanolamine is an antihistamine and diet aid, with epidrine-like action. Propylhexedrine is found in decongestant inhalers (for example Dristan). Nicotine is contained in tobacco products (cigarettes, cigars, pipes and smokeless tobacco). There are also two stimulant plants – betel nut and khat. There are five active alkaloids in betel nut; khat's main ingredient is cathinone, which is chemically similar to amphetamine.

Opiates
Opiates include some 20 alkaloids that act on opiate receptors, and generally are taken orally or injected, although they can also be inhaled. Some are derived from the opium poppy, whereas others are synthetic. Opiates include **morphine, codeine** and **thebaine** (all of natural origin); heroin, hydrocodone, hydromorphine and oxycodone (all semi-synthetic); and meperdine, fentanyl and pentazocine (all synthetic). Intoxication generally includes slurred speech, analgesia, slowed respiration, drowsiness, euphoria and possibly itching. The effects of one dose may last around three hours. There are approximately half a million opiate **addicts** in the United States alone.

Hallucinogens
Hallucinogens generally are taken orally and include indole (serotonin-like) alkylamines such as LSD, DMT (N, N-dimethyltryptamine) and psilocybin ('magic mushrooms': 4-phosphoryloxy-N, N-dimethyltryptamine); and catecholamine-like phenylalkylamines such as **mescaline** (peyote: trimethoxy-phenethlamine) and DOM (di-methoxy-methamphetamine, also known as STP). There are more than a hundred natural or synthetic hallucinogens. Intoxication generally includes sensory changes experienced as visual illusions and hallucinations, alteration of experience of external stimuli and thoughts, and can involve paranoia and thoughts of losing one's mind. The effects of hallucinogens may last an average of twelve hours (for LSD). Street substitutions include amphetamines, PCP, strychnine (strong stimulant used in rat poison) and anticholinergic hallucinogens that are rarely sold directly on the 'street' (scopolamine and stropine; for example, belladonna or deadly nightshade, jimsonweed).

Cannabis
Cannabis (delta-9-tetrahydrocannabinol) generally is smoked, though it can be taken orally, and it produces a sense of well-being and relaxation, loss of temporal awareness and impairment of short-term memory. Cannabis also can produce anxiety and a sense of derealization. Effects may last around five hours for a single dose. The lethal to effective dose is 1000:1, although lung damage and short-term memory problems are documented consequences of use. Marijuana occurs in leaf and resin (hash, hash oil) forms, and a synthetic form of THC-9, marinol, which is used as an oral pill clinical adjunct for glaucoma and cancer.

Other

There are many drugs that could be considered as additional categories of use. One might call these 'other' categories. Perhaps these categories will become 'official' by the DEA or other organizations. The **anabolic-androgenic steroids** are one such 'other' category. It is a recognized and separate category in the US DEA/National Coast Guard and Julien's schemes, though not in the DSM-IV, ICD-9 or Sussman/Ames schemes. These approximately eighteen different products exert their effects by overwhelming the hypothalamic-pituitary hormonal system, creating abnormally high testosterone hormone levels that lead to such peripheral effects as increased muscle mass and aggression. These drugs generally are taken orally, but they also may be injected intramuscularly. These drugs may be useful in **recovery** from trauma. There are, however, numerous negative consequences of use, including high blood pressure, potential heart attacks, liver tumours, transient infertility, tendon degeneration, acne and severe mood swings. Between 4 and 11 per cent of teenage males and 1 to 3 per cent of teenage females in the United States had tried steroids in the mid-1990s; this is a drug category on which to keep an international watchful eye.

Also among the 'other' categories, there are different types of drugs that have become popular in public circles, and are referred to as **designer drugs**. Some of these drugs may have been newly synthesized, but probably most of them have been around for a while, have received renewed popularity, and may or may not have become associated with one of the above-presented established drug use classification categories (for example see NIDA 1999a). For example, GHB (gamma-hydroxybutrate) is a drug that was synthesized in 1960 – perhaps for use as an anaesthetic, and at present is considered a treatment option for narcolepsy. GHB acts on the dopaminergic system by stimulating **dopamine** production and by preventing release at the synapse. It comes in a powder or liquid form, generally is taken orally (1.5–3 grams powder) and it provides alcohol-like CNS depressant effects, including sedation, subjective relaxation and possibly increased gregarious behaviour. It also has growth hormone releasing effects. It may produce **psychotic symptoms**, coma and seizures, and is a recent nightclub-goer 'date rape' type drug (NIDA 1999a). It can be lethal when mixed with other depressants, and 'home made' forms tend to be mixed with trace poisons (for example heavy metals, lye and 'industrial' solvents).

As another example, **Ketamine (Special K)** is an anaesthetic that has been approved for human use since 1970. It is produced in liquid form or as a white powder that is injected, snorted or smoked with marijuana or tobacco. At high doses it can produce dream-like states, hallucinations, delirium, impaired motor functions, depression and potentially fatal respiratory problems (NIDA 1999a). The US DEA currently anticipates future synthetic drugs of abuse (Cooper 2000: http://designer-drugs.com/synth/index.html), including derivatives of LSD, tryptamines, phenylakylamines (for example mescaline), PCP, stimulants, sedatives-depressants and analgesics.

Consequences of taking drugs of abuse

We shall discuss some of the drugs mentioned above in subsequent chapters. For the purposes of this chapter, it is sufficient to mention that some of these drugs are very likely to have lethal consequences, whereas others are not; some produce recognizable withdrawal symptoms whereas others do not; some drugs seem to have a high addiction-potential, whereas others do not. However, all of these drugs can be abused. All of these drugs can lead to drug abuse. Table 1.1 shows thirteen direct consequences of the Sussman/Ames categories of drugs (plus the anabolic steroids). All of these drug types are associated with the production of psychotic symptoms (for example paranoid ideation) and injury (accidents, violence). At least five of eight categories are associated with cardiovascular diseases or financial problems. Otherwise, each drug class is associated with a unique but deadly set of potential consequences. The next section provides a working definition of drug abuse.

Drug abuse and drug dependence

Drug use pertains simply to use of a drug. A drug may be injected, smoked, sniffed, huffed (inhaled), swallowed or sometimes absorbed through the skin. Drug misuse means not using a drug in the manner in which it was intended or prescribed. For example, one may use a pain medication for fun rather than for pain control, one may use too much, or one may use too often. Drug abuse may be defined as the accumulation of negative consequences resulting from drug misuse (Newcomb and Bentler 1989; APA 1994; Sussman *et al.* 1997a).

A formal definition of **substance abuse** disorder is provided by the DSM-IV (APA 1994). Drug abuse is a maladaptive pattern of drug use leading to clinically significant impairment or distress, as manifested by one or more of four symptoms or criteria occurring within a 12-month period.

1 Recurrent drug use may result in a failure to fulfil major role obligations at work, school or home. Repeated absences, tardiness, poor performance, suspensions or neglect of duties in major life domains suggest that use has crossed over into abuse.
2 Recurrent drug use in situations in which it is physically hazardous is a sign of abuse. Operating machinery, driving a car, swimming or even walking in a dangerous area while under the influence indicate drug abuse.
3 Recurrent drug-related legal problems, such as arrests for disorderly conduct or DUI ('driving under the influence') arrests, are indicative of abuse.
4 Recurrent use despite having persistent or recurrent social or interpersonal problems, caused or exacerbated by the effects of the drug, is indicative of abuse. For example, getting into arguments or fights with others, passing out at others' houses, or acting inappropriately in front of others is indicative of abuse.

Table 1.1 Long-term consequences of different categories of drugs of abuse

Drug type	Consequences												
	Withdrawal	Dementia	Memory	Psychosis	PNS[1]	Seizure	Digestion	Excretion	Cancer	Cardiac	Lung	Injury	Money
Depressants	x	x	x	x	x	x	x	x	x	x		x	x
PCP				x		x		x	x	x			
Inhalants		x	x	x	x		x	x			x	x	
Stimulants	x			x		x	x			x	x	x	x
Opiates	x			x								x	x
Hallucinogens				x								x	
Cannabis	x		x	x					x	x	x	x	x
Steroids				x		x	x	x	x	x		x	x

Note:
1 PNS stands for peripheral nervous system; as with other consequences, indicates damage to the PNS.
For additional reading see APA 1994; Julien 1998

In summary, drug use that leads to decrements in performance of major life roles, dangerous action, legal problems or social problems indicates abuse.

There are seven other criteria that, if met, constitute **substance dependence**. A diagnosis of substance dependence, a more severe disorder, would subsume a diagnosis of substance abuse. The criteria for substance dependence provided by the DSM-IV (APA 1994) include a maladaptive pattern of drug use, leading to clinically significant impairment of distress, as manifested by three or more of the following seven symptoms occurring in the same twelve-month period.

1 **Tolerance** is experienced. There is either a need for markedly increased amounts of the drug to achieve the desired drug effect or a markedly diminished effect with continued use of the same amount of the drug.
2 Withdrawal is experienced. Either a characteristic withdrawal syndrome occurs when an individual stops using the drug, or the same or a similar drug is taken to relieve or avoid the syndrome.
3 The drug is often taken in larger amounts or over a longer period than was intended. For example, an alcohol-dependent woman may intend to drink only two drinks on a given evening but may end up having fifteen drinks. Alternatively, she may decide to 'party' over the weekend; however, the party lasts for two weeks until she runs out of money.
4 There is a persistent desire or unsuccessful efforts to cut down or control drug use. For example, an alcohol-dependent man may decide to become a controlled drinker. He may intend to drink only two drinks every evening; however, he ends up having fifteen drinks on some evenings, maybe two drinks on some evenings, and maybe twenty drinks on other evenings – to his own dismay.
5 A great deal of time is spent on activities necessary to obtaining the drug, use the drug, or recover from its effects. For example, a person may travel long distances or search all day to 'score' a drug, may use the drug throughout the night, and then may miss work the next day to recover and catch some rest. In this scenario, two days were spent for one 'high'.
6 Important social, occupational or recreational activities are given up or reduced because of drug use. For example, the drug abuser may be very high, 'passed out' or 'hung over' much of the time, and thus may not visit family and friends as they did before becoming a drug abuser.
7 The drug continues to be used despite knowledge of having a persistent or recurrent physical or psychological problem that is likely to have been caused or worsened by the drug. For example, someone who becomes very paranoid after continued methamphetamine use, and is hospitalized but continues to use it, shows this last symptom.

The definitions of drug abuse and dependence provided above were developed primarily to identify adult drug abusers, individuals from the ages of 18 to 65 years.

Withdrawal symptoms, also known as the **abstinence syndrome**, consist of adjustment in physical functioning and behaviour attributed to overactivity of the nervous system. These symptoms are experienced when physically dependent persons cease their drug use. Withdrawal symptoms vary from drug to drug. *Alcohol, sedative, hypnotic or anxiolytic withdrawal* may involve autonomic reactivity, increased hand tremor, insomnia, nausea or vomiting, transient illusions or hallucinations, psychomotor agitation, anxiety, or grand mal seizures. *Amphetamine or cocaine withdrawal* includes fatigue, unpleasant and vivid dreams, insomnia or hypersomnia, increased appetite, or psychomotor retardation or agitation. *Opioid withdrawal* includes dysphoric mood, nausea or vomiting, muscle aches, tearing, rhinorrhea (that is runny nose), sweating, diarrhoea, yawning, fever or insomnia. *Nicotine withdrawal* includes depressed, anxious or irritable mood, insomnia, difficulty concentrating, restlessness, decreased heart rate, constipation, sweating and increased appetite. *PCP* has no or few withdrawal symptoms, although its use is associated with anxiety, rage, seizures and induction of psychotic disorder. *Caffeine* has few withdrawal symptoms, except perhaps for some fatigue, difficulty concentrating, and headache. While not recognized until recently by researchers (APA 1994), even to the dismay of generations of chronic users (Marijuana Anonymous 1995), *cannabis* has a few withdrawal symptoms – fatigue, difficulty concentrating, stomach pains, some agitation, perhaps anger, and vivid dreams, especially among chronic users (Zickler 2000). *Hallucinogens* are not known to have withdrawal symptoms, although flashbacks (high-like states) occur in some people who have stopped using these drugs.

The next few sections examine terms associated with drug abuse (for example **craving** and **addiction concern**). Finally, the physical appearance of the drug abuser is mentioned as an applied social psychological issue.

Craving

While noted by the DSM-IV as central to drug abuse, the concept of craving is not officially a separate indicator of drug abuse. Perhaps it should be, though it may be difficult to measure. Craving refers to the myriad of urges and obsessions that drug abusers may talk about regarding obtaining and using a drug. But what does this phenomenon reflect? Craving may be the result of classical conditioning to **drug-related stimuli** (Sussman *et al.* 1990b), **post-synaptic neurotransmitter supersensitivity**, or may reflect interpretations of the experience of withdrawal or implicit cognitive processes (a cognitive construct), but it does seem central to differentiating the drug user from the drug abuser. For example, the alcohol drinker may drink a glass of wine, but not finish it. They may comment on the flavour, but other topics are important. The alcohol abuser tends to drink all of the wine in the glass; if not, they may have noted salivating on that occasion and feeling badly about not finishing the wine. They may not remember other events, but may recall not finishing the glass of wine long after the event.

While craving is associated with drug abuse, it is not clear whether or not craving is associated with relapse. Littrell (1991) completed a careful review of the alcohol craving literature. In sum, she found that craving was related to expectancies regarding alcohol, demonstrated conditioning-like characteristics (for example salivation when seeing alcohol-related **cues**), but that craving-related relapse was highly correlated with negative affectivity. In other words, as opposed to being some innate phenomenon, craving may reflect an anticipatory reaction, classically conditioned or involving higher-order cognitive processes, to diminishing negative affect by drinking.

Research on craving continues. Conditioned craving and cue exposure have received interest in drug relapse prevention research (for example Sussman *et al.* 1990b). Most simply stated, conditioned craving refers to classical conditioning to drug-related stimuli. Drug cues (exteroceptive or interoceptive) that have been repeatedly paired with drug-taking experiences may come to serve as conditioned stimuli. Unless extinction of the responses to these cues occurs, exposure to the conditioned stimuli will elicit a conditioned anticipatory response (craving), leading to potential use or relapse. Repeated exposure to drug cues without any use occurring (flooding) can result in extinction of the conditioned response. Researchers have assessed conditioned craving or flooding efficacy primarily in small-scale studies (see Sussman *et al.* 1990b). Some research evidence suggests that cue-conditioned responses (CCRs) may be more important than outcome expectancies in determining subsequent drinking in alcoholics, at least relative to non-alcoholics (Cooney *et al.* 1987, 1991). However, some researchers have questioned the relative importance to relapse of CCRs versus expectancies of positive alcohol use outcomes.

The relevance of cognition

One impediment to appreciating the potential importance of CCRs has been making traditional Pavlovian theory the explanatory focus. Reactivity is elicited upon the sight of preferred alcohol beverages or of other related stimuli through stimulus generalization. How could such a process explain the complexity of relapse, including relapse that might begin under conditions where no drug cues are obviously available? Consideration of cognitive representations of drug cues and drug-related concepts are relevant here. Indeed, a crucial factor in subjective urges and thoughts about alcohol or other drugs may be the set of key cognitive concepts (categories of drug-related stimuli) that elicit the urges and thoughts. Concepts that are potent in causing urges and thoughts regarding alcohol or other drugs are ones that are retrieved frequently, and with ease. Ease and frequency of retrieval are brought about by the fact that the key concepts have become imbedded in over-determined cognitive structures, in which each of many related concepts can invoke the retrieval of the key concepts (Sussman *et al.* 1990b). Given current lack of clarity regarding the notion of craving, this term will continue to be considered an important feature of drug abuse, but not one that can be considered an objective criterion.

Addiction concern

Does the person who is abusing drugs recognize that they have a problem? Some treatment providers may believe that the drug abuser does not recognize the severity of the problem, and does not recognize the value of a sober life (Littrell 1991). Alternatively, drug abusers may recognize that they have a problem, but fail to recognize the extent of damage they are inflicting on themselves or others, know how to cope with life stresses without using drugs, or lack **self-efficacy** to change. An individual's recognition that they may have a drug problem is viewed by the recovery movement (for example **Alcoholics Anonymous** or **AA**), as well as those in **behaviour therapy** oriented cessation practice (for example De Leon *et al.* 1994), as the first step in recovery. In other words, once someone contemplates that their drug use may become a serious problem – that they may have become a drug abuser, addict or alcoholic – attempts at **cessation** are more likely to occur. The earlier a drug abuser attains that awareness, the sooner recovery can begin. One may refer to this drug abuse awareness as an *addiction concern.*

Three variables have been found to be strong correlates of addiction concern (Sussman and Dent 1996). First, the greater the level of someone's current drug use, and expectation that they will continue to use drugs, the greater the level of addiction concern. Apparently, drug abusers do not exhibit a simple, invariant **denial** of their problem. Rather, they hold a more equivocating stance regarding the consequences of their drug use (see also W. Miller and Rollnick 1991). Second, a lack of general assertiveness may influence drug use through inhibiting creation of new prosocial, anti-drug-oriented bonds leading to greater addiction concern. Finally, individuals who place lower importance on health as a value are relatively likely to be concerned about becoming an addict or alcoholic. They do appear to be equivocating in their thinking. On the one hand they do not think that health is an important value. On the other hand, they worry more about aspects of their health (that is their drug use). One may speculate that anti-drug, pro-health social influences might help 'raise the bottom' (that is stop continued use) among those with relatively high addiction concern.

Social psychology and drug abuse: do they look like drug abusers?

One interesting **social psychological** issue is whether or not one can tell that a person is a drug abuser just by looking at them. Drug abuse is often masked as something else. The drug abuser may come into contact with the treatment system through a variety of channels – as a comatose or psychotic patient at a hospital, an employee who is having work relationship problems, or as the perpetrator of a car accident, as examples. It would be helpful to treatment agents if there were some visual signs that the person might be abusing drugs. In most cases, the drug abuser is not likely to look like a movie portrayal of some crazed derelict. Alternatively, arguably, everyone at a rave who sucks on a pacifier may look like an ecstasy addict.

What physical features are telltale signs of drug abuse? Facial features are strongly related to prolonged alcoholism. Redness of the eyes and nose and wrinkles on the face and neck are commonly associated with sustained alcohol abuse. The most pronounced effects of chronic alcohol use include dilation of the vessels of the skin, a chronic flushed appearance and thinning of the skin due to serious liver damage. Heavy and chronic use of alcohol can also precipitate a condition called 'rosacea', which includes flushing and inflammation especially of the nose and middle portion of the face. Small blood vessels with a corkscrew shape may also fill the whites of the eyes.

With respect to body features, an awkward posture, being underweight or overweight, and poor grooming may also be present in drug abusers. However, these body features are not exclusive to drug abusers. They are also seen among schizophrenics and those who are severely or moderately depressed. It is important to emphasize that these body characteristics are a consequence of specific behaviours that, when performed (for example maintaining clean clothes), result in positive changes in appearance.

Sussman *et al.* (1990a) investigated changes in appearance among a group of drug abusers observed at admission and six weeks later as they stood individually in front of the nurses' station (getting ready to get their blood pressure checked) at a private inpatient chemical dependency facility. These drug abusers were from middle-class backgrounds. They did not demonstrate the low-bottom characteristics of the skid-row drunk. Features that seemed unique about them included a slightly leaned over posture, wrinkles under the eyes and a frozen facial expression. The only changes that were observed over the six-week period – six weeks of **sobriety** – was an improvement in posture and reduction in wrinkles under the eyes. In some cases, weight changes were also observed, but not for a majority of the sample. One interesting physical feature that was not observed as a change was the existence of a neutral but frozen facial expression. It is not clear whether such a lack of animation is due to the impact of drug use, lack of socialization, confusion over the inpatient experience, typical behaviour near a nurses' station, or other reasons. However, it is likely that if their lack of expression remained constant as these patients were discharged into the community, it might lead them to be ignored by others – and could precipitate relapse. Education in how to smile may be an important pre-discharge learning modality for drug abusers.

Summary

Drug use is drug use. Using drugs for unwarranted reasons is drug misuse. Using drugs as a means to learn how to live life is drug abuse. Decrements in performance of major roles, dangerous action and legal and social problems may be indicators of drug abuse. Drug dependence is being described when tolerance and withdrawal are experienced, when someone loses the ability to predict and control their drug use, and when consequences pile up. People in Alcoholics Anonymous and **Narcotics Anonymous (NA)** often say that the person takes the drink or drug, then the drink or drug takes the next drink or drug, and then the drink or drug takes the person.

2

Is drug abuse a disease?

To ask if drug abuse – that is, continuing to use drugs while failing to fulfil major role responsibilities, in dangerous situations, or while suffering legal or social consequences – is a disease, one must first understand how the word 'disease' is defined. 'Disease' is a word. Words can be defined in two ways. First, an **intentional** (rule-based) **definition** can be applied. There is great economy to this type of definition. For example, using simple maths one can 'consider whole even numbers between 0 and 7'. The numbers are identified through a summary rule. Likewise, a disease can be defined through use of a summary rule. A disease may be defined as an outcome condition that involves impairment of bodily functions, resulting from exposure to a living or non-living object, that is mediated by some causal mechanism. For example, the flu is an outcome condition that involves antibody buildup and a high temperature. The sufferer often feels terrible and may not be able to work for a few weeks. It results from exposure to particles in the air or on surfaces, and is mediated by intake of a virus or bacteria. As another example, cardiovascular disease involves a closing up of vital cardiovascular organs. The sufferer may suffer a variety of consequences such as strokes or heart attacks that grossly restrict participation in daily activities. This disease results from intake of fatty foods, lack of exercise and cigarette smoking, among other factors. The operation of these factors on cardiovascular disease are mediated by some process that involves preparedness to wear down the cardio-vascular system (heredity) and elicitation of gradual plaque buildup. If drug abuse is a disease, one may define drug abuse here as an outcome condition that involves negative social, legal, physical or functional consequences, that results from intake of a drug. Processes that involve heredity, changes in neurotransmitter homeostatic function or other unknown factors may mediate drug abuse.

The other definitional framework is the **extensional** (listing-type) **definition**. Using the same simple mathematical definition presented in the preceding paragraph, instead of presenting a rule one would list '2, 4, and 6'. In other words, the numbers identified by the rule are listed rather than the rule itself. The numbers are said to be elements of the same class or set. To discern whether or not any word is an 'element' of a 'class' word, one considers similarities and differences among the proposed 'members' of the class word. The class word here is disease. Relevant element words might consist of a listing of disease labels such as flu, cardiovascular disease and drug abuse.

Is the element word 'drug abuse' a member of the set 'disease'? From an extensional perspective, drug abuse would be defined as a disease (as a member of the class, disease) based on its familial resemblance to other examples of a disease. For example, one might ask if the flu *is any more* a disease than drug abuse. Some may tend to think of disease as acute, infectious types; however, many now consider chronic, non-infectious types of diseases. Most people would consider a cardiovascular disorder as a disease. Well, then is cardiovascular disease any more a disease than drug abuse? As we look at the characteristics of these different disease labels some seem to overlap, such as symptoms of tiredness, and impairment of daily functioning. Other symptoms seem different, such as the exhibition of grossly inappropriate behaviour.

There is great economy to an intentional definition, but a rule-based definition is most useful if one can truly offer necessary and sufficient conditions for the word; that is, solid boundaries. Unfortunately, many words do not have clear boundaries. They are defined primarily by their use in the language; there is a familial resemblance learned from use (Wittgenstein 1958). One sees a complicated network of similarities of detail. For example, cognitive psychological research has shown that people view a robin as a real bird. However, some would question whether or not a penguin is a bird because it cannot fly. But it is every bit as much a bird as is a robin, isn't it (Rosch 1978)? Likewise, while a virus-born disease seems like a real disease, some may question whether or not drug abuse belongs in the same class. How is drug abuse used in the language now? Is it considered similar to other words generally accepted as being diseases?

Where does drug abuse 'fit' in current thinking about diseases?

Epidemiology is the field that studies the incidence and prevalence of disease in humans. According to Timmreck (1998), in an introductory text of epidemiology, disease is

> an elusive and somewhat vague concept and is defined socially and culturally as well as scientifically. Any disruption in the function and structure of the body can be considered a disease. Disease is defined as a pattern of responses by a living organism to some form of invasion by a foreign substance or injury, which causes an alteration of the organism's

normal functioning. Disease can be further defined as an abnormal state in which the body is not capable of responding to or carrying on its normally required functions. Disease is also a failure of the adaptive mechanisms of an organism to counteract adequately the invasion of the body by a foreign drug, resulting in a disturbance in the function or structure of some part of the organism.

(Timmreck 1998: 28)

Timmreck goes on to suggest that diseases may be acute or chronic (time course), and may be infectious or non-infectious. Heart disease, cancer, paralysis, diabetes and alcoholism are included as chronic and non-infectious diseases. Genetic, behavioural and **environmental influences** may cause a disease. Thus, Timmreck defines drug abuse as a disease. Also, Timmreck seems to be trying to provide an intentional definition of a disease; however, the all-inclusiveness of the definition plus the use of a classification scheme suggest the operation of an extensional notion of a disease.

It is clear that epidemiology, the American Medical Association and World Health Organization view drug abuse as a disease entity, and that most lay people also do perceive drug abuse as a disease or an addiction (Littrell 1991; Cunningham *et al.* 1996; Timmreck 1998). Thus, drug abuse appears to be a member of the class word 'disease', as considered by the definition of its current use in epidemiology, medicine and everyday language. Arguably, drug abuse would appear to be a disease notion by use of an extrinsic definition, but it may fail to qualify as an intrinsic definition of a disease because of a lack of knowledge about the 'rules' that govern it.

What led to the endorsement of a disease label?

Before the mid-1800s, when a wide-sweeping social reform movement was in operation (for example against slavery and child labour, in favour of supportive treatment of mental illness), people with drug problems tended to be considered weak in character or self-control. The clergy or the criminal justice system were given the charge of dealing with drug abusers. The disease concept began to be used with drug abusers with the intention of changing public **attitude** from one of blame and punishment to one of concern and treatment (Cunningham *et al.* 1996). For example, the American Association for the Cure of Inebriates was established in 1870. This organization attempted to define drug abuse as a disease, and to place drug abuse within the charge of hospitals for scientific treatment.

Unfortunately, it remains unclear whether or not the disease label has helped decrease perceptions of the immorality of drug abusers. Appeals to religious or morality-based cures abound. Also implications of 'tough love' for drug abusers in the *denial* of their disease may include punishment as treatment (Littrell 1991). Further, the emphasis on need for continuing treatment may lead to a perspective among drug abusers that they are incapable of helping themselves much (Littrell 1991; Cunningham *et al.* 1996). Drug abusers' self-efficacy for change may decrease. Thus, the social utility of using a disease label has not been optimal.

On the other hand, there is a perspective that drug abusers become more willing to take responsibility for self-care if they view their drug abuse as a disease (Vaillant 1983, 1990). More work is needed to discern the pluses and minuses of considering drug abuse as a disease (for example regarding self-efficacy versus responsibility for self-care).

Problems with the disease label

There are at least four problems when trying to define an abnormal behaviour, such as drug abuse, as a disease (see Table 2.1). First, a common criticism of a disease notion of abnormal behaviour is that the clinician has no independent means of verifying the existence of the disease. In several conditions, the factors producing certain symptoms can be assessed. For example, a viral infection can be measured through a throat culture, antibody production and a high temperature. Also, the factors can be assessed independently of the resulting symptoms (for example one may determine that either a poison, virus or bacterium produced the temperature). However, it is often difficult to separate factors from symptoms in behavioural disorders (Davison and Neale 1990). Among drug abusers, one can say that intake of a drug preceded the behaviour that appeared to be 'under the influence'.

Table 2.1 Four limitations of a disease notion of drug abuse

- *No independent means of verifying the existence of the disease*
  Neither drug use nor subsequent behaviour identifies the key factors that produce the behaviours.
- *Variation in disordered behavioural symptoms*
  Drug abuse appears to fall along a continuum of disordered behaviour: not a binary (yes/no) perspective often used to define a disease.
- *Variation in behavioural symptoms may not reflect the same underlying processes*
  There are many different patterns of drug abuse: from single-use catastrophes, to periodic use, to heavy regular use. Do all these variations reflect the same causes?
- *Aetiologic factors for drug abuse as a behavioural disorder are not known*
  Maybe both quantitative and qualitative differences in susceptibility factors exist, but predictive influences are not fully known or integrated. Defined as a disease, each addictive behaviour is considered qualitatively distinct; common underlying processes across problem behaviours are not considered. Defined as a disease, some individuals may not feel responsible for their actions. Also, defined as a disease, treatment options may be limited; moderation goals may not be preferred, and this may inhibit some individuals from seeking treatment.

For additional reading see Littrell 1991; Peele and Brodsky 1991

However, neither the drug intake nor subsequent behaviour identifies the factors producing these behaviours. It is difficult to separate drug abuse behaviour from the 'ism' (that is alcoholism or drug abuse-ism). Of course, if the problem were merely one of behaviour, then drug use cessation would stop the problem, right? However, relapse rates never fall to zero, and in fact are 65 per cent the first year post treatment, and perhaps halve each subsequent year, no matter whether or not the person is involved in use of heroin, alcohol, marijuana or cigarettes (Sussman *et al.* 1996c). High relapse rates imply underlying factors; currently, however, there are no independent measures of **assessment** of underlying factors of drug abuse. This may be more of a problem when an intrinsic definition is considered.

A second problem is that behavioural symptoms may be defined as more or less disordered depending on the social environmental context. A person who becomes drunk and obnoxious once a month may be perceived as an alcoholic in a church-going population, but may be considered a fun person in a college dormitory. As a corollary, drug abuse appears to fall along a continuum of disordered behaviour, as opposed to a binary (yes/no) perspective often attempted to define a disease. In other words, the observable characteristics are subject to many variations. Drug use behaviour may show many variations and still be referred to as reflecting drug abuse disorder – or not. Of course, coronary heart disease also falls along such a continuum, leading to an occasional inaccurate diagnosis (Vaillant 1990). This is a problem whether or not an intrinsic or extrinsic definition is considered.

A third, related problem is that variations in behavioural symptoms may or may not reflect the same underlying factors (Littrell 1991). For example, it is not clear whether or not a person who drinks alcohol seldom and gets into trouble once in a lifetime, a person who exhibits a periodically problematic drinking pattern, and a person who never drank in a controlled fashion, are subject to the same aetiologic forces.

A fourth problem is that the aetiological factors for drug abuse as a behavioural disorder simply are not known (the intrinsic definition problem). To define drug abuse as a disease may involve a leap of faith that a drug abuse proneness-specific underlying defining process is in operation. There are alternative underlying processes. For example, it is plausible that drug abusers have abnormal wiring that is not specific to drug abuse behaviour. Indeed, drug abuse is correlated with a variety of problem behaviours including crime, violence and poor diets, which may precede abuse of drugs (Hawkins *et al.* 1992). If so, one does not suffer from drug abuse as a disease. Rather, drug abuse is an example of another disease such as a **sensation seeking** disorder (see Chapter 3).

Another alternative underlying process is that drug abuse may be considered an abuse of someone's normal wiring (Rodgers 1994; Hovarth 1999), rather than some pre-existing qualitative difference among individuals. One may overuse, or artificially play with, one's natural reward system. There are at least seven examples of theories that consider drug abuse as only a 'quantitatively' different phenomenon. These theories are not mutually exclusive, but they are illustrative of drug abuse as an abuse of normal wiring. First, drug abusers may have irreversibly damaged their previously normally wired brain through continued use ('chronic injury model'). Second, drug abuse may reflect the norms of deviant social learning (Akers *et al.* 1979). Third, drug abusers simply may strongly desire to avoid withdrawal symptoms ('physical dependence model'). Fourth, they may enjoy the feeling of withdrawal so much that they go through repeated use – withdrawal cycles ('hurts so good model'). As a fifth alternative, they may come to enjoy immediately pleasurable effects of use relative to delayed destructive effects, or perceived lifestyle alternatives (**positive reinforcement** model). Sixth, through continued heavy drug use, they may become subjected to automatic memory processes that encourage continued drug use (an 'implicit **cognition** model').

Finally, Peele and Brodsky (1992), like Hovarth (1999) and Rodgers (1994), present a seventh alternative underlying process that suggests drug abuse is only quantitatively different from drug use (see also Peele 1998). They argue that drug abuse is a means of coping with oneself and one's environment ('coping model'). Peele and Brodsky label their model as the **life process model**. Their perspective is that addiction stems from other life problems the person has. It can be outgrown.

Peele and Brodsky (1991) state that the disease model of addiction does more harm than good because it undermines one's capacity for self-management: to problem solve, adapt to changes and feel accountable for actions taken. They claim that the 'disease model' argues that addiction is inbred and biological, is a binary condition (versus a continuum of problem behaviour), is permanent and is progressive. They then argue against this perspective by saying that it is not clear how important genetics is to the aetiology of drug abuse, not all drugs abused are addictive, and abuse may cease without treatment. Drug abuse can be progressive *per se* only if the person continues to abuse drugs (Littrell 1991; Rodgers 1994).

Unfortunately, Peele and Brodsky and others are apparently raising a fuss based on their understanding of a specific type of drug abuse disease model. As we discussed above, it is not necessary for a disease model to refer to inbred and biological mechanisms, or to be defined as a binary construct, to lead drug abuse to be labelled a disease according to an extrinsic perspective. In addition, the life process model has its own theoretical gaps. A coping explanation does not identify why some maladaptive habits are selected over others. For example, an ingrained habit of extreme, repetitive behaviour may be reflected through a variety of symptoms (different drugs, overeating). Drug use appears to work as a coping mechanism for some people but not others. The factors that differentiate among such people remain unexplained. Also, it is not known why some people appear to be better at coping than others, such that 'poor copers' are vulnerable to drug abuse. It is not certain that any of the alternative explanations of drug abuse are clearly separable from a disease notion.

Another look at the disease label: on a disease continuum

Conceptually we could examine drug abuse as a continuum in which individuals at one end of the continuum are relatively 'disease-free' but tend to engage in maladaptive behaviours over which they have choice and control. These individuals may repetitively use drugs (for example they experiment and 'party') and over time they may abuse drugs. However, they choose to live a certain life, resulting in seriously maladaptive behaviour, which may or may not result in other disease states associated with use (for example hepatitis C, cirrhosis of the liver). If these individuals are stopped or prevented from continuing to engage in this negative cycle, they can then choose to engage in more prosocial activities and, perhaps on their own, learn alternative coping mechanisms and self-efficacy. On the other hand, individuals at the other end of the continuum literally may have no choice or control over their use. Some individuals use for the first time and appear to lose control of their use. These individuals can be likened to a toggle switch that is either on or off; they must abstain because they have no control processes once the switch is in the 'on' position. They will use until they die unless someone else can turn their switch off and keep it off. There is no logic to their behaviour and no choice, and these individuals will destroy their lives and the lives of those around them in order to use their drug of choice. For these individuals, there is no 'grey'. Everything is 'black or white'. Seemingly, as one moves towards a more 'at risk' end of the continuum, the degree of choice and control processes disappear.

What causes the difference in **loss of control** among those at different points of the continuum? Researchers do not understand the process very well. They do know that other factors may exacerbate drug abuse. These factors include biologically based differences in metabolic processes. For example, there are differences in activity of alcohol dehydrogenase, the primary enzyme involved in the metabolism of alcohol, which might make some persons more vulnerable to alcohol abuse (see Chapter 5). These factors also include differential susceptibility to the reinforcing effects of drugs (for example variation in differences in neurochemistry), presence of dissociative experiences (for example perhaps related to trauma such as sexual abuse), **co-morbidity** (for example personality disorders or depression along with drug abuse) and differences in tolerance for frustration or emotional discomfort. Some processes are under individual control but many are not, and it does appear that the less control the individual has over these types of processes, the more likely the individual is to behave as if they are experiencing a 'real' disease-notion of drug abuse. This notion of drug abuse is conceptually similar to a continuous, normal distribution (that is the bell-shaped curve). At one end of the curve a small percentage of the sample exhibits maladaptive lifestyles, and, at the other end of the curve, a small percentage of the sample exhibits a 'disease state', but the majority of individuals are distributed in the middle along the continuum.

Stereotyping and drug abuse

Perceptions of outgroups (persons perceived as members of a different group from one's own), especially outgroup minorities, tend to be more extreme and negative than perceptions of one's own group (ingroup perceptions). In addition, the ingroup may tend grossly to overestimate the frequency of deviant behaviour associated with the outgroup (Fishkin et al. 1993). Furthermore, the ingroup is relatively likely to be accurate regarding its own behaviour. For example, Fishkin et al. (1993) found that youth who self-identified with low-risk groups perceived that their high-risk peers engaged in fewer school and non-school low-risk activities, more high-risk activities, and greater drug use than did high-risk ingroup members, themselves. Apparently negative social **stereotyping** processes were in operation on the high-risk youth. It is not surprising that the general population defines the 15 per cent of the population (a minority) labelled as 'drug abusers' in unflattering terms. Certainly, both drug abuse ingroup members and non-abuser outgroup members tend to define drug abusers as engaging in deviant acts. However, outgroup members are likely to overestimate the frequency of such acts relative to the abusers. Whether or not drug abuse is defined as a disease or as something else, explanations of why people suffer repeated drug use consequences do not preclude the operation of negative stereotyping processes. As soon as someone is given a name, such processes can occur. For example, lepers have tended to be labelled quite negatively even though they are victims of a disease. Cancer victims often are avoided by friends after they are diagnosed. Drug abusers also are subject to such processes and may need the assistance of disability activists.

One other point is worth considering. Regardless of whether or not we view drug abusers as 'diseased', we do view them as in need of help. One may speculate that it does not matter anymore whether or not one uses a disease label, or a behaviour disorder label, or some other term. Most people agree that drug abusers are in need of treatment or other supports.

Summary

One may begin to understand drug abuse as a disease – based on its use in our society and its resemblances to other conditions referred to as diseases. Drug abusers often report that they do not use drugs in a way that provides them with their desired lifestyle; they do report several problems while using that they wish did not happen. Drug abusers may (or may not) be distinguished from others based on a loss of control over use and extreme behavioural changes while using compared to when sober (Alcoholics Anonymous 1976). Adaptive mechanisms appear to fail. Numerous consequences occur over a course of years. Sometimes drug use behaviour may appear to be under control or in remission, and at other times it appears to progress with awful results. Heredity, opportunity and social influences all have been posited as contributing to drug abuse disorders (for example Timmreck 1998). Drug abuse appears to share characteristics that could place it in a disease class, shared with other chronic lifestyle disorders such as heart disease. The 'concept' of a disease has 'scientific use' if it provides information about what undelies a behavioural syndrome. Merely using or not using the term 'disease' might *cause* researchers to look in the right or wrong direction, depending on a slew of contextual factors (Alan Sussman, personal communication).

A word is a word. People use words and give them meaning through the usage of the word. Some words have fairly precise meanings, such as nouns of common objects (for example ball or car), although even these words are subject to interpretation (for example What is a car? Is a 'box car' a car? Is a toy model car a car? Is a hatchback a car?). It is not even that the disease label would add much information once a causal mechanism for drug abuse is fully known. The main point, perhaps, is that drug abusers would like some acknowledgement that they did not aspire to end up the way they did.

Drug abuse once was used to describe acts of immoral individuals who disobeyed the law and used drugs at the expense of family and friends. Even so, it was also understood that the drug abuse seemed to go beyond this person's self-control, once this person used the drug long enough. Nowadays it is understood that drug abuse is used to describe a *diseased* individual who disobeys the law and uses at the expense of family and friends. While this person is understood to be sick, this person also is pressured to admit that they are a 'liar, thief, and a cheat'. What may have really changed is the primary and secondary emphasis on what it is to engage in drug abuse. We not only feel sorry for this victim, but also view this person as immoral. Such is the nature of the social psychology of words. We are left with a social diagnosis, and the poll currently defines drug abuse as a disease of immorality. How might it be defined a hundred years from now?

3

Drug abuse and other problem behaviours

This chapter addresses the issue of whether or not one should consider drug abuse as one element of a larger class of problem behaviours, or as a distinct, different phenomenon. There is evidence that drug abuse often does not occur as a solitary manifestation of an individual's behaviour, but that drug abuse is often one facet of a cluster of behaviours and attitudes that form a syndrome or lifestyle of problem behaviours (Newcomb and McGee 1991; Hovarth 1999). However, drug abuse demonstrates a unique behavioural topography. In this chapter we also discuss drug-related problem behaviours (violence, accidents and risky sex) and compulsive problem behaviours that may or may not have underlying processes similar to drug abuse (see Table 3.1). Regarding compulsive problem behaviours, we consider substance addictions (food and drugs) and **process addictions** (gambling, work, exercise and spending). Finally, we grapple with the question of overlap and non-overlap of drug abuse with other behaviours.

Drug-related problem behaviours

Some problem behaviours are obviously directly drug related. Drug-related problem behaviours include dangerous or illegal activities used as a means of obtaining drugs – such as drug production and sales, fraud, robbery or violent crimes. Other drug-related problem behaviours include methods of using drugs – such as needle sharing among intravenous drug users. Finally, drug-related problem behaviours include those actions exhibited while under the influence – such as foolish behaviour while drunk or high, unsafe sexual behaviour, or driving under the influence (resulting in fatal and non-fatal vehicular accidents). In this section, we briefly mention three such drug-related behaviours: violence and **victimization**, accident proneness and risky sex.

Table 3.1 Matrix of twelve problem descriptions by eight problem behaviours

Problem descriptions	Problem behaviour							
	Drugs	Food	Gambling	Work	Violence	Sex	Exercise	Spending
'Immoral'	X		X		X	maybe		
Obsessions	X	X	X	X	X	X	X	X
Compulsions	X	X	X	X	X	X	X	X
Loss of control	X	X	X	maybe	X	X		X
Craving	X	X	X	?		X	X	?
Relapse	X	X	X	?		X		X
Stimulus bound	X	X	X	?	X	X		X
Financial problems	X		X			X		X
Social problems	X	X	X	X	X	X	maybe	maybe
Legal problems	X		X		X	X		X
Physically dangerous	X	X			X	X	X	
Not fulfill life roles	X	?	maybe	?	?		?	

Notes: X = problem description applies to this problem behaviour
maybe = sometimes this problem description applies to this problem behaviour
? = it is not clear whether or not this problem description applies to this problem behaviour
left blank = this problem description probably does not apply to this problem behaviour
For additional reading see Schaef 1987; Hovarth 1999

Drug abuse, violence and victimization

Non-alcohol drug use and sales are responsible for approximately 25–50 per cent of property crimes and 4–5 per cent of violent crimes, whereas alcohol use is responsible for about 25–30 per cent of violent crimes and 3–4 per cent of property crimes. In England, the All-Party Group on Alcohol Misuse (advised by the British Medical Association) found alcohol use to be a factor in 60–70 per cent of all murders, 75 per cent of all stabbings, 70 per cent of all beatings and 50 per cent of all fights and domestic assaults (Institute on Alcoholic Studies Factsheet 1995). Chemically dependent women are often victims of traumatic events, such as child abuse, sexual abuse, incest, rape and domestic violence (for example Teets 1997). The drugs most frequently implicated in domestic violence are stimulants, because their use can increase paranoia and lead to pre-emptive violence, alcohol, because its use diminishes impulse control, and anabolic steroids (Irons and Schneider 1997).

Goldstein (1985, 1998) developed the **tripartite conceptual framework** to examine drug-related violence. This framework consists of the *psychopharmacological model*, the *economically compulsive model*, and a *systemic model*.

The *psychopharmacological model* postulates that 'individuals as a result of short or long term ingestion of drugs, may become excitable, irrational and may exhibit violent behavior' (Goldstein 1985: 495). This model hypothesizes that drugs may contribute to both violent behaviours and to the likelihood that a person may become a victim of such behaviour. This hypothesis also holds out the potential for some psychoactive drugs to reduce violent behaviour.

The *economically compulsive model* suggests that 'some drug users engage in economically oriented violent crime (for example robbery) in order to support costly drug use' (Goldstein 1985: 496). Goldstein notes that heroin and cocaine, because of the 'compulsive patterns of use' and relative costs associated with use, are especially relevant to this model.

The *systemic model* suggests that 'violence is intrinsic to involvement with any illicit drug' (Goldstein 1985: 497). Goldstein (1985: 497) defines systemic violence as 'traditionally aggressive patterns of interaction within the system of drug distribution and use.' For example, violence may be used to block competition, to punish drug dealers for selling poor quality drugs, to collect unpaid debts or to intimidate potential informants. According to this model, involvement in drug distribution could increase the likelihood of perpetrating or being victimized by violence.

Drug abuse and accident proneness

Alcohol abuse has been implicated in approximately 48 per cent of all motor vehicle crashes and 40 per cent of fatal crashes in the United States. Additionally, alcohol use is responsible for more deaths involving car accidents, suicides and homicides than any other single chronic disease among adults (Williams and Knight 1994). Approximately 50 per cent of the deaths caused by fire, 50 per cent of home accidents and 70 per cent of drowning incidents are alcohol related (Williams and Knight 1994). The use of other drugs, especially marijuana and methamphetamine, has also been implicated in reckless driving arrests and accidents (Sussman *et al.* 1996c). Accidental lethal overdoses are well-known consequences of the use of such drugs as heroin or alcohol mixed with barbiturates.

Drug abuse and risky sex

Drug abuse is related to child sexual abuse, prevalence of sexually transmitted diseases, prostitution and sexual decision-making (that is safe sex). The relationship between risky sexual behaviour and drug use has been conceptualized as first, a result of the disinhibiting effects of drugs consumed and subsequent diminished decision-making and judgement (for example Leigh and Schafer 1993), and second, as a behavioural manifestation of a more general problem behaviour orientation (Donovan and Jessor 1985).

Risky sex not only is a drug-related behaviour, but also can be a compulsive problem behaviour (a process addiction). The DSM-IV provides diagnoses for sexual disorders and dysfunctions. However, debate continues regarding the notion of sexual addiction (Carnes 1996). There may be commonalities between sex addiction and drug abuse thoughts and behaviours, including obsessions, loss of control, compulsive behaviour, continuation despite adverse consequences, escalation of behaviours and high relapse rates after treatment. In addition, many drug abusers also report being addicted to sex (Schneider 1994). Several competing twelve-step groups, for example Sex Addicts Anonymous (SAA: www.saa-recovery.org), Sex and Love Addicts Anonymous (SLAA: www.slaafws.org), Sexaholics Anonymous (SA: www.sa.org), Sexual Compulsives Anonymous (SCA: www.sca-recover.org) and Sexual Recovery Anonymous (SRA: ourworld.compuserve.com/homepages/sra), as well as cognitive behavioural-related approaches, such as **Rational Recovery** (**RR**: www.rational.org) and Positive Realism (www.sexualcontrol.com), exist as a means of support for people who identify as sex addicts. Other compulsive problem behaviours are discussed in the next section.

Compulsive problem behaviours

There are other problem behaviours that show behavioural patterns like drug abuse, but are not necessarily associated with drug use situations. They might be colloquially referred to as **compulsive problem behaviours** and would include eating disorders, **pathological gambling**, compulsive exercise, compulsive work and compulsive spending. Compulsive problem behaviours can be characterized by

- a loss of control over the behaviour once initiated
- difficulty in regulating the behaviour
- relatively automatic responses to environmental or physical events, in other words, stimulus bound (for attributes of compulsive drug use, see Tiffany and Carter 1998).

There is the possibility that all such compulsive problem behaviours, drug abuse included, have an underlying common function, such as fulfilling sensation-seeking desires or self-medicating.

On the other hand, one might draw a major distinction between a compulsive problem behaviour (or **addictive process**) and an obsessive-compulsive process. Individuals usually derive some pleasure from engaging in an addiction-related activity and may wish to resist it only because of its negative consequences (APA 1994). In other words, individuals get a good feeling from using a drug, gambling, exercising or working excessively, or manipulating their eating patterns. (After several years of practice, these behaviours may offer little pleasure.) Typically, however, people suffering from obsessive-compulsive disorder (OCD) are subjectively driven to perform their compulsions in response to an obsession, or according to rigid rules aimed at preventing distress or some dreaded event. The entire behavioural sequence may be experienced as unpleasant, both as the symptomatology develops and as it maintains itself. Thus, compulsive problem behaviours apparently are conceptually separable from OCD. The next section looks at the pool of compulsive problem behaviours, and examines them as composing a possible two-category typology.

Substance and process addictions

Schaef (1987) proposed a typology to attempt to differentially classify various addictive behaviours. **Substance addictions** involve all mood-altering products, including drugs (for example caffeine, nicotine, alcohol and cocaine, heroin, and so on) and food-related disorders (for example **anorexia nervosa**, **bulimia nervosa**, overeating, and so on). *Process addictions* consist of a series of actions that expose the person to 'mood-altering events' on which they become dependent (for example gambling, **workaholism**, excessive exercise and sex, excessive spending, excessive television watching, and so on). This distinction between substance and process addictions could reflect different underlying causal mechanisms. Substance addictions involve direct manipulation of pleasure through use of products that are taken into the body. By intake of these products, perhaps a direct effect on neurotransmitter systems occurs. Process addictions involve a more indirect manipulation of pleasure though situational and physical activity manipulations. The subsequent sections of this chapter describe the phenomena of substance and process addictions.

Substance addictions

Through ingestion of a substance, an individual may attempt to achieve a desired or expected state. Repeated use of a substance may lead to a variety of consequences. Many individuals lose control over their drug use and engage in compulsive use, as discussed in Chapter 1. The ingestion of substances other than drugs of abuse (for example food) might also change one's mood. Numerous individuals have difficulty managing their food consumption. We shall focus on food disorders in this section. Food addiction is a disorder characterized by preoccupation with food, the availability of food and the anticipation of pleasure from the ingestion of food. Food addiction involves the repetitive consumption of food contrary to an individual's wishes, resulting in loss of control and preoccupation with the restriction of food, body weight and body image. Characteristics associated with eating disorders include concern about body shape, chronic dieting, impaired social and work functioning, low self-esteem, emotional problems such as depression and anxiety, general psychopathology, lack of family cohesion and drug abuse among family members, and drug abuse (for example Kerr *et al.* 1991). It is not uncommon for individuals with eating disorders to misuse alcohol and other drugs, as well as substances such as laxatives, diuretics, diet pills and ipecac (Mitchell *et al.* 1997). Compulsive eating, anorexia nervosa, bulimia nervosa and dieting failure affect millions of people (perhaps 8 per cent of the world population). Thousands of people suffer from eating disorders, cycles of dieting, bingeing, starving, persistent weight problems and food and weight obsessions. Many individuals attempt to control their weight by fasting, overexercising, purging or by using slimming pills, diuretics or laxatives. The result is often rebound weight gain, cravings, feelings of failure, and damage to social, emotional and physical well-being.

Compulsive overeaters

Compulsive overeaters use food inappropriately, eventually losing control over the amount of food they consume. Obesity is related to a variety of negative health outcomes including high blood pressure, cardiovascular disease, some cancers, diabetes and 5.5 per cent of all health-care costs. In the United States, as assessed through use of the body mass index (BMI; that is a ratio calculated by dividing the weight in kilograms by the square of the height in metres), 25–30 per cent of the population are overweight (31 per cent of males, 24 per cent of females) and 12 per cent of the population are severely overweight (> 30 lbs). Obesity is related to size and number of adipose cells, the number of which can change in childhood and maybe in adulthood. There is evidence that humans may not be born with a predisposition to select a healthy diet (that is there is a tendency to eat what tastes good, such as sweets, and anticipated consequences and ideational factors being learned: (Wadden and Brownell 1984; Brownell and Wadden 1992). Twelve-step self-help programmes for overeaters exist (that is Overeaters Anonymous (OA): www.overeatersanonymous.org; Eating Addictions Anonymous (EAA): www.decregistry.com/users/eatingaddictions/main.html), with a focus on an individual's powerlessness over their food consumption.

Anorexia nervosa

Anorexia nervosa is an eating disorder characterized by

- a refusal or inability to maintain a minimally normal weight for age and height, leading to maintenance of body weight 15 per cent below expected
- an intense fear of gaining weight or becoming fat
- a significant disturbance in body image (always seeing oneself as fat)
- in females, at least three consecutive missed menstrual cycles that should otherwise be expected to occur.

There are two subtypes – restricting type and **binge**-eating/purging type. Among individuals carrying a diagnosis of anorexia nervosa, those who binge/purge are more likely to abuse drugs and alcohol, to be sexually active and to exhibit more mood lability (Jonas *et al.* 1987; APA 1994).

Bulimia nervosa
Bulimia nervosa is characterized by

- repeated episodes of binge eating, including eating an amount of food that is larger than most people would eat during a similar period of time, and experiencing a sense of lack of control over eating during the bingeing episode
- recurrent inappropriate compensatory behaviours to prevent weight gain (for example misuse of laxatives or diuretics, diet pills, very vigorous exercise, self-induced vomiting)
- concern with body image
- at least two binge eating and purging/severe compensatory behaviour episodes per week for a minimum of three months.

(APA 1994)

These episodes do not occur only during a course of anorexia nervosa. There are two subtypes – purging type and non-purging type. The purging type of bulimic usually engages in self-induced vomiting and/or misuse of diuretics or laxatives, while the non-purging type does not usually self-induce vomiting or misuse diuretics or laxatives. The non-purging type engages in compensatory behaviours, such as fasting for a day or more or excessive exercise. Approximately one-third of individuals with bulimia nervosa also abuse drugs, mainly alcohol and stimulants (APA 1994).

Process addictions

In the previous section we considered food disorders. People who suffer food disorders show a pattern of abuse not too dissimilar from drug abuse. Many people with food disorders also suffer from drug abuse. In this section we consider four process addictions: pathological gambling, workaholism, excessive exercise and excessive spending. (Previously, we also discussed sex as not only a drug-related behaviour, but also a potential process addiction.) These problem behaviours also show drug abuse-like behaviour patterns and are associated with drug abuse.

Pathological gambling
Gamblers whose repeated losses lead to serious financial and psychological problems are increasingly being labelled compulsive or pathological (that is the individual has a disease). Pathological gambling can disrupt personal, family and/or vocational pursuits. The essential features of pathological gambling are as follows (APA 1994): first, persistent and recurrent maladaptive gambling behaviour as indicated by five (or more) of the following:

- preoccupation with gambling (for example preoccupation with reliving past gambling experience, handicapping, planning the next venture or thinking of ways to get money with which to gamble)
- need to gamble with increasing amounts of money in order to achieve the desired excitement
- repeated unsuccessful efforts to control, cut back or stop gambling
- restlessness or irritability when attempting to cut down or stop gambling
- gambling as a way to escape from problems or relieve a dysphoric mood (for example feelings of helplessness, guilt, anxiety, depression)
- after losing money gambling, often returning another day to get even ('chasing' one's losses)
- lying to family members, therapist or others to conceal the extent of involvement with gambling
- committing illegal acts such as forgery, fraud, theft or embezzlement to finance gambling
- jeopardizing or losing a significant relationship, job or educational or career opportunity because of gambling
- relying on others to provide money to relieve a desperate financial situation caused by gambling.

Second, the gambling behaviour is not better accounted for by a manic episode.

Several similarities have been reported between compulsive gambling and drug abuse. For example, the states of arousal and euphoria sought by gamblers seem similar to the high derived from using drugs. Compulsive gamblers tend to increase the size of their bets or the odds against them to increase excitement, analogous to drug tolerance effects (Spunt *et al.* 1998). Researchers also have found the equivalence of drug withdrawal symptoms in compulsive gamblers (for example irritability, depressed mood and obsessional thoughts). Roy *et al.* (1988) found biological differences between gamblers and controls in the noradrenergic neurotransmitter system; specifically, that pathological gamblers show greater concentrations of by-products of norepinephrine that are associated with the facilitation of arousal, excitement and thrills (sensation seeking).

Prevalence estimates of pathological gamblers in the United States range around 1–3 per cent of the adult population (APA 1994). Males are more likely than females to be pathological gamblers. Alcohol and other drugs commonly are consumed by individuals when gambling. Drugs are often used to stay awake while gambling, free drinks are served in many casinos, and most racetracks have bars (Spunt *et al.* 1995, 1998). Pathological gamblers report higher rates of alcoholism and other drug misuse than that of the general population. Among women pathological gamblers participating in Gamblers Anonymous (www.gamblersanonymous.org), a twelve-step self-help programme for gamblers, the rate of alcohol and drug misuse is approximately two to three times higher than the general female population. Rates of pathological gambling are four to ten times higher for drug misusers than for the general population. Some heroin addicts are able to support their habits through gambling or hustling at gambling games. In a study of 462 individuals in a methadone maintenance treatment programme in New York City, 59 per cent of the pathological gamblers reported using heroin, almost half reported using alcohol, and 23 per cent reported using cocaine more than 50 per cent of the time or always while gambling (Spunt *et al.* 1998). Researchers have also reported a relationship between pathological gambling and participation in criminal activity (mainly property crimes), as well as drug dealing to obtain money to gamble and pay debts (Spunt *et al.* 1995, 1998).

Workaholism
Workaholism is an addiction to working. It is not currently formally recognized as a mental disorder in the DSM-IV or ICD-9 or ICD-10, however, work can be a compulsive behaviour similar to other process addictions. Workaholism is characterized by feelings of being driven to keep working, as well as perfectionism, non-delegation of responsibility and job stress. Workaholic behaviour interferes with other life domains (Spence and Robbins 1992).

Working long hours is certainly a relatively prosocial activity and possibly a **harm reduction** strategy for individuals coping with other compulsive or addictive behaviours. For instance, pathological gamblers, when not gambling, may be workaholics (APA 1994), or addicts in recovery may choose to work excessively as they change their lifestyles. If one's working behaviour results in lack of fulfilment in other life roles, such as effective interpersonal relationships, effective parenting or necessary life skills (for example how to purchase a car), then one might consider strategies for engaging in a more balanced, healthy life. Workaholism may be associated with poorer emotional and physical well-being (R. Burke 2000). Compulsive work is recognized as a problem behaviour in the recovery movement (for example Workaholics Anonymous: wawso@media.mit.edu).

Excessive exercise
Participation in exercise or physical activity is often negatively associated with addiction (Donovan *et al.* 1993). Exercise tends to exert many positive effects, including decreasing low-density lipoprotein (LDL) and heart rate, and increasing high-density lipoprotein (HDL), oxygen utilization and metabolism. It is often used in the treatment of drug abuse. However, even exercise can become a craving for some people when it is compulsively engaged in (for example going jogging three times per day), when other life roles are neglected, when not exercising leads to depressed mood and when it leads to repeated injuries (Thaxton 1982; Griffiths, 1997). Compulsive runners have been likened to anorexics in that 'their behavior becomes pathological as a result of an extreme degree of constriction, inflexibility, repetitive thought adherence to rituals and need to control themselves and their environment' (Peele and Brodsky 1991: 42). One may speculate that

injuries, which lead to an inability to exercise, may be replaced by drug use. Since exercising may stimulate endorphin turnover, other drugs that provide a similar function may be used once exercise is not a viable option. Currently, no widely publicized support groups exist, although compulsive exercise is an issue that has been addressed by eating disorder support groups.

Excessive spending
Participation in excessive buying behaviour (for example **compulsive shopping**), which leads to unsecured debt, is also not recognized as an official mental disorder by the DSM-IV (APA 1994). However, one out of every twelve residents of the United States is overwhelmed by debt. This process addiction is associated with its own twelve-step programme composed of at least 400 groups, worldwide, Debtors Anonymous (DA) (Mundis, 1986: www.solvency.org). DA was founded in 1976 by a man who had been sober in Alcoholics Anonymous for 27 years. Compulsive spenders repeatedly incur debt despite negative emotional, social and financial consequences. They tend to value money greatly as a solution to problems (Hanley and Wilhelm 1992), and they are also relatively likely to suffer from drug abuse, eating disorders and pathological gambling (for example Schlosser *et al.* 1994).

Summary

After reviewing a sample of problem behaviours associated with drug use and abuse, the question remains – is drug abuse an element of a class of problem behaviours or a distinct phenomenon? The information provided above suggests that drug abuse is but one behaviour associated with a syndrome of problem behaviours – that compulsive behaviours represent behavioural manifestations of similar underlying processes (for example Hovarth 1999). Certainly drug-related problem behaviours are part of using drugs for a long period of time. However, the fact that many persons who engage in other compulsive problem behaviours also report drug abuse strongly suggests some common impulsive-compulsive aetiology. Of course, there is considerable variation here. There are many individuals who exhibit only one compulsive problem behaviour. After they quit that behaviour, no 'substitution behaviour' occurs. There are other individuals who engage compulsively in several behaviours at once (for example drugs, overeating, sex, gambling). There are still others who engage in one behaviour at a time, but always seem to be battling one compulsive problem behaviour after another. What can explain such variations?

In Chapter 2 we examined drug abuse as a continuum in which individuals at one end of the continuum are relatively 'disease-free' but tend to engage in maladaptive behaviours over which they have some control. At the other end of the continuum, there are people who seem to have no choice or control over their use. We conjecture that individuals at the 'choice' end of the continuum will show only one compulsive problem behaviour. When they are finally able to gain control over that behaviour, they may be fine. However, at the other end of the continuum are individuals who, no matter what activity they choose to engage in – gambling, working, exercise, shopping, or drug use – will excessively engage in that activity. They may try substitute drugs (for example 'marijuana maintenance') and compulsive problem behaviours (for example sex addiction) in order to stay off another drug they consider more dangerous at that time (for example alcohol, heroin). Alternatively, they may try to combine several drugs or behaviours in an attempt to feel all right. Perhaps, for them, drug addictions, substance-related problem behaviours and process addictions are relatively indistinguishable as a means to an end. That is, as one enters the 'no-control' end of the continuum, the breadth of problem behaviours fans out. Of course, this is our conjecture. To increase our understanding of addictive processes, continued research focused on various compulsive problem behaviours and their co-morbidity is a reasonable pursuit.

4

Assessment of drug abuse

This last chapter in the first part of the book pertains to assessment of drug abuse. There are at least three assessment domains that one would want to cover in an evaluation of potential drug abusers. First, one would like to know whether or not a pattern of use qualifies as drug misuse, abuse or dependence, as discussed in Chapter 1. Second, one would like to know the details of the extent to which someone's drug use pervades the rest of their life; that is, where on the continuum of loss of control one falls, as discussed in Chapter 2. Finally, one would like to know the co-morbidity of drug use with other psychological difficulties (for example character disorders, depressions and other compulsive problem behaviours), as discussed in Chapter 3.

Let us suppose we all agree on what drug abuse is; perhaps we use a DSM diagnostic scheme (APA 1994). Still, assessment of drug abuse can be problematic and challenging. Drug users may under-report use because of the perceived and actual negative stigma associated with a drug abuse diagnosis and the illegal nature of many drugs that are used. Alternately, some drug users may over-report use to avoid punishment by legal agencies, or may try to receive financial assistance (for example service connection). Also, there are wide variations in the topography of drug use behaviour for specific drugs. For example, some marijuana smokers use marijuana once a week, some once a day, and others several times per day. Differentiating drug misuse from drug abuse may not always be certain. Finally, there are variations in the manifestation of problem drug use across different types of drugs. Some drugs of abuse are 'tissue' addictive and others are not. Some are very highly rewarding because of their pharmacological effects and influence on reinforcing **neurobiological processes**; some are less so. Some drugs of abuse quickly increase an individual's risk for negative consequences while other drugs of abuse may not be as noticeably detectable. For example, individuals may abuse alcohol for many years and not experience negative consequences of their use, whereas other individuals may have used heroin for only one or two months and become physically dependent on the drug, making them unable to participate as a functional member of society. Additionally, the **metabolites** of some drugs are stored in body tissues for long periods of time, and may be detectable in biochemical testing for weeks, while the metabolites of other drugs are not detectable after a few days. With these limitations in mind, we shall examine methods used to assess drug abuse and dependence, establish location on the drug abuse continuum, and assess co-morbidity. The chapter is organized as the following sections: **clinical interviewing**, **drug use history**, formalized alcohol and other drug use inventories, and laboratory testing/**biochemical validation**.

Clinical interviewing

Many current assessment practices rely on clinical judgement and the use of semi-structured interviews. The initial goal in assessment is to determine the nature of an individual's involvement with drugs of abuse and to assess psychological and medical status, **psychosocial functioning**, **social supports**, attitudes towards drug use, and **motivation** for initial **abstinence**. Detailed information is obtained regarding one's drug use history and related consequences, and co-morbidity. Due to response demand problems, it is helpful to use corroborative methods of assessment, including family members' reports or biochemical methods. Of course, some differences in judgement as to whether or not one is a drug user or abuser is dependent on such variables as the age of the drug user (see Table 4.1).

Mental status examination

A **mental status examination** generally is conducted as a systematic means of gathering psychological and behavioural data. The purpose is to provide an initial screening of an individual's health status, and to help suggest other means of assessment to determine whether or not a diagnosis of a formal psychiatric disease should be made. The mental status examination includes the assessment of appearance, attitude and behaviour, speech, mood and affect, thought and language, perceptions and cognitive functioning, and insight and judgement (Schottenfeld 1994).

When performing a mental status examination, the following questions are examples of those that help to provide a guideline to determine whether or not an adolescent or adult is suspected of drug abuse or other psychopathology. Does the individual appear to be hostile, uncooperative, seemingly withdrawn, socially isolated, undernourished, agitated or depressed, tired, unable to concentrate, or having had lost interest in pleasurable activities, or physical appearance? Is the individual evasive or defensive, and are there any discrepancies in reports of autobiographical events (that is lies, missing information)? Are any delusions or visual or auditory hallucinations reported? If so, what were the circumstances? Was the individual under the influence

Table 4.1 Indications of drug abuse among adolescents versus adults

Adolescents	Adults
Situations in which testing is appropriate for adolescents • Employment (for example lifeguards, delivery personnel, driving vehicles, babysitters) • Individuals with a history of use • To obtain a driving licence • Student athletes • Parental discretion/suspect of social problems related to drug use	*Situations in which testing is appropriate for adults* • Individuals in the health-care professions • Individuals suspect of criminal activity or for legal reasons • Prisoners • Individuals operating equipment (for example bus drivers, pilots) • Individuals working with children • Athletes • Law enforcement candidates/officers • Pregnant women (controversial)
Reasons for misreporting use among adolescents • Athletic coaches, for star players • Students to maintain scholarships • To avoid problems with the law • Students to appear 'cool'; peer acceptance • To avoid conflict at home	*Reasons for misreporting use among adults* • Protection of current status • Memory impairment • Don't want to get caught • To get a job • To avoid being sacked from a job • For insurance purposes • To escape legal problems and obtain psychological treatment • Pregnant women
Reasons for biochemical confirmation of drug use among adolescents • To confirm accuracy of self-reports • Screening for potential problems • Early initiation of treatment • Fair play in sports/scholarship/personal health • Legal reasons to prove innocence • To rule out other possible illness • When individuals are brought to the emergency room	*Reasons for biochemical confirmation of drug use among adults* • To confirm accuracy of self-reports • Screening for law enforcement agents/motor vehicle operators/health-care workers • For those charged of crimes (may minimize or maximize the charges) • People in rehabilitation or treatment facilities (to stay in or get out) • For childcare workers to ensure the safety of others • To rule out other possible illness • When individuals are brought to the emergency room
Important questions to ask adolescents during assessment • Have you taken or tried any drugs? • What do you use?	*Important questions to ask adults during assessment* • Prior treatment history • Last time you drank or used drugs

Table 4.1 (*cont'd*)

Adolescents	Adults
• How much (quantity)?	• Why biochemically tested (motivation, ordered, as a condition of something)?
• Do your peers use any drugs? Does your best friend use drugs?	• Any convictions
• Do your parents use drugs?	• Last physical examination
• Ask about their beliefs; attitudes about drugs of abuse	• Any history of failure to quit
• How did you get into using drugs?	• Family history
• How old were you?	• Are you on any medications or over-the-counter drugs? If so, what (how many) and for how long?
• Have you experienced any legal or social problems from drug use?	• Ever failed a drug test?
• What do the drugs do for you? How do they make you feel?	• Ever terminated from a job for substance abuse?
• Have you gone to a psychiatrist?	• Whether they had a clean motor vehicle driving record
• Any potential suicidal or homicidal ideation or sexual, physical abuse? (need to report)	• Do you have any hobbies?
• How much control do you think you have over your drug use? How long do your using episodes last? What happens?	• Any potential suicidal or homicidal ideation or sexual, physical abuse? (need to report)
• Do you seem to lose control over any other areas of your life? How about gambling? Sex? Spending? Eating? Exercising a lot? Studying or working long hours?	• How much control do you think you have over your drug use? How long do your using episodes last? What happens?
	• Do you seem to lose control over any other areas of your life? How about gambling? Sex? Spending? Eating? Exercising a lot? Studying or working long hours?

For additional reading see McLellan *et al.* 1980; Rychtarik *et al.* 1998

of mood-altering drugs at the time? After answering these questions, the individual might be assessed through a more specific interview assessment.

The SCID

The *Diagnostic and Statistical Manual of Mental Disorders* of the American Psychiatric Association (DSM-IV) is widely used in establishing whether or not an individual has a drug abuse disorder (APA 1994), as introduced in Chapter 1. This manual also contains specific criteria sets for substance abuse, dependence, intoxication and withdrawal applicable across different classes of drugs. The **Structured Clinical Interview for the DSM-IV (SCID)** is a broad-spectrum instrument that adheres to the DSM-IV decision trees for psychiatric diagnosis, and encourages multiple paths of exploration, clarification and clinical decision-making. It can be tailored to a variety of populations (Spitzer *et al.* 1990 for DSM-III-R version; First, *et al.* 1995 for DSM-IV Axis I Disorders). This interview is a primary measure of substance abuse disorder and substance dependence, with clarification particularly regarding efforts to decrease or control use, continued use despite problems, specific withdrawal symptoms of a drug, and assessment of co-morbidity.

Drug use history

Drug use recovery battles

The use of interviews or self-reports that elicit information regarding an individual's prior involvement in drug treatment programmes, psychiatric facilities, self-help support groups (for example twelve-step programmes) or public sanctions (for example court, prison) can be quite useful. Such data can assist in understanding people's level of addiction (where individuals fall on the drug abuse continuum), occurrence of other compulsive behaviours and psychiatric difficulties, and motivation to stop using. It is also useful to assess the longest period of abstinence endured with the help of a structured environment, and without the help of a structured environment. Many individuals will disclose that while in prison, or while in treatment, they can remain abstinent, but when in the community, without some structure, they are unable to remain abstinent.

Frequency, quantity, and method of drug use, and family drug use

Although questioning individuals about the *frequency* and *quantity* of drug use may not be essential in making a diagnosis of substance abuse, it is none the less associated with drug-abuse-related dysfunction (Rychtarik *et al.* 1998, 1999). Of course, there are some individuals who experience severe consequences while using relatively low levels of drugs (for example experiences of some Asian groups with alcohol) and there are some individuals who appear to experience few consequences on relatively high levels of regular use. However, high quantities of intake are highly correlated with occupational, social and medical impairment. *Frequency of use* indicates how often individuals are using a drug. Frequency of drug use can be measured through self-reports of lifetime estimates of use, yearly estimates of use, monthly use and/or daily estimates of use. Unfortunately, this type of assessment lacks precision because of memory biases, social desirability, denial and other response demands. *Recency of use* does not indicate the length of time or the extent of the addiction, but it helps disclose the most current autobiographical events. *Quantity of use* is more predictive of problems or disruptive drug use than frequency (for example binge drinking versus small amounts of daily use) (see Annis 1984; Newcomb and Felix-Ortiz 1992). According to the *National Household Survey on Drug Abuse*, binge drinking is defined as consuming five or more drinks on one occasion at least one day in the past thirty days. Alternatively, heavy drinking is defined as drinking five or more drinks on the same occasion on five or more of the past thirty days. Given these definitions, 30 per cent of the United States population engaged in a drinking binge in 1997 (Substance Abuse and Mental Health Services Administration (SAMHSA) 1998). Bingeing behaviour may lead to a greater likelihood of cardiovascular disease and advanced liver disease, adjusting for average weekly consumption, due to periodic 'shocks' to the body (Kauhanen *et al.* 1999; Sussman *et al.*, under review a). Bingeing can also apply to other drugs, though little research is currently available. Anecdotally, bingeing on heroin may account for several drug-overdose-related deaths.

The assessment of the *method of drug intake* may help to understand the level of addiction for those drugs that vary in means of use (for example cocaine and heroin). For instance, many crack addicts originally began their use with powdered cocaine. Eventually, they may smoke crack that is cheaper, readily available in small quantities, and immediately potentiates dopamine transmission in the nucleus accumbens. Conversely, individuals snorting cocaine may use it daily, but have used it only for the past year and have not suffered comparable social or personal consequences (for example loss of job, home and relationships) as the individual using crack cocaine. Likewise, many heroin injectors begin use by sniffing the drug in some countries, and by smoking it or smoking opium in other countries. They may have progressed to injecting the heroin for more intense effects.

Assessment of *family history of drug use* may further help to assess the level of addiction, perceived problems and consequences, attitudes towards drug use, and probability of relapse. Current use among significant others, and perceptions that drug use is simply a part of normal behaviour, would lead one to expect future struggles with drug use.

Formalized alcohol and other drug use inventories

Several formalized inventories have been tested regarding their ability to assess alcoholism and drug abuse. The list of formalized assessments is becoming longer every day, and is way beyond discussion in the scope of this text. We do, however, present several well-known means of assessment in this section of the chapter.

Assessment of alcoholism

The *Alcohol Use Inventory* (AUI) (Horn *et al.* 1990; Littrell 1991; Rychtarik *et al.* 1998) is a 228-item multiple-choice self-report inventory. It was systematically developed to measure alcohol problems. There are 24 subscales with

17 primary scales characterizing individuals along various dimensions. The dimensions are grouped according to benefits from drinking, drinking styles, drinking consequences, and concerns about and recognition of a drinking problem. The primary scale factors include: (1) drinking to improve sociability, (2) drinking to improve mental functioning, (3) drinking to manage or change mood, (4) drinking to cope with marital problems, (5) gregarious versus solitary drinking, (6) obsessive-compulsive drinking or constantly thinking about drinking, (7) continuous, sustained drinking, (8) loss of behaviour control when drinking, (9) social-role maladaptation, (10) perceptual withdrawal symptoms (alcohol hallucinosis, delirium tremors), (11) somatic or physical withdrawal (shakes, hangovers, convulsions), (12) drinking provokes marital problems, (13) quantity of alcohol used, (14) post drinking worry, fear and guilt, (15) external support to stop drinking, (16) ready to quit, and (17) recognition of drinking problems.

The AUI primary scales often identify three general profiles of problem drinkers (Rychtarik *et al.* 1998, 1999). First, there are low impairment problem drinkers. They are likely to show a later onset of problem drinking and seek treatment as outpatients. They are also likely to be relatively successful in their social and vocational lives. Second, there are medium impairment drinkers. They are similar to the first type of drinker in that they show relatively good social adjustment. However, they are more likely to report a history of physical, emotional or sexual abuse, and depression. Finally, there are high impairment drinkers. They show the greatest social and vocational impairments, high levels of previous physical, emotional or sexual abuse, highest levels of sustained drinking, and highest levels of psychopathology (depression, anger or sociopathy).

The *CAGE questionnaire* (Ewing 1984) is a self-report screening instrument that uses the mnemonic CAGE to assess problems with alcohol. It is a relatively sensitive four-item instrument that assesses attempts to Cut down on drinking; Annoyance with criticisms of drinking; Guilt feelings about drinking; and use of alcohol as a morning Eye opener. When someone answers 'yes' to two or more questions, that individual is suspected of having alcohol problems. These questions could be adapted for other drug use, as well, by replacing the word 'drinking' with 'drug use', and 'a morning eye opener' with 'the drug to get you started in the morning.'

The *Comprehensive Drinker Profile* (W. Miller and Marlatt 1984) is a structured interview. Detailed information is obtained on an individual's alcohol consumption history, motivation, behaviour and self-efficacy. This interview was developed to determine treatment modality.

The *Michigan Alcoholism Screening Test (MAST)* (Selzer 1971) is a 25-item questionnaire used to screen for consequences of problem alcohol use and perceptions of alcohol-related problems. This questionnaire was established to identify abnormal drinking by addressing social and behavioural consequences (Selzer 1971). This measure can be used to place drinkers into early (mild impairment), middle (moderate impairment) and late (severe impairment) stages (or levels of impairment) of alcoholism. The Brief MAST is a shortened ten-item version that is relatively effective in discriminating alcoholics from non-alcoholics. The items are designed to describe extreme drinking behaviours, and to establish the presence of negative consequences of excessive alcohol consumption. Examples of discriminating items are as follows: have you ever attended a meeting of Alcoholics Anonymous? Have you ever gone to anyone for help about your drinking? Have you ever been in a hospital because of drinking?

The *MAC/MAC-R (MacAndrew Alcoholism Scale/Revised* (MacAndrew 1965, 1989) is a subscale of the Minnesota Multiphasic Personality Inventory (MMPI), a standardized questionnaire developed by Hathaway and McKinley (1943). This inventory can be used to help rule out possible psychopathology. Some profiles characterize alcohol and/or drug abuse as a form of self-medication for depression (for example the 24/42 scale). The MAC/MAC-R consists of 49 items that differentiate between alcoholic patients and non-alcoholic psychiatric patients (Clopton 1978; Clopton *et al.* 1980; Svanum *et al.* 1982). The scale has also been found to help to identify individuals who are at risk for developing alcohol-related problems (McCourt *et al.* 1971). One limitation of the scale is that it does not effectively differentiate alcohol abusers from other drug abusers (H. Burke and Marcus 1977). Additionally, female alcoholics consistently obtain higher scores than males with similar difficulties (Butcher and Owen 1978). Higher scores suggest potential drug abuse, but are also suggestive of extraversion, assertiveness, risk taking and the possibility of having experienced blackouts and difficulty concentrating. Low scores are suggestive of introversion, conformity and low self-confidence, as well as being contra-indicative of drug abuse.

The *Alcohol Expectancy Questionnaire (AEQ)* (Brown *et al.* 1980) was developed to evaluate anticipated effects of alcohol consumption. This inventory addresses expected effects in several domains including global positive changes, sexual enhancement, physical and social pleasure, increased social assertiveness, relaxation and tension reduction, arousal and aggression (Brown *et al.* 1987). An *Adolescent AEQ* form was subsequently developed (Brown *et al.* 1987). The adolescent AEQ addresses the following expectancies: global positive changes, changes in social behaviour, improved cognitive and motor abilities, sexual enhancement, cognitive and motor impairment, increased arousal and relaxation and tension reduction.

The *Comprehensive Effects of Alcohol (CEOA)* questionnaire (Stroot and Fromme 1989; Fromme *et al.* 1993) was developed to assess positive and negative alcohol effects and the subjective evaluation of those effects. This measure consists of several expected positive effects including factors that address sociability, tension reduction, liquid courage and sexuality, and several negative effects, including factors addressing cognitive and behavioural impairment, risk and aggression, and self-perception.

The *Inventory of Drinking Situations (IDS)* (Annis 1982) assesses the contextual aspects of alcohol use and provides information about relapse situations.

This inventory consists of eight subscales to evaluate drinking situations, including unpleasant emotions, physical discomfort, pleasant emotions, testing personal control, urges and temptations, conflict with others, social pressures, and pleasant times with others.

The *Alcohol Abstinence Self-Efficacy Scale* (DiClemente *et al.* 1994) consists of temptation and self-efficacy items that are self-rated to assess an individual's confidence to resist use in several drinking situations.

Assessment of other drugs of abuse

The *Addiction Severity Index (ASI)* is a structured clinical research interview designed to provide information about various areas of an individual's life in which there often exists dysfunction associated with drug abuse. Problem areas assessed include medical, legal, drug abuse, alcohol abuse, employment, family and psychiatric problems. Reliability and validity data for the ASI have been extensively reported (McLellan *et al.* 1980, 1985; Rounsville *et al.* 1986). McLellan and colleagues developed a strategy for obtaining a composite score based on the sum of several individual questions within each problem area.

The *Substance Dependence Severity Scale (SDSS)* (Miele *et al.* 2000) is a clinician-administered structured interview that was developed to assess severity and frequency of dependence across a range of drugs, based on the DSM-IV. The test–retest, joint rating and internal consistency reliabilities across alcohol, cocaine, heroin, marijuana and sedative users is good.

The *Drug Use Screening Inventory (DUSI)* (Tarter 1990) is a self-report inventory and is used to quantify problems in several areas, including drug use, psychiatric disorders, behaviour, family, peer, work, school, social skills, leisure and recreational time, and health. Both adult and adolescent versions exist.

The *Chemical Dependency Assessment Profile (CDAP)* (Harrell *et al.* 1991) is a 235-item multiple-choice and true–false self-report instrument used to assess substance use, dependency problems and treatment needs among adolescents and adults. Domains addressed include quantity/frequency of use, physiological symptoms, situational stressors, antisocial behaviours, interpersonal problems, affective dysfunction, treatment attitudes, impact of use on life functioning, and expectancies.

The *Inventory of Drug Use Situations* (Annis and Graham 1992) assesses the contextual aspects of drug use and provides information about relapse situations. This inventory consists of eight subscales to evaluate drug use situations including unpleasant emotions, physical discomfort, pleasant emotions, testing personal control, urges and temptations, conflict with others, social pressures and pleasant times with others.

The *Adolescent Diagnostic Interview* (Winters and Henly 1993) is a 15-minute evaluation used to assess the need for treatment of drug use among adolescents. This interview includes the evaluation of various cognitive, interpersonal, and school functioning factors that may contribute to alcohol or drug use.

The *Personal Experience Inventory* (PEI) (Winters *et al.* 1993) and the *Personal Experience Inventory for Adults* (Winters 1999) are comprehensive questionnaires used for detection of problem consequences and potential **risk factors** believed to predispose individuals to use or maintain drug use. These questionnaires help to quantify level of involvement with a variety of drugs and the severity of problems in personal, family and psychosocial domains.

The *Adolescent Drug Abuse Diagnosis (ADAD)* (Friedman and Utada 1989) is a comprehensive structured interview consisting of 150 items used to assess substance abuse and other problem areas. The format is adopted from the ASI. This interview addresses nine life areas including medical, school, work, social relations, family relationships, legal, psychological, alcohol use, and drug use.

Comprehensive Addiction Severity Index for Adolescents (CASI-A) (Myers *et al.* 1995) is an instrument designed to provide an in-depth, comprehensive assessment of the severity of adolescents' addiction and problem consequences. Ten domains are assessed, including psychological, peer relationships, family history and relationships including sexual and physical abuse, significant life changes, use of free time, substance use effects and treatment experiences, leisure activities, educational experiences and plans, legal history and psychiatric status, including prior treatment experiences.

Inventories for other problem behaviours exist (for example Clinical Screener for Compulsive Buying (CSCB): Faber and O'Guinn 1992). However, there is a paucity of formalized means simultaneously to assess multiple compulsive problem behaviours.

Laboratory testing/biochemical validation

Blood serum and urine **toxicology** screening play an important role in the assessment and treatment of individuals with drug use disorders. These tests need to be properly conducted and the results need to be properly interpreted to minimize errors when analysing samples collected. False-negative results (saying that someone is using drugs, but the test fails to detect use) or false-positive results (saying someone is not using drugs, but the test detects use) may be obtained as a result of the methods of sampling and the accuracy of the laboratory. Positive test results for any drug should be confirmed by a second test on the same sample using a different analytic method (Kapur 1993). Factors contributing to false-positive, false-negative and inconclusive results include appropriate specimen collection, specimen handling, and testing of specimens (for example urine, blood, hair or saliva).

False-positive tests are sometimes referred to as 'cross reactivity' and may occur as a result of ingestion of closely related compounds in various medications and foods. In other words, other drugs may mimic biochemical readings that are obtained with illicit drugs, using some analyses. For instance, poppy seeds found on bagels can produce detectable amounts of morphine in urine, yielding a positive urine test for opioid use. Of course, heroin use can be analysed with a heroin metabolite that cannot come from eating poppy seeds. For amphetamine use, false positives can result from over-the-counter medications containing high concentrations of decongestants. Also, phenylpropanolamine and ephedrine found in over-the-counter diet pills and cold remedies are similar in chemical structure to amphetamines and can produce a false-positive result in immunoassays. Additionally, secondhand marijuana smoke or passive inhalation of marijuana smoke can result in a false-positive result for marijuana. Although positive toxicology screens may indicate past exposure to psychoactive drugs, they do not indicate when the exposure occurred and the extent of the exposure, or whether or not there were social or behavioural consequences or impairment as a result of use.

Drugs and metabolites are excreted in all body fluids – urine, faeces and sweat – and are sequestered into hair and nails. A variety of chemical assays can be used to detect drug use. Urinary excretion by the kidney is the most prevalent route of excretion; excretion by the liver into bile and faeces is also a major route of elimination. Urinalysis or urine toxicology screening for the detection of drugs is non-invasive, relatively easy and inexpensive. Urine samples can be tested for specific drugs and for different drug categories.

The most commonly used screenings for collected samples involve use of radioimmunoassay (RIA), enzyme immunoassay (EIA) and fluorescence polarization immunoassay (FPIA) for initial screening. Immunoassays involve the measurement of labelled and unlabelled antigen (drug or metabolite) and antibody interactions. The label utilized in such procedures may be a radioisotope (radioimmunoassay), an enzyme (EIA) or a fluoraphone (FPIA) (Goldberger and Jenkins 1999). In **drug testing**, the antigen is a drug or metabolite and its corresponding labelled analogue, and the antibody is a protein grown in an animal and directed towards a specific drug metabolite or group of similar compounds.

Comparable testing techniques that are more selective screening assays for confirmation include gas chromatography/mass spectrometry (GC/MS), gas chromatography (GC) and high performance liquid chromatography (HPLC). Chromatography consists of a variety of techniques used to separate physically mixtures of drugs, their metabolites and other chemicals, into individual components based on differences in relative affinity for a mobile phase and a stationary phase. The stationary phase requires that the mixture to be separated be placed on an immobile medium (for example a narrow tube or column). The mobile phase consists of a liquid, gas or fluid that passes through the stationary phase. For example, in gas chromatography, the mobile phase is inert gas, such as nitrogen or helium, and the stationary phase is a high-boiling liquid bound to fine particles packed in a glass column. Both the stationary and mobile phases compete for components of the mixture to be separated (that is the mobile phase dissolves components and the stationary phase absorbs, adsorbs and dissolves). Components that have little or no affinity for the stationary phase, and/or are particularly soluble in the mobile phase, move on and are separated. The presence or absence of a component can be determined once separation is completed (http://chemistry. rutgers.edu/genchem/chrom.html).

The length of time a drug or its metabolites can be detected in urine is called the *retention time*. Detection of drug metabolites is dependent on the sensitivity of the assay. Drug concentrations are highest several hours after drug use and decrease to undetectable levels over time. Retention times differ according to

- the amount of drug consumed
- whether use is occasional or chronic
- the method of drug use
- individual metabolic rates and excretion
- diet
- acidity of the urine
- fluid intake
- the time of day.

Alternative drug-monitoring methods include hair and saliva analyses. Hair analysis supposedly detects drug use for months, as long as the individual's hair has been growing. Hair may provide a longer detection time, but will be positive only after chronic drug use because hair is a minor route of elimination. Also, hair tests seem to be sensitive to cocaine use, but their sensitivity to marijuana usage has not been well established to date (Baumgartner *et al.* 1989).

Generally, the length of time drugs spend in the body varies from class to class. For example, cocaine and some hallucinogens (for example LSD) are present in the body for 12–48 hours. Drugs that are present in the body for 1–3 days include methadone, opiates (heroin, morphine, codeine), proposyphene (Darvon), methaqualone (Quaalude), barbiturates (for example Phenobarbital) and amphetamines (crystal, ice, crank, methamphetamines: 1–2 days). Phencyclidine (PCP) when used occasionally remains present in the body for 1–8 days, whereas when chronic use is present, PCP remains in the body for up to 30 days. Finally, cannabinoids (marijuana) used occasionally are present in the body for 1–7 days, whereas daily chronic use causes cannabinoids to remain present in the body for 1–6 weeks.

Regarding tobacco use, expired carbon monoxide (CO) air samples can be analysed immediately upon collection, with a relatively short half-life (3–5 hours). Thiocyanates (SCN) are found in body fluids, partly as a result of detoxification of hydrogen cyanide in cigarette smoke (Luepker *et al.* 1981), and have a half-life of 10–14 days. However, SCN levels can be inflated by cyanogenic foods, such as cabbage, and can be influenced by factors that change intercellular fluid volume. The measurement of cotinine, a major metabolite of nicotine, is a more precise measure of nicotine intake and has a half-life of 30 hours (2–4 day detection period). A positive test with CO paired with a negative cotinine test could indicate marijuana use.

Summary

Unquestionably, the assessment of substance abuse is essential in evaluating an individual's treatment needs. However, different cut-off levels may be used by different clinicians when deciding whether or not drug users are abusing drugs. Some clinicians may err on the side of caution for the individual – to protect the individual's privacy. Other clinicians may err on the side of caution for society – to protect the society from harm. We speculate that most clinicians err on the side of protecting society. Certainly, some consequences of drug use are given more weight in eliciting a label of drug abuse and ushering people into treatment. For example, being arrested for an income-generating crime, such as armed robbery as a result of a heroin addiction, is obviously a societal, legal problem – one that is placed on the public record, and one in which the perpetrator is likely to be restrained by agents of the public. On the other hand, if an individual has experienced no legal consequences related to their use, and no obvious interpersonal problems, they are less likely to become diagnosed as a drug abuser.

To date, many interview and self-report assessment tools have been developed and implemented to help quantify drug use behaviour and the severity of consequences associated with drug use behaviour. Still, the assessment process remains challenging, and a strong reliance on clinical judgement – guided by public demand – remains the main determinant of whether or not drug users are labelled as drug abusers, drug abusers are deemed able to maintain relative control over their drug use, and co-morbidity with other compulsive problem behaviours or psychiatric diagnoses are determined to be present.

Part **2**

Predictors of drug use and abuse

Extrapersonal predictors of drug abuse

Introduction to predictors of drug use and abuse

The first part of this book presented the general problem of drug abuse – what it is and how to measure it. The second part of the book examines what leads to drug abuse. Drug abuse is a multifactorial biopsychosocial process. The diversity and complexity of factors contributing to the initiation and perpetuation of drug use makes its study particularly challenging. Current theoretical discussions of drug abuse development are based in environmental, social, learning, cognitive/affective and physiological arenas, as well as an integration of these arenas (for example Niaura *et al.* 1988; Petraitis *et al.* 1995; see also Chapter 7 of this book). There are multiple influences and causal pathways that lead to drug abuse. Many suspected influences contributing to the maintenance of drug use are not readily changeable (for example genetics, though the future of genetic engineering looks very promising), whereas many other influences are more amenable to change (for example social influence, unstructured time). Some influences place individuals at risk for future abuse and some influences appear to be protective – that is, help to counteract or inhibit the effects of risk factors of drug abuse (see the discussion on risk and **protective factors** in Chapter 7).

Obviously, not all individuals choose to experiment with drugs of abuse, and not all individuals who experiment with drug use progress to abuse. An individual is exposed to numerous life events, generally over a period of many years (though not always), before experimental use progresses to abuse (Wills *et al.* 1996). There has been a great deal of research and attention focused on drug use behaviours, and there is now some consensus about correlates of drug use, abuse, and dependence. A *correlate* is a variable that tends to co-occur with, vary with, or is associated with the behaviour of interest in a way that is not expected simply on the basis of chance. For example, a relatively obvious correlate of drug abuse is someone's quantity of drug use consumption. The greater the level of current drug use, the greater the likelihood that problems will result (Newcomb and Bentler 1989; Stacy *et al.* 1991).

Prospective studies (that is studies in which a group of individuals who do not use drugs are followed forward in time until they develop a substance use disorder) permit establishment of the order of precedence between drug use and its correlates. If a correlate predicts subsequent drug use, controlling for prior level of drug use, one is somewhat confident that this *predictor* could cause drug use, statistically unconfounded by the converse possibility.

ABCs framework

The *ABCs framework* is an aspect of learning theories that can be applied to the functional analyses of many behaviours (Elder and Stern 1986; Sussman *et al.* 1995a). The idea is that when attempting to understand a behaviour, one can evaluate the **antecedents** or the precursors of the behaviours of interest (A), the topography of the behaviours (for example drug abuse: B) and the consequences or results of the behaviours (C). For example, **peer pressure** to use certain drugs (A or antecedent) can lead to IV drug use (B or behaviour of interest), which can lead to becoming HIV seropositive or drug dependent (C or the consequence of the behaviour). Drug abuse researchers tend to focus on relationships between the antecedents and the behaviour of interest and/or the behaviour and its consequences.

Extrapersonal/intrapersonal domains

An array of *antecedents* preceding drug use and abuse can be roughly broken down into two general domains. The first domain consists of **extrapersonal factors**, including **demographic influences**, environmental, cultural and social variables. These factors or characteristics are exogenous to the individual (that is external to or outside the individual). Extrapersonal factors include interactions with others in different locations and the learning of social behaviours from significant others, especially parents, close friends and role models. It is often difficult to disentangle various *extrapersonal* influences, since many of these influences overlap (for exmaple environmental, **cultural influences** and social influences may be intertwined). The second domain consists of **intrapersonal factors**, which include genetics, **personality** (for example as correlates of neurobiological processes), **affective states** and cognitive factors. These factors or characteristics are endogenous to the individual (that is are influences within the individual). These variables affect the manner in which individuals interact with their environment and influence developmental and socialization processes. It is sometimes difficult to differentiate among intrapersonal influences (for example a sensation seeking personality from one's genetic make-up). Also, it is sometimes difficult to differentiate extrapersonal influences from intrapersonal influences. For example, certain characteristics of role models (extrapersonal: for example alcoholic parents) interact with individual reactivity to the role models (intrapersonal: for example individuals may react to having alcoholic parents by using drugs to cope with emotional distress, or they may seek out positive supports). Research is ongoing to clarify overlap and nonoverlap among these factors.

In this chapter, we address four types of extrapersonal factors that are correlated with, or predict, drug use and abuse: *demographic, environmental, cultural* and *social* influences. Chapter 6 will examine intrapersonal factors, which can account for individual differences affecting drug use and abuse. Chapter 7 will describe different ways that various factors have been included in integrated models that predict drug use and abuse.

Demographic influences on drug use

Generally, demographics are labelled as extrapersonal variables, especially as considered from socio-environmental, sociological or intergroup perspectives. However, demographics also can be construed as intrapersonal factors since they are also inextricably related to genetics studies (for example Newcomb and Earleywine 1996). Examined as extrapersonal variables, as we do in this chapter, how can demographic variables (characteristics of a population) such as gender, age and **ethnicity**, influence one to use or abuse drugs? Demographics most likely reflect associations between *other* predictors and drug use (Newcomb and Earleywine 1996).

Gender

Drug use generally is more prevalent among males than females (Barbor 1994; Johnstone 1994). For example, in most surveys and studies of problematic opiate use, males outnumber females by a ratio varying around 2:1 to 4:1 (Grant 1994). Gender *per se* is a description of group differences, not an explanation of why these group differences exist. Gender differences in drug use might be explained by a consideration of sex-role expectations and differential stigma associated with drug use.

Males are often taught to deal with problems by engaging in goal attainment (instrumental orientation), rather than by talking about difficulties (expressive, nurturing or nurture-seeking orientation). Taking drugs might be one way for men to take action to cope with stress. Women, on the other hand, might be more likely to seek out social support. The magnitude of gender differences currently observed may change among younger cohorts of more recent decades, given changing sex-role expectations. As females pursue more instrumental goals and decrease in tendency towards expressiveness (for example seeking social support), drug use and abuse may increase in prevalence as a maladaptive coping option. On the other hand, women who have multiple roles, such as being a wife and working outside the home, tend to have lower rates of alcohol-related problems than those who do not have multiple roles (Wilsnack *et al.* 1986). Possibly, taking on both instrumental and expressive sex-roles (androgyny) may serve a protective function among women.

There also may be a worldwide expectation that women do not use drugs, that drug use among women may be more stigmatizing than drug use among men. Relatedly, women tend to be under-represented in traditional alcohol and drug treatment programmes, worldwide (US DHHS 1998). Women drug users may fail to seek treatment because they fear loss of custody of their children or access to childcare, they may fear reprisal from authorities, spouses or boyfriends, and they may lack health insurance (Chasnoff 1991).

Gender differences among drug abusers

Women who are drug abusers are different from men who are drug abusers in at least three ways. First, among women in drug abuse treatment, 70 per cent report having been sexually abused in their lifetimes. This is a much higher prevalence of sexual abuse than in the general population. Sexual abuse appears to be a risk factor that affects drug initiation and maintenance of drug use among women. Additionally, female drug users are more likely to be subject to physical victimization than their male counterparts (Brooner *et al.* 1997).

Second, while males have more alcohol-related problems and dependence symptoms than women (Malin *et al.* 1982; Wilsnack *et al.* 1984), *among heavy drinkers*, women are equal to or surpass men in the problems resulting from their alcohol use. Consequences of alcohol consumption appear to be accelerated in women, and chronic alcohol abuse seems to exact greater physiological impairment (for example alcohol-related organ damage) earlier in females, despite consuming less alcohol than males (S. Hill 1984; Tuyns and Pequignot 1984). Female alcoholics (and abusers of other drugs) have death rates 50 to 100 per cent higher than those of male alcoholics, and a greater percentage of female alcoholics die from suicides, alcohol-related accidents, circulatory disorders and cirrhosis of the liver (S. Hill 1982). One may conjecture that women who are heavier users of other drugs may also present relatively greater problems from their drug use.

Third, females have to deal with foetal health risks related to drug use during pregnancy. Several foetal health risks associated with drug use have been identified. For example, cigarette smoking has been associated with low birth weight infants and slowed growth. Foetal Alcohol Syndrome (FAS) is a syndrome associated with high levels of alcohol exposure, and is characterized by facial anomalies, growth retardation and central nervous system deficits. Also, female drug users who are HIV seropositive, or who have hepatitis C, risk transmitting these viruses to their foetuses. Among the total cases of paediatric AIDS in the USA, 54 per cent are related to either maternal injection drug use or maternal sex with an injecting drug user. Additionally, pregnant female drug users are at increased risk for miscarriage, stillbirth, low weight gain, anaemia, thrombocytopeia and hypertension (Hershow *et al.* 1997).

Age

Age is a consistent predictor of alcohol and other drug use. Alcohol use tends to peak between 26 and 34 years of age, and illicit drug use tends to peak between 18 and 25 years of age (Johnstone 1994). This critical period of young adulthood and drug use may reflect the taking on of adult roles, including new jobs and responsibilities, independence in decision-making, and the freedom to purchase alcohol and smoke cigarettes legally. Becoming an adult, without familial constraints, may result in the escalation of use.

Age differences among drug abusers

Teenage drug abuse differs from adult drug abuse in several ways (see Sussman *et al.* 1997a). First, regular use may or may not be considered abuse in adults, whereas it might be considered abuse in youth because of the potential of such use to interfere with developmental growth and adjustment tasks. Second, adolescents may exhibit less physical dependence and fewer physical problems related to use (alcohol, in particular) and consume a lower quantity overall. Alternatively, adolescents may engage in more binge use type behaviour. Third, high-risk situations may differ between adolescents and adults. In particular, adolescents may be relatively likely to use drugs in situations in which they are not responsible for the care taking of others; that is, aside from serving as car drivers (in which they are at highest risk among age groups for fatal accidents). Finally, adolescents have a higher likelihood of suffering social consequences specific to adolescence (for example problems at school, statutory difficulties and truncated development such as early involvement in family creation and divorce: Newcomb and Bentler 1988).

Prescription medication misuse (especially of benzodiazapines, barbiturates and anti-inflammatory drugs) is the most common form of *drug abuse among elderly people.* Many elderly persons frequently ingest two or more prescription medications and may obtain medication from more than one physician. In fact, individuals over age 65 average thirteen prescriptions each year. Physicians are not always aware of medications prescribed by others or alcohol use patterns. The rate of elderly drug misuse and abuse of prescription medications is approximately twice as high as that for other adult age groups, but drug problems may be underestimated or not detected because elderly people are stereotyped as non-users. Drug abuse estimates among individuals over age 55 in the United States range from 500,000 to 2.5 million. This relatively low prevalence may reflect a cohort effect (lack of involvement in drug use for a generation), the reduced survivorship of drug abusers or a maturing-out phenomenon. On the other hand, drug abuse in elderly people may increase threefold over the first quarter of the current millennium as those who began use in the 1960s and thereafter continue to remain users into old age.

Relatively lower quantities of use among elderly people may qualify as abuse because of the potential for drugs of abuse to exert life-threatening consequences. Drug effects on elderly people may be more long lasting because of relatively slower metabolic rates. Slowing metabolic rates, coupled with ingestion of many medications, may result in an increase in the likelihood of harmful drug interactions. Older adults are subject to many significant life changes that put them at risk for drug dependency. These stressful life changes include retirement, excessive leisure time and loss of significant others (that is loss of social networks and social support). Other life adjustments that place elderly people at risk for drug abuse include potential functional loss and deterioration of physical and mental well-being, resulting in increased rates of use of prescription medications.

Ethnicity

In the United States, several researchers have found white ethnicity to be associated with relatively greater drug use among adolescents and adults (Newcomb and Earleywine 1996; Galaif *et al.* 1998; Johnston *et al.* 1999). Perhaps whites achieve less extended familial support, leading to greater drug use as a means of coping. On the other hand, among those with a lifetime history of dependence, African Americans are significantly more likely than Whites to report twelve-month dependence duration. Possibly, once dependent on drugs, disadvantaged minorities have less access to health care, leading to a more sustained period of drug dependence.

These data are not as simple to interpret as they may seem. Ethnicity also interacts with other demographic variables such as age and gender in predicting prevalence of drug abuse. For example, the prevalence of use of alcohol, marijuana, hallucinogens and cocaine among adolescents in the United States tends to be highest among Latino and White males, followed by Latino and White females, then African American males, and then African American females. Alcohol use disorders tend to decline with age among males in White and African American ethnic groups, but increases among African American women as they reach 30 to 44 years of age. Also, across genders among adults, rates of current use of cocaine are approximately 1.4 per cent for African Americans, 0.8 per cent for Latinos and 0.6 per cent for Caucasians. Perhaps taking on, or giving up, key adult responsibilities (jobs, parenthood) may be associated with such apparently complex patterns of drug use.

Asian groups report lower rates of alcohol abuse and dependence than other ethnic groups in the United States. Among some Asian ethnicities, individuals experience what is called a **flushing response** after consuming alcohol. Researchers attribute some observed ethnic differences in the incidence of alcoholism to variation in acetaldehyde degradation and polymorphisms (that is different forms) of the alcohol metabolizing enzymes, alcohol dehydrogenase (ADH) and aldehyde dehydrogenase (ALDH) (responsible for alcohol-induced flushing) (Wall *et al.* 1992). This alcohol sensitivity reaction that many flushers experience is believed to contribute to lower alcohol-related problems (for example they need to drink less alcohol to achieve intense effects). Researchers who examined the relationship between the flushing response and drinking behaviour found that flushers reported drinking significantly less than non-flushers with respect to both frequency and amount (Suzuki *et al.* 1997). On the other hand, Native Americans in the United States, many of whom also exhibit a flushing response, have relatively worse alcohol and drug problems than other groups. Thus, a socially disadvantageous position may contribute to differences in problem use as a function of ethnicity.

Environmental influences on drug use

Environmental antecedents describe the influence of an individual's physical surroundings, including geographical location, dwelling contexts and changes occurring in these contexts (for example disorganization, modernization). Environmental influences that are associated with, and perhaps motivate, experimentation with drugs include neighbourhood disorganization, economic deprivation and availability of drugs (Hawkins *et al.* 1992).

Neighbourhood disorganization refers to a lack of centralized authority, or rapid changeovers of authority, such as to produce insufficient methods or degree of monitoring and regulating behaviours in the community. In a disorganized neighbourhood, one is relatively likely to be exposed to unsanctioned instances of social disobedience, such as public drunkenness, drug dealing and gang-related activities (Skogan and Lurigio 1992). Building structures that provide many enclosed public areas (lack of defensible space), as well as abandoned buildings, lend themselves to a greater incidence of crime perpetration and drug use, and tend to be prevalent in dense, urban, disorganized neighbourhoods.

Adverse socio-economic conditions may limit access to prosocial recreational opportunities (for example money for cinema tickets). Additionally, adverse environmental conditions might also expose one to relatively greater drug-related criminal activity, such as drug sales, as an alternative means of generating income. Relatively low socio-economic status (SES) tends to be associated with greater drug use among adults (Wills *et al.* 1996). For example, the use of crack cocaine is prevalent among economically deprived groups and ethnic minorities who reside in large metropolitan areas. There exists a perennial question: does drug abuse lead to lower SES (downward drift) or does lower SES lead to drug abuse (alternative income or self-medication)?

Among adolescents, influences such as family dynamics and peer group association may affect the relative importance of **socio-economic influences** on drug use. One may conjecture that familial and other social influences protect children from pro-drug influences. However, as young people grow older, these protective influences fade. As adults, lower SES may be associated with a myriad of challenges to self-worth and security. Some young adults may seek out means of self-medication under these disadvantaged circumstances. Conversely, young adults who are successful economically may be able to afford to purchase large quantities of expensive drugs, may become addicted, and then may suffer a rapid descent in SES. Probably, both self-medication and downward drift operate as explanations of the relations of SES with drug abuse.

The *availability* of drugs in a person's environment includes ease of distribution, access and acquisition. *Ease of distribution* refers to the establishment of a 'business' structure, with relatively little resistance to transporting drugs in and out of a location. *Access* refers to an individual's knowledge on where to tap drug supplies along the distribution route. Finally, ease of *acquisition* refers to someone's ability to obtain the drug (for example through establishment of trust, provision of services, or through money). An obvious example of availability would be the presence of drug use in an apartment upstairs from where one lives. Near proximity of drugs in an individual's environment may result in frequent exposure, and may suggest means to acquire the drugs. As a second example, observed regional variation in drug use prevalence has been found within the United States. In particular, residents of communities in the Northeast or West are more likely to use drugs than residents of the Midwest or South (Adams *et al.* 1989; Almog *et al.* 1993; Warner *et al.* 1995). It is likely that differences in use frequency are related to distance from major points of drug distribution (for example New York City and Los Angeles).

Variation in drug abuse worldwide

Worldwide there exists variation in areas of production, distribution, and access, affecting use and abuse. For example, drugs that are strictly controlled in one country might be readily available over-the-counter in another country. In addition, environmental influences overlap with cultural and social influences, affecting the learning of social behaviours. For example, different cultures adopt different building plans that may affect social learning (modelling) of drug use behaviours.

As previously mentioned, the main drugs of abuse worldwide are tobacco (approximately 25 per cent of the population), alcohol (approximately 10 per cent of the population) and marijuana (approximately 2.5 per cent of the population). Approximately 0.5 per cent of the population abuse stimulants, 0.3 per cent abuse cocaine or opioids and up to 0.8 per cent abuse other drugs (for example inhalants, depressants or hallucinogens). About 80 per cent of drug abusers smoke cigarettes and 40 per cent of cigarette smokers abuse other drugs (Sussman 2001b). Points of drug production (for example opium fields), manufacturing (for example heroin creation) and distribution routes tend to identify regions at high risk for abuse. The prevalence of abuse of cocaine, heroin and cannabis, according to summaries of statistics on treatment admissions, drug arrests and self-report surveys are as follows (US DEA 1996; US DEA-NNICC 1997; US DHHS 1998; White 1999; see also Table 5.1).

1 Most cocaine is currently produced and manufactured in Colombia. For distribution, it travels through Mexico and the Caribbean to different markets; generally first throughout the Americas, then onward to Europe. Cocaine-type drugs dominate in North and South America. Cocaine-type drugs (cocaine, crack-cocaine and basuco (coca paste)) are predominant in all countries in the Americas (nineteen countries). Cocaine-type drugs are responsible for close to 60 per cent of all treatment cases in the Americas. Among the larger countries in the Americas (United States, Mexico and Brazil), approximately 30 per cent of treatment demand is related to cocaine abuse. In Europe, 3 per cent of treatment admissions are for cocaine abuse. Traffickers based in South American countries, Japan, United States and Nigeria bring cocaine to Asia. Thus, abuse of cocaine is spreading out all over the world, though highest abuse is along the production centres and distribution routes.

2 Currently 95 per cent of opium is grown in Myanmar (Burma) and Afghanistan. Much of the opium travels out from Myanmar into China and into Canada and the United States. It also travels from Myanmar, through Malaysia and into western Europe. Opium leaves Afghanistan through Turkey, northern Pakistan, Central Asia and Russia, then to Europe or the United States. The majority of treatment admissions in South Asia and East Asia are for heroin abuse. In most parts of Europe, the main problem drugs are opiates (mostly heroin abuse). Approximately 70 per cent of treatment demand in Europe is linked to opiates.

3 Cannabis is grown all over the world. However, major hot spots of production and distribution are California in the United States, Mexico, Jamaica, Amsterdam, Cambodia (from where it makes its way to Europe through Malaysia) and the Philippines. In America and Europe, cannabis is the second largest drug creating treatment demand (9 per cent of treatment admissions in Europe are for cannabis abuse). In Asia, cannabis is the third largest problem drug. Treatment for cannabis abuse is quite diffusely spread out around the world.

Cultural influences on drug use

Cultural precursors of behaviour include intergenerational, geographically derived group differences that impact their members. Examples of cultural

Table 5.1 International drug abuse: a sampling of eight regions ('ballpark' per cent primary drugs of abuse)

Location	Heroin	Alcohol	Cannabis	Other opiates	Stimulants	Depressants	Inhalants	Cocaine	'White pipe'[a]
East Asia	57	14	8	5	5				
South Asia	61	18	6	11					
Australia		70	13		2				
Canada	6	70	23		1	4			
Mexico		23	42				20	6	
Central America		70	16					13	
Western Europe	60	10	20		10	15		15	
South Africa		75	7						7

Note: [a] 'White pipe' consists of Mandrax, a tranquillizer, which is sprinkled on marijuana and smoked; multiple categories can be endorsed within each location
Source: extrapolated from US DHHS 1998
For additional reading see Petraitis *et al.* 1995; Wills *et al.* 1996

antecedents that might affect drug use include life habits and rituals that are important and meaningful to the group, normative structures and expectations (cultural morality), and beliefs and attitudes about reasons for drug use and drug effects. Culture might help determine which drugs are available, preferable and highly valued at a given time, whether experimentation is acceptable, and what one's expectations about the effects of a drug might be (Heath 1999).

An example of a 'life habit' and 'normative structure' is the regular use of wine with meals in France. Some children in France learn that wine is a food rather than merely an alcoholic beverage; they learn to drink wine with meals and are able to buy wine in stores. On the other hand, in the United States, it is illegal for individuals less than 21 years old to buy alcohol and children are not supposed to drink any alcohol. Another example of a normative structure pertains to the acceptance, availability and recreational use of marijuana and hashish in the Netherlands (as part of a harm reduction approach: see Chapter 9), whereas in the United States even the medical use of marijuana is highly controversial. As an example of a 'ritual' which involves 'beliefs pertaining to drug use', one unique cultural influence is the use of peyote, a hallucinogen, by certain groups of Native Americans in the Church for Spiritual Enlightenment (in the United States: Julien 1998). Cross-culturally, looking across several countries, a defining characteristic of whether or not people suffer from drug abuse appears to be their ability to perform their culturally specific roles. If they are viewed as unable to carry out their life roles because of drug use, they are considered to be a drug abuser (Quintero and Nichter 1996).

Another important cultural construct is acculturation (Diaz-Guerrero 1984). This construct pertains to *changes* in cultural rituals, norms or beliefs. New cultural influences may interface with a person's native culture, or the person may move to a location that provides a new host culture. Generally, acculturation is defined as the degree to which individuals adopt or prefer a culture to which they are more recently exposed. The degree to which a group or individual distance themselves from their native culture increases as more time is spent in the environment of a different culture (that is acculturation can be construed as a social learning process: Szalay *et al.* 1993). Level of acculturation in the new environment can affect drug use through exposure to cultural attitudes towards use or expectations of drug effects. Drug use or abuse might also occur when individuals are separated from traditional cultural groups that might discourage drug use. Alternatively, the stress resulting from failure to bond successfully to a new culture may increase the probability of drug use.

Finally, an important macro-level sociocultural influence affecting drug use initiation and experimentation is the increasing role of the media and worldwide access to information. The worldwide web now provides incredible access to information about drugs of abuse and means of producing these drugs. Different cultures may influence others' beliefs regarding drug use to the extent that they use a shared language on the web (for example www.legalize.org/global/). Also, television and films may inadvertently promote drug use by conveying images of role models or idols, such as rock stars, romancing heroin addiction, models who are tough chain smokers, film stars happily addicted to alcohol, or rappers who like to sing about marijuana (Sussman *et al.* 1996c). Cinema images, in particular, are likely to be viewed internationally, and influence the host culture within which they are viewed. Even if an individual does not attend to images portrayed by the media, the *mere exposure* to these images has been shown to affect preferences for objects (for more about the mere exposure effect and preference literature, see Kunst-Wilson and Zajonc 1980; Zajonc 1980). But do these preferences influence choice behaviour? Should the media be required to reduce the glamorization of drug use in the movies and on television? Should the media be required to provide more realistic portrayals of consequences of use, abuse or dependence?

Clearly the media are important sources of information and, as such, influence behavioural options. Researchers have shown that repeated exposure to images affects reactions and preferences (Theus 1994). For example, advertisements that associate smoking with excitement-seeking cues and social popularity have been shown to be important influences in the onset of smoking (see Wills *et al.* 1996). Media coverage of health risks or benefits associated with drug use may influence use patterns among large groups of individuals. For instance, media reports of beneficial health effects of wine drinking may rouse changes in beliefs among the population, and change or increase patterns of drinking. The media have the ability to diffuse information quite rapidly affecting large groups. The potential international cultural impact of the media cannot be overstated.

Media exposure makes available information that may have been formerly unavailable. For example, repeated exposure to alcohol advertising may render drinking or drug use behaviour more accessible in memory. Repeated exposure to advertising coupled with images of idols or role models who use drugs can be a toxic combination. Those predisposed or at risk to use or abuse drugs, and those already using, may selectively attend to or expose themselves to advertisements, images and media programmes for reinforcement of their beliefs and behaviours. Consequently, awareness of the range of drug use or drinking options and stimuli may increase. Conversely, they may tend to ignore other anti-drug use information that is portrayed through the same or other channels.

Social influences on drug use

Social antecedents of drug use include the characteristics of the people in an individual's support system, and describe the various effects the group has on the individual. The values and behaviours of parents, siblings, friends, peers and role models affect the learning experiences of individuals. *Social support* pertains to the assistance that people in social networks give each other. *Social networks* describe connections among individuals – that is, different relationships (for example friends, colleagues). There are various types of social support individuals can offer each other (for example companionship, instrumental, conformity, informational), all of which may be important in the development of drug use and abuse. For example, observing friends who seem to be enjoying drug use may make one more curious about drug use; friends may provide an 'informational' type of support. Also, one may want to use drugs in order to have others with whom to spend time ('companion' type of support). Alternatively, social support may directly influence an individual's behaviour (for example peer pressure to use drugs; 'conformity' type of support; drugs may be purchased by friends or family; 'instrumental' support).

Differential socialization refers to the channelling of the development of beliefs, intentions, expectations, perceptions and modelling of social behaviours. For instance, socialization processes may lead to beliefs and perceptions that drug use is tolerable by others in one's social environment (Akers *et al.* 1979). This may affect an individual's intention to initiate use. Family conflict, poor supervision or drug-use tolerance by parents, family modelling of drug-using behaviour and deviant peer group association are processes of differential socialization that have been found to be influential in experimental drug use (for review, see Hawkins *et al.* 1992).

Researchers in social psychology report two main types of pressure the peer group exerts on its members (see Sussman *et al.* 1995a). First, **normative social influence** is described as wanting members to act consistently with the group to gain or maintain acceptance of other group members. Second, **informational social influence** is described as wanting members of the group to share similar attitudes about the frequencies of various behaviours and their social meanings. In turn, for yielding to normative or informational social influence attempts, the group provides social reinforcers. These reinforces are various social supports. Researchers have consistently demonstrated that one of the strongest predictors of drug use among teens is friend and peer use of drugs (Barnes and Welte 1986; Kandel and Andrews 1987). The deviant peer group tends to use drugs, will offer drugs at times, and will role model drug use. Social influence is especially important as a predictor of drug use and abuse among teens.

Social cognitive/learning theory

One theory that is, perhaps, a specification of informational social influence, is social cognitive/learning theory. According to social cognitive/learning theory (Bandura 1986), drug use can develop through vicarious learning, modelling and/or through reinforcing pharmacological drug effects. In other words, role models act as teachers of where and when, how much, and how a drug is used. For example, one might learn that it is acceptable to drink alcohol at celebrations on weekends. Role models also teach the probable outcomes of drug use (for example that moderate alcohol use enhances social interaction) and how to use certain drugs (for example to drink wine from a wine glass and beer from a beer mug). Social/cognitive learning theory also helps explain how involvement with deviant peers (that is modelling of peer norms and other social agents) affects beliefs about drug use and consequences. It is important to note that processes of social learning (for example watching others use drugs within a different culture) affect cultural perceptions and meanings; cultural antecedents overlap with social antecedents.

Summary

This chapter addressed a variety of extrapersonal influences that contribute to drug use – demographics, environmental factors, cultural factors and social factors. Many of these extrapersonal influences overlap. And, while exposure to numerous extrapersonal influences might place an individual at risk for use, they alone cannot explain why some individuals who use drugs go on to abuse them and others do not. Disentangling the aetiologic web of drug use and abuse, understanding the diversity and various levels of influence of correlates and predictors, is a daunting task. The need to continue exploring prediction models of use and abuse, and to identify at-risk individuals among diverse populations, exists because of the implications for the health and well-being of individuals and society. The next chapter considers the set of intrapersonal predictors of use and abuse – those factors that operate within individuals.

6

Intrapersonal predictors of drug abuse

Processes contributing to individual differences in drug use include **physiological susceptibility** as measured in studies of **genetic heritability** and neurobiological processes, personality traits, affective states, cognition, including expectancies as a motivation to engage in drug use behaviour, and memory processes. Relative to extrapersonal factors, intrapersonal factors likely play a more active role following initiation of drug use and help explain why some individuals who use do not go on to abuse while others do.

Physiological susceptibility

Genetic heritability

Research on the genetic heritability of numerous drugs of abuse is ongoing (for example opiates, marijuana: Kendler and Prescott 1998; Reich 2000), although a majority of this work has focused on genetic predisposition to alcoholism. Genetics may determine metabolic processes involving differential effects of drugs. Alternatively, genetics may indirectly influence drug abuse through its influence on such precursors as individual temperament or personality, such that one becomes vulnerable to alcohol or other drug abuse (for example Schuckit 1987). Although research suggests that genetic heritability may be a possible explanation for intergenerational familial alcoholism or other drug problems, it is difficult to disentangle genetic-environmental interactions (Sher 1993; Sher *et al.* 1997). In other words, individuals who seem genetically predisposed to drug abuse may also live in social environments that are conducive to drug abuse (for example have family members who use). It has been argued that adoption studies, in which genetic factors are investigated among family members who are reared in different social environments, may help control for non-genetic factors. Adoption studies reveal that approximately 30 per cent of sons of alcoholic fathers themselves become alcoholic and that approximately half of all individuals hospitalized for alcoholism have a family history of alcoholism (Hawkins *et al.* 1992). Interestingly, other genetics work suggests that brother–brother co-occurrence of alcoholism may be as high as 50 per cent – higher than the father–son association (Reich 2000). Thus, there would appear to be a genetic component to alcoholism, or other drug abuse, although there are other factors that operate as well.

Researchers have not yet identified one gene or an inherited quality that single-handedly leads to alcoholism or drug abuse (although currently there is some suggestion that Chromosome 1 peculiarities may signal risk for alcoholism: Reich 2000). However, significant strides have been made in understanding the actions of addictive drugs on neuronal circuitry and neurotransmitter systems. Animal researchers also have contributed to our understanding of the role of genetics by breeding rodent strains that willingly self-administer certain drugs at high rates (Li *et al.* 1993). Still, animals do not self-administer all drugs, and some drugs they administer inconsistently. For instance, animals do not tend to self-administer cannabinoids and inconsistently self-administer phencyclidine (that is PCP) (Brust 1999). Continued research addressing heritability of individual variation in neurobiological processes of reinforcement, dependence, tolerance and sensitization or reverse tolerance may help increase our understanding of the heritability of a variety of drugs of abuse (Blum *et al.* 1997; Brust 1999).

Neurobiological processes

Variations in neurochemical systems may influence individual differences in reinforcing effects of drugs (Olson *et al.* 1992; Cloninger *et al.* 1993; Zuckerman 1993; Cloninger 1994; Hegerl *et al.* 1995). Susceptibility to the reinforcing effects of drugs may be governed by an interaction of the dopaminergic and serotonergic systems, as well as the endogenous opioid system (Olson *et al.* 1992; Kranzler and Anton 1994). Although the exact nature of the interaction has not been clearly defined, drugs may potentiate the dopaminergic reward system (neurons ascending from the substantia nigra and ventral tegmental area or mesolimbocortical pathways: Wise 1988; Gray 1990; Kuhar *et al.* 1991). Regulation of the serotonergic system may be altered by drug use, and serotonin may be implicated in the maintenance of pleasure. A dysregulation of the opioid system may influence individual differences in reinforcing effects of drugs (Olson *et al.* 1992; Cloninger *et al.* 1993; Zuckerman 1993; Cloninger 1994; Hegerl *et al.* 1995).

Dopamine has been thought to be of primary importance. The neurotransmitter, dopamine, through interactions with various neuronal systems, affects aspects of addictive behaviours including arousal, reward and motivation. Dopaminergic activity is associated with pleasure (Phillips 1984; Wise and Bozarth 1984; DiChiara 1998), and the encoding and processing of proximal stimuli associated with pleasurable or rewarding experiences

(Montague *et al.* 1996). Increased dopamine transmission in the nucleus accumbens reinforces the repetition of behaviours, influencing learning and strengthening associations of reinforcing effects. There is evidence that rewarding affective experiences are mediated by mesolimbic dopaminergic neurons (Phillips 1984; Melis and Argiolas 1995; Pfaus *et al.* 1995; Van Furth and Van Ree 1996) and that the nucleus accumbens is a brain region associated with reward, motivation, addiction and learning (Setlow 1997).

Personality traits

There is some agreement that *sensation seeking* is important as a personality trait, manifested in individuals likely to be susceptible to the reinforcing effects of pleasurable stimuli, including drug effects. Zuckerman (1994) conceptualized sensation seeking as 'a trait defined by the seeking of varied, novel, complex, and intense sensations and experiences, and the willingness to take physical, social, legal, and financial risk for the sake of such experience' (Zuckerman 1994: 27). Of course, a willingness to take such risks entails potential consequences, including that of drug abuse. Sensation seekers may be more eager to seek out and adopt any new behaviours, even when those behaviours carry potential negative consequences, because of a biologically derived preference for stimulation. Sensation seeking as a construct has been found to be positively related to and predictive of alcohol use (Stacy *et al.* 1993), smoking (Zuckerman *et al.* 1990), sexual behaviour, and other drug use (Newcomb and McGee 1991; Ames *et al.* 1999). Additionally, sensation seeking has been shown to be a significant predictor of problem consequences of alcohol consumption (Stacy *et al.* 1991) and early-onset alcoholism (Zuckerman 1987; Cloninger *et al.* 1988). Stacy *et al.* (1993) found that sensation seeking and certain cognitive motivation indicators independently predicted driving under the influence and predicted alcohol use. Early drug use experiences – whether they involve experimentation with drugs or mere exposure to drug use behaviours (for example in media messages, observations) – may be highly enticing for individuals high in sensation seeking.

Childhood and adolescent personality characteristics associated with drug use include not only sensation seeking, but also several other personal dispositions. One such personality trait is **impulsivity** or lack of behavioural inhibition (Jessor and Jessor 1977; Earleywine and Finn 1991). Impulsivity refers to the tendency to act immediately in response to stimuli without consideration of consequences or various behavioural options. Individuals may continually choose drug use as a behavioural choice, to achieve initial positive effects, if they do not give delayed negative consequences much thought. Another trait is *lack of regulation*, such as behavioural undercontrol (Sher 1991). While individuals may be able to think before they act, they may seem unable to regulate the extent of their behavioural responses. They may over-react or under-react to circumstances, leading them to seek means to regulate their reactions (for example through drug use). A third trait is the *inability to bond*, relate or connect with institutions and significant others (Newcomb and Earleywine 1996). While individuals may be able to think before acting, and may be able to regulate the extent of their reactions, they may still have difficulty obtaining a sense of belonging to institutions or groups of people because of academic problems, a unique pattern of interests, or access to resources. They may lack a sense of coherence about their lives (see Antonovsky 1984). Drug use may provide a superficial means of bonding to others. Finally, dispositional attitudes such as *unconventionality*, rebelliousness and tolerance of deviance are obvious correlates of counternormative behaviours such as drug use.

Affective states

The relief of a negative affective state or the expectancy of a desired affective state may motivate an individual who has engaged in drug-taking behaviour to continue to use, and for those in recovery, to lapse or relapse. Several negative affective states have been found to influence relapse among adults, including anger, sadness, boredom, anxiety, depression, guilt, apprehension and anticipation of stressful events (Marlatt and Gordon 1985; L. Miller 1991). Among at-risk young people, anger and depression have been found to be associated with substance abuse or dependence (Sussman *et al.* 1997a). Although the co-morbidity of substance abuse and some mood disorders is high (Kushner and Sher 1993; Newcomb and Earleywine 1996) the order of precedence in the **web of causation** between drug use and mood is not clear. In other words, it is not clear whether these mood states or traits generally precede or are the result of drug use. Drug use could make people eventually feel more depressed or angry, through drug effects on neurotransmitter systems, withdrawal symptom experiences, or psychological dependence (V.E. Johnson 1980). If mood states precede drug use, this may suggest biological vulnerability to drug use, that is, the existence of those who use drugs to 'self-medicate'.

The *self-medication hypothesis* of addictive disorders has been advanced by several researchers (for example Uhlenhuth *et al.* 1981; Khantzian 1985). This theoretical approach suggests that individuals use drugs as a means of controlling unpleasant feelings. Substantial empirical evidence supports the contention that individuals seek out drugs as a means of self-medicating or averting negative affective states (Khantzian 1985; Deykin *et al.* 1987; Teichman *et al.* 1989; Swanson *et al.* 1992; Henry *et al.* 1993). Further, this notion suggests that individuals' drug of choice is the result of an interaction between a perceived negative affective state and the psychopharmacologic action of the drug (for example people may use cocaine to achieve different effects than alcohol). This other aspect of the self-medication hypothesis has as yet not received much support.

Cognitive motivation or expectancies as behavioural motivators

Since Rotter (1954) first proposed expectancy theory, variations of the formulation of expectancy as a cognitive construct have been applied to research on alcohol and drug use (for a review, see Leigh 1989). Expectancy as a construct (more specifically outcome expectancies) is generally conceptualized as the anticipated consequences of behaviour or beliefs held about alcohol and other drug effects (Brown *et al.* 1980; Goldman *et al.* 1991; Leigh and Stacy 1991; Stacy *et al.* 1991; Leigh and Stacy 1993). For example, an expected consequence or outcome of alcohol use may include feeling more relaxed. Expectancies have both cognitive (that is informational) and motivational components (that is affective incentive: Marlatt and Gordon 1985). Expectancies as a cognitive mediator of behaviour have been used to explain both volitional and non-volitional behaviours (Stacy *et al.* 1990b). Several researchers have provided evidence that outcome expectancies are correlated with alcohol use and contribute to the initiation and maintenance of alcohol use (for example Leigh and Stacy 1993; Rather and Goldman 1994; Sussman *et al.* 1996a). Moreover, positive expectancies appear to be more proximal and more reliable predictors of drug use than negative expectancies. In other words, when individuals initially observe drug use or experiment with drugs, it is more likely that they will experience a positive outcome than a negative outcome (Stacy *et al.* 1990a, 1990b; Fromme *et al.* 1997). Information about the use of alcohol and other drugs and their effects can be gathered among youth based on individual differences in exposure to drug-use-related situations, through observational learning, and through early personal experiences with use (Goldman *et al.* 1991; Dunn and Goldman 1996). Please note that extrapersonal variables, such as social experiences, can influence the development of an intrapersonal variable such as outcome expectancies.

Expectancies as components of memory processes

Various researchers have conceptualized cognition involving outcomes of drug use (that is expectancies) as components of a memory process thought to influence decisions about alcohol and drug use (for example Stacy *et al.* 1990b; Goldman *et al.* 1991; Rather and Goldman 1994; Stacy 1995). In this perspective, the motivation to perform a behaviour at a given moment may be a function of one's memory of the anticipated consequences of the behaviour. As an example, in an implicit cognition approach to drug use, outcome expectancies are predictive associations that are stored in long-term memory between the concept of alcohol or drug use and associated outcomes (Stacy *et al.* 1994; Weingardt *et al.* 1996).

Theoretical perspectives of memory processes and drug use motivation

Cognitive models developed during investigation of general memory processes have been applied to addiction research. These models propose that memory is a key mediator of alcohol and drug use (Tiffany 1990; Goldman *et al.* 1991; Earleywine and Martin 1993; Rather and Goldman 1994; Roehrich and Goldman 1995; Stacy 1995; Dunn and Goldman 1996; Stacy *et al.* 1996; Weingardt *et al.* 1996; Stacy 1997). In addiction research, assessment of cognition frequently entails use of judgements of perceived alcohol and drug effects, such as outcome expectancies, beliefs, reasons and reports of urges (for example Stacy *et al.* 1990b; Rather *et al.* 1992; Earleywine and Martin 1993; Fromme *et al.* 1993; Rather and Goldman 1994). However, these variables do not necessarily measure long-term memory processes hypothesized to influence drug use behaviour and motivation to use (Stacy *et al.* 1996; Weingardt *et al.* 1996). Measures of implicit cognitive processes have been adopted as an alternative focus in assessing long-term memory for drug use motivation (for example Earleywine and Martin 1993; Roehrich and Goldman 1995; Stacy 1995; Stacy *et al.* 1996; Weingardt *et al.* 1996; Stacy 1997; Ames and Stacy 1998).

Implicit cognition theory (ICT)

In an ICT approach, memory associations are established and strengthened through repetitive experience with alcohol or drugs (see Stacy 1995, 1997). Stacy (1995) proposed that associations of behavioural outcomes and cue-behaviour have motivational significance; a strong memory association between a behaviour and its outcome suggests that when an outcome is thought about, the behavioural option becomes salient and is strongly activated in memory. Additionally, through repeated drug use, specific cues (for example drug stimuli) automatically activate thoughts about drug use, triggering patterns of behaviour associated with use. In an ICT approach, individuals differ in the strength of associations in memory between cues (for example a party) and behaviours (drug use) and outcomes (for example feeling more relaxed). Whether or not a drug-consistent cognitive state and propensity to use drugs are easily activated in a variety of situations is determined by the strength of associations (Stacy 1995; Stacy *et al.* 1996; Weingardt *et al.* 1996; Stacy 1997). When memories of aspects of an event or a set of concepts are strongly activated, it implies that attributes of the same or related events are highly accessible. This pattern of activation of concepts in memory greatly influences a person's decision to use drugs. Individuals' thought processes, judgements and interpretations of a situation will be highly influenced by strongly activated concepts resulting in the performance of behaviours related to that concept (Stacy 1995; Stacy *et al.* 1996; Stacy 1997). Moreover, it is improbable that healthy behavioural decisions or competing concepts are activated simultaneously when a drug-consistent activation pattern has been elicited.

In an implicit cognition approach to drug use, individual differences are partially accounted for by suggesting that differences in physiological reward systems differentially influence the development of memory traces of past experiences with drug use. Specifically, the accessibility and activation of memory traces of a past experience are dependent on individuals' experiences with drug use (Wise 1988; Stacy *et al.* 1994; Stacy 1995, 1997). Stacy and his colleagues have demonstrated that manipulations of the accessibility of drug-related cognition from memory may influence drug use decisions (Stacy *et al.* 1990a). They have also demonstrated that measures of implicit memory for drug effects predict drug use cross-sectionally and prospectively (Stacy *et al.* 1994; Stacy 1995, 1997; Ames and Stacy 1998). Implicit cognition theory has recently been applied to another problem behaviour, HIV-risk behaviour (Stacy *et al.* 2000).

Various other investigators have demonstrated links between alcohol and other drug use and implicit cognitive assessments (for example A. Hill and Paynter 1992; Earleywine 1994; Doherty and Szalay 1996; Szalay *et al.* 1996; Stormack and Hugdahl 1997; Stormack *et al.* 2000). In addition, Tiffany (1990) used an implicit cognition approach to explain theoretically how automatic memory processes might motivate addictive behaviour. In Tiffany's *automaticity approach*, extended practice of a task should result in performance that requires little or no attention, concentration, or effort to execute.

Semantic network model of drug use

A theoretical framework advanced by Goldman and his colleagues involves the application of a semantic network of associations in memory to explain motivation to use alcohol (for example Goldman *et al.* 1991; Rather and Goldman 1994; Roehrich and Goldman 1995; Dunn and Goldman 1996). Goldman and his colleagues place alcohol expectancies into a 'memory framework by modeling expectancies as units (nodes) of information about specific outcomes of alcohol use located in a symbolic network' (Dunn and Goldman 1996: 209). They propose that exposure to alcohol stimuli results in spreading activation among nodes within the network. Goldman and his colleagues produced plots depicting a dimensional structure of alcohol expectancies as a function of different levels of alcohol consumption (Rather *et al.* 1992; Rather and Goldman 1994). They extended their research by empirically modelling an alcohol expectancy memory network among children (Dunn and Goldman 1996).

Summary

Although many of the factors discussed in this chapter may predispose someone to become an abuser if they use drugs, most individuals do not become

Table 6.1 Summary table of extrapersonal and intrapersonal factors affecting drug use

Extrapersonal influences	Intrapersonal influences
Demographics Age, gender, ethnicity, socio-economic status and family structure	*Demographics* Some demographics can be construed as intrapersonal factors
Environmental • Geographical location, regional variation • Dwellings and dwelling contents • Laws and norms favourable to drug use • Economic deprivation/neighbourhood disorganization • Availability of drugs including ease of access, distribution and drug acquisition	*Physiological Susceptibility* • Genetic heritability (no one gene or inherited quality single-handedly leads to substance abuse) • Variations in neurochemical systems may influence individual differences in reinforcing effects of drugs • Personality correlates of neurobiological processes (sensation seeking, impulsivity), dispositional traits (lack of regulation such as behavioural undercontrol, inability to bond, unconventionality)
Social • Characteristics of the person's support system, effects the group has on the individual • Values and behaviours of parents, siblings, friends, peers and role models; family and peer modelling of drug-using behaviour • Peer pressure to use drugs, deviant peer group association • Family conflict, poor supervision by parents or their tolerance of drug use • Lack of commitment to conventional institutions	*Affective states* • Possibly inherited, less than optimal neurochemistry (could be construed as susceptibility) • Self-medication of negative affective states or emotional distress *Cognitive Processes* • Explicit or reflective cognitive processes including judgements of perceived alcohol and drug effects, outcome expectancies, beliefs, reasons, and reports of urges • Implicit cognition theories (that is memory associations between the behaviour and its outcomes, and cues and the behaviour, are motivationally significant) • Automaticity • Semantic network models
Macro-level sociocultural • The media and worldwide access to information • Cultural habits • Acculturation processes	

For additional reading see Khantzian 1985; Newcomb and Earlywine 1996 drug abusers overnight. There are a variety of events that are likely to occur in the process or progression towards abuse. Substance abuse arises from repetitive experiences and learned associations between events that are meaningful to the individual. If an individual is physiologically susceptible, that is, if the individual gets a 'bigger bang' from the pharmacological effects of a drug (that is the pleasurable experience is relatively intense), then that person may more readily repeat the experience. An intricate interplay of physiological reward mechanisms (Bozwarth 1994; Kranzler and Anton 1994), affective and cognitive individual difference variables (Marlatt and Gordon 1985), and environmental and social influences affect the development of substance abuse and dependence. Table 6.1 presents a summary of the extrapersonal and intrapersonal variables that have been presented in this chapter and Chapter 5. The next chapter presents several theories that attempt to integrate a range of intrapersonal and extrapersonal influences.

7

Integrated theories of drug abuse

There are many means of studying the aetiology of drug abuse but no clear-cut explanations as to why some individuals who experiment with drugs go on to abuse them and others do not. Drug abuse appears to be a multifactorial process. To provide a more comprehensive understanding of the development of drug use and abuse, researchers combine single-factor type models (presented in Chapters 5 and 6) through use of various decision rules to create integrated models. That is, integrated models (or **integrated theories**, the terms 'models' and 'theories' are used interchangeably here) are defined as models that utilize two or more single-factors in a poly-factor model combined, based on some a priori rules of combination. Several different integrated substantive models have been developed. One simple means of integration has been simply to add single concepts or predictors together. This approach has been referred to as the 'risk and protective factors' of drug abuse. A second approach has been carefully to delineate non-overlapping factors, and then combine factors together. This approach has been used in different **biopsychosocial models**. A third approach has been to take a more deductive, theoretical scheme, as has been the case with **functional meanings** models, the 'problem behaviour model' or **triadic influence theory**. Other means of combining single-factor type models include **stage modelling** (predictors of onset, experimentation, regular use, abuse and dependence) and integrating variables at different 'distances' from drug use behaviour (distal/environmental–proximal/intrapersonal). Finally, one might go back to the drawing board and consider a simple, **hedonic treadmill** model as the root of drug abuse. A return to a simple model might help rectify the myriad of idiographic peculiarities in the paths leading to drug abuse. A summary of these approaches is depicted in Table 7.1.

Table 7.1 Summary table of integrative theories

Risk and protective factors model
Combines various factors that place someone at risk for future abuse and factors that are protective or counteract the effects of risk.

Biopsychosocial models
Groups risk factors according to biological, psychological and social categories.

Theoretical models
- *Functional meanings models*: individuals use drugs recreationally/socially, symbolically/ritualistically, for utilitarian purposes, or for medical purposes. These meanings may overlap.
- *Problem behaviour theory*: problem behaviours reflect problem proneness, determined by interaction of personality, behavioural and perceived environmental systems.
- *Triadic influence theory*: integrative model that groups fourteen theories into three substantive domains – interpersonal, attitudinal/cultural and intrapersonal – with distances from performance of drug use – ultimate, distal and proximal.

Stage modelling
Addresses the influence of correlates and predictors in the history of individuals' drug use, that operates at various stages – initiation, experimentation, use and abuse.

Distal and proximal factors
Proposes that predictors of drug use be at different plausible distances from drug experiences.

Hedonic treadmill model
Proposes that drug use is essentially the pursuit of pleasure, which derails. Can a good theory of drug abuse be this simple?

For additional reading see Hawkins *et al.* 1992; Kandel *et al.* 1992

Risk and protective factors model

Risk factors for drug abuse are those diverse factors that contribute to the initiation and continuation of drug use. Genetic predisposition, relatively young age of drug use, perception of risk, aggression, impulsiveness, chaotic home environments, ineffective parenting, lack of attachment to parents, failure in school, poor social and coping skills, negative peer influence and poverty – among other predictors – all contribute to the later development of drug abuse. Some risk factors are more difficult to change (for example genetics) than others (for example social influences, unstructured time).

Alternatively, protective factors are those characteristics that reduce the risk of substance abuse and promote positive development. Cooperativeness, social competence, attachment to parents, family supervision, having conventional friends, high achievement in school, neighbourhood cohesiveness and lack of drug availability are among factors that have been found to be protective against drug use (Bry *et al.* 1982; Hawkins *et al.* 1992; Smith *et al.* 1995; V. Johnson and Pandina 2001). Most of these risk and protective factors were introduced, simply as predictors, in Chapters 5 and 6.

Risk and protective factors show cumulative effects on the prediction of drug use and abuse. One can combine these factors additively, and will see that the more risk factors individuals have, the more likely it is that individuals will use and abuse drugs in the future (Bry *et al.* 1982). However, different factors may vary in importance for different groups or stages of use (V. Johnson and Pandina 2001). Depending on the outcome of interest, these factors may differ in the manner in which they affect outcomes (direct or indirect effect), in their strength of impact (low, medium or high), and in their stability (relatively stable or dynamic condition). These factors also appear to form a rough qualitative continuum. They range from simple markers (that is surface indicators including gender and race) to moderators (for example augmenting influences, such as the presence of a co-morbid disease or disorder) to mediators (primary causal mechanisms, such as exposure to drug use) of dysfunctional outcomes (Johnson and Pandina 2001).

Biopsychosocial models

These models demonstrate the attempt to group risk factors according to biological, psychological and social categories. Individuals are differentially vulnerable to drug abuse through certain genetic mechanisms, psychological attitudes and social groupings. This general type of model suggests the need to consider radically different sources of predictors, and it highlights the need for persons from different disciplines to work together to better understand drug abuse. This paradigm views dysfunctional behaviour generically as a product of not only specific neurobiological, psychobehavioural and socio-environmental factor arrays, but also as a product of the complex and dynamic interaction of factors (Johnson and Pandina 2001). This type of model helps to place different sets of predictors into different categories. The biopsychosocial notion itself is a means of grouping, a tool, a heuristic method.

Theoretical models

Functional meanings models

Some theoretical models of the aetiology of drug use and abuse are those that examine functional meanings. That is, one may come to understand the aetiology of drug use by uncovering what using drugs 'means' to individuals. Different individuals may use drugs for different or multiple reasons. Individuals use drugs for at least four general reasons. First, drugs may be used *recreationally* and to *promote social interaction*. Drugs disinhibit individuals and can enhance the speech frequency, if not quality, of social interactions. Ultimately, however, recreational or social use, including 'partying' and 'clubbing', may become a high-risk lifestyle. Drugs adversely affect judgement, including judgements that place both adults and adolescents at risk for negative consequences.

Second, alcohol and drugs may be used *symbolically* and *ritualistically*. For instance, in parts of Africa the exchange of a few cola nuts (stimulants) is a necessary prerequisite to the opening of marriage, or to assist financial and political negotiations (Pickering and Stimson 1994). In the Andes of South America, coca leaves are used as offerings to deities and to dead ancestors. Peyote is used ritualistically by the Huichol Indians of Mexico and Native American Indians in the United States for spiritual and personal revelation. The Mazatec Indians of Mexico use hallucinogenic mushrooms in religious and medically diagnostic ceremonies (Heath 1999). Wine is used in the Catholic Church as a symbol of the blood of Christ, and to promote joviality at Jewish festivals (for example at Passover). Worldwide, alcohol is frequently used symbolically to celebrate special events (for example weddings, New Year's Eve) or as a reward for achieving a goal (for example being promoted in one's job, earning a college degree).

Third, drugs may be used for *utilitarian* purposes. The use of drugs as some means to an end (that is utility) differs from recreational use. For example, truck drivers, students and various night workers have used a variety of stimulants to help them stay awake and alert. During the Second World War, stimulants were distributed to British, American and Japanese troops to raise morale and improve fighting ability (Pickering and Stimson 1994). Adolescents may use drugs to elevate status among peers (for reviews, see Hawkins *et al.* 1992; Petraitis *et al.* 1995).

Fourth, drugs may be used *medically*. For example, throughout history, amphetamines have been used for the treatment of narcolepsy and asthma, as antidepressants, to alleviate fatigue, for weight loss, and to treat attention deficit hyperactivity (Pickering and Stimson 1994). South American Indians chew coca leaves as medicine to relieve cold, hunger and thirst. Traditionally, physicians have prescribed opiates to help alleviate and manage pain. And, in elderly people, moderate alcohol consumption has been reported to stimulate appetite and promote regular bowel function, as well as to improve mood. Additionally, lower levels of drinking decrease the risk of death from coronary artery disease. Both adults and adolescents might use alcohol or drugs to self-medicate (for example to minimize depressive feelings or alleviate emotional distress).

These four functional meanings are often tested together. One may assess whether or not someone is using drugs for recreational, symbolic, pragmatic, or self-medication purposes (for example US DHHS 1994; Weiner *et al.* 1999). For example, one may conjecture that drugs are used at 'raves' (all-night dances, which is an age-old phenomenon) for all four reasons: to have fun, to express a rite of passage to adulthood, to achieve a social network, and perhaps to feel better about oneself. In principle, statistical methods could be used to assess overlap and non-overlap among these reasons for using drugs. While this approach provides a means of integrating ideas together, and seems theoretically rich, the next two theories take a more *a priori* approach to theory testing in this arena.

Problem behaviour theory (PBT)

Problem behaviour theory is a comprehensive, psychosocial framework developed by Jessor and Jessor (1977) to explain teenage behaviours that violate social and legal norms of society. They suggest that there is a general propensity to behave in deviant ways. PBT proposes that problem behaviours satisfy psychosocial functions for adolescents. These functions include:

- a display of opposition to the norms and values of conventional society
- coping mechanisms for frustration, failure and feelings of inadequacy
- demonstration of unity with one's peer group
- an affirmation of personal identity (for example being bad)
- a symbol of transition to an adult status
- an assertion of holding non-conventional values.

(Jessor 1984, 1987)

Involvement in problem behaviours is a function of 'problem proneness', which is determined by an interaction of personality (for example alienation, rebelliousness), behavioural (going to parties or to church) and perceived environmental systems (for example social approval and social support). These systems are composed of elements which help to control (inhibit) or instigate (promote) risk behaviours (Jessor and Jessor 1977; Jessor 1987; Sussman *et al.* 1995b; Newcomb and Earlywine 1996). Each system is intended to be predictive of a variety of problem behaviours.

The personality system consists of three structures. There is a motivational/ instigation structure that focuses on an individual's motivation towards goals (for example independence, health values, and academic achievement, as examples). Second, there is a personal belief structure that encompasses beliefs about oneself (for example self-esteem, depression) and society, and reflects 'rejection or repudiation of society or of a sense of isolation or separation from its normative hold over one's behaviour' (Jessor and Jessor 1977: 25). Third, there is a personal control structure that encompasses attitudinal acceptance of non-conventional activities (for example religiosity or tolerance for deviance).

The perceived environmental system consists of distal and proximal structures that affect an individual's perception of their social-psychological environment. Perceived environment explains the extent to which an individual's social environment is family- versus peer-oriented. **Distal structures** are believed to be indirectly related to problem proneness, and suggest perceived family and peer support for, and control against, involvement in problem behaviours. For instance, if one's perceived family orientation is associated with a stronger affiliation with conventional norms, there is a reduced likelihood of participating in problem behaviours. **Proximal structures** include perceptions of peer and family approval of problem behaviours and modelling of particular behaviours (for example perceived prevalence of problem behaviours among peers).

The behavioural system is composed of both conventional (prosocial) behaviours and problem (antisocial) behaviours. Jessor and Jessor (1977) consider problem behaviour to be 'behavior that is socially defined as a problem, a source of concern, or as undesirable by the norms of conventional society and the institutions of adult authority' (Jessor and Jessor 1977: 33). This includes such behaviours as alcohol and drug use, sexual activities, driving under the influence and delinquent crime (Jessor 1984; Hays *et al.* 1987; Jessor 1987; Orpinas *et al.* 1995; Sussman *et al.* 1995b). According to PBT, activities with the family, or involvement in church activities, are incompatible with drug use, gambling and other such behaviours.

Triadic influence theory

Petraitis *et al.* (1995) reviewed fourteen multivariate theories of teenage experimental drug use in an attempt to derive an integrated model. They grouped these theories into cognitive-affective (reasoned action, planned behaviour), social learning (social learning, social cognitive/learning), commitment and social attachment (social control, social development), intrapersonal theories (social ecology, self-derogation, multistage social learning, family interaction) and relatively comprehensive theories (problem behaviour, peer cluster, vulnerability, domain). The cognitive-affective theories examine attitude types and valences, perceived pressures to use drugs and motivation to comply with those perceived pressures, and perceptions of others' control of one's behaviour versus one's own control. In addition, one's intention to use drugs is examined as an immediate outcome of these other variables.

The social learning theories examine the role of observation of others, imitation of others' behaviour, social reinforcement for engaging in drug use behaviour, and the creation and maintenance of outcome and self-efficacy expectations. Outcome expectations are the beliefs that if one engages in certain behaviours, certain outcomes are likely to occur, whereas self-efficacy expectations are the beliefs that one is able to engage successfully in these behaviours. These social learning theories place a relatively greater emphasis on observational learning characteristics as opposed to attitudinal perceptions.

Commitment and social attachment theories examine lack of economic or social opportunity, disorganized neighbourhoods, inappropriate socialization, inadequate social skill development and social conflict as precursors of drug use. Commitment to institutions, attachment with significant others and social equality are key features that protect one from drug use. Intrapersonal theories examine the impact of perceived stress, low self-esteem, inadequate coping, and deviant socialization and neglect on drug use. Essentially, clinical psychological functioning is assessed. The comprehensive theories examine personal (psychological and attitudinal), perceived social environment or socialization, and activity participation structures. In addition to these three conceptual structures, the vulnerability and domain theories examine relatively more closely the biological contributions to drug abuse.

Triadic influence theory attempts to classify the elements of these other fourteen theories into three substantive domains (interpersonal, attitudinal/ cultural and intrapersonal), with differing 'distances' from performance of drug use behaviour (ultimate, distal and proximal). Within the interpersonal domain, ultimate variables include home stress, distal variables include drug use role models, and proximal variables include social-related drug beliefs (for example perceived social approval for drug use, estimates of prevalence of drug use). Within the attitudinal/cultural domain, ultimate variables include community disorganization (community stress), distal variables include development of hedonic values or alienation, and proximal variables include expectancies regarding drug use benefits minus costs. Finally, within the intrapersonal domain, ultimate variables include biological temperament (biological stress), distal variables include low self-esteem and poor coping, and proximal variables include refusal self-efficacy and intentions to use drugs. One may interpret this theory to reflect that within three domains of one's life, which involve significant others, one's (social) environment, and within one's own skin, one may suffer negative experiences or stresses. These stresses may become included in one's schemas about the nature of people, social organizations and oneself. Next, if one's beliefs, expectancies and attitudes/ intentions about drug use are favourable, drug use is inevitable.

Stage modelling

While not addressed in several of the previously presented theories, such as triadic influence theory, it is generally agreed that social, situational and environmental factors are likely to be more influential in low-level or early drug use, whereas intrapersonal factors tend to predict higher levels of use (US Office of Technology Assessment (OTA) 1994). An individual generally is subject to many events over a period of time before experimentation progresses to abuse (Wills *et al.* 1996). Obviously, not all individuals choose to experiment with drugs of abuse, and not all individuals who experiment with drug use progress to problematic use or abuse. So, what reinforces the continuance of a maladaptive behaviour like drug use? Some individuals are more susceptible to the addictive process than others as a result of numerous risk factors, and those who are susceptible vary in the *drug* or *drugs of choice* they abuse. Despite the potentially reinforcing pharmacological effects of drugs, some individuals who might be considered highly susceptible or at-risk never abuse drugs. Only one thing is for sure – if individuals never use drugs, then they do not abuse them.

The fact that different predictors may operate at different points in the history of individuals' drug use suggests the operation of stages. One *can* begin to delineate stages before the person has ever tried a drug (Levanthal and Cleary 1980; Flay *et al.* 1983; Sussman *et al.* 1995a). The first stage might be characterized as a preparatory phase in which an individual's personality, family and peers are highly influential. The next stage might involve drug use initiation or experimentation and may be highly influenced by peers and other social influences. Some intrapersonal factors such as high susceptibility to peer influence and subjective feelings of discomfort may also make individuals vulnerable to suggestions of peers. Individuals tend to experiment with cigarettes, alcohol and marijuana first, which is why they are known as **gateway drugs** (Kandel *et al.* 1992). During the times that role models are viewed using drugs, and during experimentation, use outcome expectancies are formed (for example does it feel good or bad to use drugs). Habits may begin to develop, and physiologically reinforcing effects of the drugs may become increasingly influential. Some individuals are highly susceptible to the reinforcing effects of various drugs while others are not. At a third stage, regular drug use may develop; then at perhaps a fourth stage, continuing reinforcing effects, self-identification as a drug user, and addiction processes begin to dominate. Continued use and expectancies also may result in the construction of memory associations (that is established associations in long-term memory). Exposure to a variety of cues may automatically activate memory associations related to use and direct individual behaviour. As a drug use habit becomes increasingly internalized, behavioural options that are incompatible with or are alternatives to drug use behaviour may become increasingly less salient and accessible. Regular use may or may not lead to addiction. Intrapersonal factors seem to dominate the process towards addiction (Levanthal and Cleary 1980; Flay *et al.* 1983; Sussman *et al.* 1995a).

One example of a stage theory: are there stages of alcoholism?

Jellinek (1952) developed the notion of four phases of alcoholism based on questionnaires administered to 2000 members of Alcoholics Anonymous. These phases were developed among adults to be applicable to adults and to assess abuse development *after* regular use has begun. The first phase, pre-alcoholic, is characterized by increasing tolerance to alcohol and drinking to self-medicate. The second, prodromal stage involves suffering blackouts, gulping drinks and having a strong life focus on obtaining drinks. The third crucial stage involves loss of control over drinking and one's behaviour while drunk, and the suffering of numerous life consequences. Finally, the chronic phase involves ethical deterioration, drinking binges and possibly serious withdrawal.

Milam and Ketcham (1983), writers influenced by Jellinek's work, define alcoholism as a chronic, perhaps hereditary, eventually fatal disease that progresses from early physiological susceptibility into an addiction characterized by tolerance changes, physiological dependence, and loss of control over drinking. Early-stage alcoholism applies when persons are embedded in a drinking-related lifestyle and some significant others do not like it. Middle-stage alcoholism applies if persons regret their drunken behaviour, and try to regain control over drinking, with little success. These individuals might try to stop drinking for a period of time, break promises to stop or cut down on drinking, may drink much more than when they first started, and report blackouts (no memory for some events that occurred while drinking). Late-stage alcoholism applies if persons crave alcohol much of the time, have lost control over drinking, and report withdrawal symptoms or health problems due to drinking.

Littrell (1991) provides a fine review of the empirical study of progression (also note Polich *et al.* 1981; Vaillant 1983; W. Miller 1992; W. Miller *et al.* 1992). Littrell (1991) cites several studies that show that approximately 60 per cent of adolescent problem drinkers remit to non-problematic levels of drinking when they reach their twenties; also, 25 per cent of young adults remit to non-problematic levels of drinking before they reach 35 years old. Indeed, there is no inevitable progression. Also discussed by Littrell (1991), a total of 40 per cent of those persons who consensually appear to be 'social' drinkers experience blackouts, and 21 per cent have experienced some alcohol related problems – so not all prototypic symptoms of problem use are all that sensitive and specific to defining clear cases of drug abuse.

In studies that examined data on a total of between 700 and 60,000 adult alcoholic inpatients and outpatients, who consensually appear to be 'real alcoholics', a general profile of outcomes emerges over follow-up periods of between one and over fifteen years. These data are not totally 'clean' and variations in data collection, samples and follow-up rates dampen conclusions one may wish to make. However, a somewhat consistent pattern appears. Abstinence rates vary from 25 to 35 per cent in the long run. An additional 15–25 per cent will be abstinent most of the time, with some lapse periods. Approximately 6–9 per cent will actually become non-problematic drinkers (particularly those persons who are lighter drinkers, have suffered fewer consequences, and who tend not to report gross behavioural changes while drinking: see W. Miller 1992). Another 20–33 per cent will maintain a stable level of problem drinking. Finally, 15–25 per cent will die.

Those who progress in their drinking tend to be heavier drinkers to begin with, report more drinking-related problems and life problems, are more likely to report a tendency to sneak their drinks and drink in the morning, and are more likely to report loss of control. Thus, while progression is a heuristic phenomenon, it is not a teleological reality. Jellinek's work with members of Alcoholics Anonymous included a fairly select sample, and the data were not free from retrospective bias. These stages described above are not inevitable; they are a heuristic. In other words, they provide a conceptual scheme that can promote research studies. There probably is some validity to a notion of progression, but much more longitudinal work is needed to learn for whom this notion is appropriate, and what this notion means. For example, progression might simply express the accumulation of consequences one endures the more times one takes a chance by drinking.

A note on identifying at-risk persons

If one could identify at-risk individuals who do not use or abuse drugs, perhaps much could be learned by their experiences. One would hope to prevent some of the consequences that drug abuse can bestow (Antonovsky 1984). Even in difficult environments, in which drug use seems overdetermined, not all young people begin using drugs. A non-use or low-use trajectory among high-risk young people should be modelled into stage notions of drug use development. There do seem to be constituents of personal 'resilience' against drug use. In particular, those youth and young adults who take on responsibility for caring for others, who adaptively emotionally distance themselves from problem others, and who take on prosocial pursuits where they can find them, seem resilient against drug use. Also, those who maintain a hopeful outlook, have good communication skills, and who seek out prosocial support when needed, tend to be resilient against drug abuse (Hawkins *et al.* 1992; US OTA 1994). Perhaps a developmental trajectory into resiliency could be better refined into a drug use non-development model.

Distal and proximal factors

The distal and proximal factor notions were presented in discussion of theoretical models (problem behaviour theory and triadic influence theory). Distal factors provide the background for potential drug use. Distal factors include those variables that reduce access to or interest in other activities, or increase access to, or vulnerability for, drug use. Proximal factors are those variables that tend to operate just prior to, or during, drug use experiences. A stage model notion seems to overlap with the distal–proximal perspective. Certainly, a preparatory stage is more distal to drug use than an initiation stage, for example. However, these perspectives still are separable, because both distal and proximal factors could be placed into the same stages. For example, poverty generally is considered a distal drug use variable, whereas peer dares to use drugs generally is considered a proximal variable. Both poverty and peer dares could influence drug use initiation. Likewise, the long-time experience of poverty and proximal variables such as physiological reinforcement from drug use could influence regular drug use. Certainly, more research is needed to better integrate stages of use with distal–proximal notions.

Summary: the hedonic treadmill

Several integrative theories were discussed in this chapter including combinations of risk and protective factors, biopsychosocial models, deductive/ theoretical models, stage modelling and distal–proximal notions. These ideas can get complicated. Some day, perhaps, an Einstein of drug abuse aetiology will come along and propose an overall theory of the development of drug abuse that 'really works'. Alternatively, perhaps there are so many different pathways to drug abuse that all one can say is if a drug user discontinues use, abuse will not result. Of course, we could also argue that we make things more complicated than they need to be. Perhaps, drug abuse is simply a matter of 'hopping on the hedonic treadmill' without learning how to get off and stay off.

The philosopher Aristippus was one of the disciples of Socrates (435 BC). He was founder of the Cyrenaic school of hedonism, the ethic of pleasure. He believed that pleasure was the highest of human values. He did believe that good judgement and self-control were important to temper the pursuit of pleasure. Otherwise, people may become victims of an endless, uncontrolled pursuit of pleasure-related goals. In other words, individuals may become more and more obsessed with obtaining pleasurable objects, regardless of the obstacles and negative consequences in their paths. This notion is the basis of the 'hedonic treadmill'. While discussed in psychology for a long while, this notion is not well studied. We do know that social images including 'to have fun' have been associated with drug use for some time (for example Sussman *et al.* 1996c; Weiner *et al.* 1999). Others have found that valuing pleasure over wisdom determines whether or not people engage in problem versus healthy behaviour (Rokeach 1973; Schwartz and Inbar-Saban 1988). One uses drugs essentially for the pleasurable effect. One wants to repeat that effect. One especially wants to repeat that effect if other aspects of one's life are stressful or anhedonic. Drug use provides a relatively easily obtainable means to *feel good very quickly* in the context of various stresses or challenges. Drug use may seem like a viable option. Pleasure has side-effects – and then negative consequences begin – one may not know how to replace the drug as a means of obtaining pleasure – and abuse begins. Could a good theory of drug abuse be that simple? Well, maybe not.

Part 3

Drug abuse prevention and cessation programming and the future

8

Drug abuse prevention programmes

This chapter will discuss various aspects of drug abuse prevention programming. First, prevention and cessation terminology will be presented. Next, parameters of drug abuse prevention programming will be discussed, including breadth of prevention programming (single drug or multiple drugs), modalities of prevention programming (contexts of delivery), contents of programming (process and substantive material) and target populations of programming (general versus high risk). In particular, the later part of this chapter will address what type of programming might be more or less suitable for which population.

Prevention and cessation terminology

Traditionally, public health researchers and practitioners have divided the field of prevention programming into three levels. These levels are primary prevention (before the problem behaviour starts), secondary prevention (before the disease starts) and tertiary prevention (before death is likely). New terms are now taking hold. Prevention may be considered 'universal' (designed to affect the general population), 'selective' (designed to affect subgroups at elevated risk for developing a problem, based on social, psychological or other factors) or 'indicated' (designed to affect high-risk subgroups already identified as having some detectable signs or symptoms of a developing problem: Gordon 1987). The key difference in meaning of these prevention vocabularies pertains to whether the focus is on the *chronology* of the problem or on the *target population*. While there is, perhaps, an implication of chronology in the second definition, the direct focus is on fitting programming to a target group. Arguably, a universal prevention programme could have a secondary prevention goal. For example, a programme designed for the general population could hope to affect those at higher risk for drug abuse. Thus, there is a possibility of some crossing of these terms.

A third set of terms to describe levels of an intervention is 'cessation' versus 'prevention'. The notion of tertiary prevention generally is similar to the notion of cessation in that both terms do involve a focus on prevention of premature death. Also, both prevention (at all levels) and cessation approaches encourage adoption of new, healthy behaviour. However, the central focus of cessation work is on stopping a current behaviour to arrest ongoing consequences and permit recovery of health, whereas the central focus of prevention work is on antecedents of the behaviour, to anticipate and prevent future negative consequences from occurring. Cessation often deals with coping with psychological dependence on a drug and with physiological withdrawal from a drug. Prevention generally does not assist drug users through such hurdles. Cessation often deals with adult and child populations. Prevention tends to focus on youth populations, although it could (in theory) deal with adult populations, as well. The choice between using a cessation or prevention approach is not always clear. Which approach would be most successful in assisting the highest number of teenagers not to use drugs? There are high relapse rates in adult cessation programmes; perhaps prevention might halt the addiction process that makes cessation so difficult. Alternatively, young people at highest risk may not benefit by prevention programming. They may benefit only when they perceive some costs occurring to them, making them appropriate candidates for early cessation efforts.

Parameters of drug abuse prevention programming

Breadth of prevention programming

Drug abuse prevention could involve addressing use of a single drug, use of any of several drugs, or behaviour that pertains to drugs and healthy lifestyles, more generally (for example including diet and exercise). Arguments that favour focusing on a single drug include being able to provide a sufficient amount of drug-focused preventive information, the possibility that different drugs might be used for different reasons, and the need to keep programming to a reasonable length. In addition, funding often comes from agencies that address specific drugs. One main argument that favours the concurrent prevention of multiple drugs is that different drugs serve similar underlying functions (for example problem proneness, peer group solidarity). Information can be efficiently provided that counteracts use of any one of several drugs by focusing on common underlying functions. Also, agencies might fund a programme if it addresses its drug of focus along with other drugs. Even more inclusive, one may argue that unhealthy lifestyles in general reflect common underlying functions. Sedentary living, fatty diets and drug use might best be counteracted together as a joint expression of a lack of wellness or problem proneness (Sussman *et al.* 1995b). One review study suggests that prevention programmes with a wide breadth are nearly as effective as narrow focused programmes (C. Johnson *et al.* 1996).

Modalities of prevention programming

School-based drug abuse prevention programming is a central modality for provision of drug abuse prevention education because young people are captive audiences to this type of programming and evidence indicates that school-based programming can be successful (for example Botvin *et al.* 1995). However, maintaining a consistent and rigorous programme at schools over many years is a challenge. Teacher training and compensation are key issues in dissemination of effective school-based programming. *Family involvement* is a relevant means of providing prevention material outside of school. However, the young people at highest risk for drug use are relatively unlikely to have parents who will take on the responsibility of teaching prevention material to their children, or serving as support persons (see Richardson *et al.* 1989). Involvement of *community agents*, such as dentists, paediatricians, youth club leaders, local health service personnel or city leaders, can assist prevention efforts. While their time availability generally is limited, and the effects they exert consequently are small, they are well respected by youth and may come into contact with many young people. Their advice not to use drug products and provision of self-help social influence-oriented material could be useful. Likewise, the *mass media* (TV, radio, film, print) can reach many young people, and can be used to counteract other media glorification of drug use, as well as to provide simple anti-drug use messages. Generally, the mass media are used to supplement other programming because only small effects may be achieved, and social interaction previously has not been possible between the media as treatment agent and the target audience. The use of interactive CDs and chat rooms on the worldwide web currently is helping to remedy this latter difficulty, however.

Finally, *legislative means* can be used to curb drug use among young people. For example, tax increases on cigarettes can curb young people's intention to begin smoking, though perhaps only very large increases will decrease prevalence noticeably once people begin regular smoking (Chaloupka and Grossman 1996). Warning labels placed on tobacco or alcohol products using clear language in ways that cue prudent behaviour may be helpful. Also, enforcement of access laws might decrease purchase of tobacco and alcohol products by young people, at least if applied across multiple (home, school, store) contexts (Wakefield *et al.* 2000). Other legislative and enforcement means of providing drug abuse prevention is described by Pentz *et al.* (1996). Many of these supply-side type approaches to drug abuse prevention fail (for example interdiction of illicit drug distribution or sales). Combined with demand reduction approaches (for example education), however, supply reduction approaches might receive greater cooperation from relevant gatekeepers. Perhaps institutionalization of multiple prevention modalities to deliver both demand and supply reduction programming will provide powerful and long-lasting preventive effects. Much research remains to determine which modalities and programme exposure durations are needed to provide the most cost-effective programming.

Comprehensive social influences programming: the hallmark of primary or universal prevention

The target population for most drug abuse prevention efforts is an adolescent age group (sixth to tenth grade, ages 10–15: Flay 1985; Glynn 1989). Although a health education curriculum can be tailored to the development and skills of youth of various ages (for example preschool children: Hendricks *et al.* 1989), adolescence is a 'critical period', that is, risk behaviours increase dramatically during this age bracket (for example Sussman *et al.* 1995a). During this time period, drugs begin to be used as a function of social influences and social use contexts. Therefore, the delivery of comprehensive social influence programming, including an awareness of social influences and **social skills training**, is most important during adolescence to be able to maximize the likelihood of achieving successful preventive effects (Flay *et al.* 1983).

Social influence programmes were developed beginning in 1976, based on McGuire's (for example 1964) work, by Richard Evans and colleagues at the University of Houston, Texas (Flay 1985). The basic assumption was that 'inoculation' to resist those social pressures that precipitate use during this critical period of young adolescence would help prevent use. Traditional drug effects and consequences information-oriented programmes had not been found to be successful; comprehensive social influences programmes have reduced tobacco, alcohol and marijuana use by as much as 50 per cent up to six years post-programme (Bell and Battjes 1985; Flay 1985; Botvin *et al.* 1995; Sussman *et al.* 1995a; Tobler *et al.* 2000).

Contents of comprehensive social influences programmes

Generally, a social influences drug abuse prevention 'curriculum' refers to a collection of instructional activities or lessons containing several thematic topic areas, typically five to twenty single-hour lessons, which can be integrated into a semester-long health education class (Glynn 1989; Sussman *et al.* 1995a). A good social influences prevention curriculum is well planned, sequentially developed and includes a variety of classroom learning experiences.

Comprehensive social influences programmes can be grouped into three main divisions. The first is basic information. Basic information lessons include listening skills/involvement (which motivates involvement in the curriculum), physical consequence information instruction, and decision-making and public commitment (which ends the curriculum). The second main division is normative social influence-oriented lessons, which counteract social pressure to achieve approval by using drugs. These lessons include normative restructuring (for example taking a class poll regarding whether or not peers approve of drug use, and learning that most peers disapprove of use), assertion refusal learning, and assertion refusal practice (to refuse direct offers of drugs).

The third main division is informational social influence-oriented lessons, which counteract social pressure to share similar and favourable opinions about drug use. These lessons include modification of drug use prevalence overestimates – for example, taking a class poll, which compares self-reported use among classmates to estimates made about use among classmates. The latter tends to be much higher. These lessons also include provision of social awareness of adult and media influences that tend to unduly glamorize drug use. Finally, these lessons include use of activism activities (for example letter writing to film producers that request that they provide accurate portrayals of drug use consequences). Many social influence programmes include most of these types of components as applied to different prevention issues (for example Glynn 1989; Pentz *et al.* 1989b; Hansen and Graham 1991; Hansen 1992; Sussman *et al.* 1995a).

One key in successful social influences programming is a focus on provision of interactive dialogue between instructor and students ('Socratic' dialogue – trying to ask pointed questions to get students to generate the answer) and interaction among students through use of games and group discussion. Didactic, lecture-like instruction is not likely to be effective (Tobler and Stratton 1997). Thus, prevention programming should allow its target population to discuss the material, ask questions about it, and thereby digest it into their memory retrieval structures and belief systems.

Relative lack of importance of refusal assertion training

The hallmark social influence activity, particularly in drug abuse prevention programmes and campaigns of the 1970s and 1980s (for example the **Just Say No Campaign**), has been **refusal assertion training**, in which young people are instructed on how to say no to drug use offers (Hansen 1992). More recent work suggests that refusal assertion skills training is not of major importance in the prevention of drug abuse, especially among those who have any intention to try drugs (for example MacKinnon *et al.* 1991; Donaldson *et al.* 1994; Donaldson 1995; Sussman *et al.* 1995a). In fact, when instructed without other activities, refusal assertion training may lead to higher estimates of the likelihood that a drug offer will be made in the future, may lower persons' refusal self-efficacy, and may increase prevalence estimates of use (Donaldson *et al.* 1994; Donaldson 1995). Drug prevalence overestimates reduction, and perceived peer approval reduction (that is 'normative restructuring') are known to be mediators of drug abuse prevention programme effects. Refusal assertion training should be used only in conjunction with the normative restructuring and prevalence overestimates reduction methods.

Will comprehensive social influences programming work with high-risk young people?

Most young people who experiment with drugs do not abuse drugs later in life (Newcomb and Bentler 1989). Perhaps prevention programmes focused on those youth at high-risk for drug abuse would provide a maximal social payoff. In other words, it may be more cost-effective to target young people who are most likely to abuse drugs in the future than to target much larger numbers of young people, many of whom will not abuse drugs. Thus, it is not surprising that one of the most difficult but important tasks in the minds of many drug abuse prevention researchers and practitioners is to treat young people at highest risk for future drug abuse (for example Newcomb and Bentler 1989; Resnik and Wojcicki 1991; Eggert *et al.* 1994).

Drug abuse prevention researchers are not decisive regarding whether or not social influence prevention programme effects differ as a function of risk of target group. Some researchers have not found effects of social influences school-based (Hansen *et al.* 1988) or community programmes (C. Johnson *et al.* 1990) to vary as a function of risk (Chou *et al.* 1998) and even favour those who are more disadvantaged in some instances (Graham *et al.* 1990). On the other hand, other researchers have provided evidence that social influences-oriented prevention programming could result in reactance effects (regarding cigarette smoking as a function of behavioural risk but not socio-economic risk: Ellickson and Bell 1990). These other researchers also have found that such programming is less likely to affect those at highest risk for drug abuse (for example Tobler 1986; Newcomb and Bentler 1989).

Generic social influences programming could be effective among high-risk young people assuming that actual or perceived social influence processes still operate and serve as the primary antecedents of use (Sussman *et al.* 1995a). However, older age life difficulties, school context interference and academic limitations may make it especially difficult to engage high-risk young people in any programming. In addition, one may speculate that, in high-risk contexts, some basic information lessons have little meaning. Perhaps few would state a commitment not to use, presenting a weak impact against drug use on oneself and others in the class. Normative social influence lessons also may exert a weak impact. Among high-risk young people, perhaps few will state disapproval of drug use. Also, these young people may not want to learn refusal assertion training, which assumes that someone refuses drug offers because they do not want to use drugs. Finally, informational social influence lessons may exert a weak impact, as well. A prevalence overestimates modification lesson may not be successful in a high-risk context if there are many users and, consequently, relatively little overestimation of use. Also, it may be less likely in a high-risk environment that young people will take an activism stance (to provide corrective social information) which requires acting on a difficult environment; they may feel less hopeful than others that they can act to change their social environment.

Need to consider motivation

According to theories of motivation (for example Emmons *et al.* 1995), there are two components that underlie young people's decisions to engage or not engage in drug use. First, youth consider why they should not engage in drug use, and should engage in some other behaviour ('the direction'). Resnik and Wojcicki (1991) note that high-risk youth must believe that prevention programming offers better life alternatives than past self-destructive patterns. Young people may become motivated to change in a particular direction when they make explicit their future goals (if their future goals are consistent with a prosocial achievement orientation).

Second, young people consider how much effort they are willing to exert to avoid drug use ('the energy': Bindra and Stewart 1966; Emmons *et al.* 1995; Sussman 1996). Perhaps, to understand the energy that youth would exert not to abuse drugs, one should consider, as further stated by Levanthal and Keeshan (1993: 266), 'the various routes perceived as available to attain those [nondrug] goals and satisfy those needs.' More specifically, young people may become motivated to work to change when intrapersonal or extrapersonal obstacles are made explicit and individuals are instructed on how to surmount them (see also Chapter 9 of this book).

Project towards no drug abuse: an indicated prevention programme for older high-risk young people

Young people in California, in the United States, are required to receive education until they are 18 years of age. Those young people who are unable to remain in the comprehensive (regular) high school system for functional reasons, including drug use, are transferred to a continuation (alternative) high school. Continuation high school students report much higher levels of drug use than do traditional/comprehensive high school students. For example, weekly use of marijuana is 36 per cent versus 9 per cent, respectively (DeMoor *et al.* 1994; Sussman *et al.* 1998a). Continuation high schools *as such* do not cause young people to continue to use drugs. To the contrary, these specialized schools may provide the additional personal attention needed to help youth correct deficiencies in life skills, increase bonding with social institutions, and otherwise help them to surmount several risks for drug abuse (that is build resiliency: Hawkins *et al.* 1992). However, continuation high school students are also exposed on a daily basis to numerous other students who use drugs, and attitudes favourable to drug use are likely to be shaped and supported by other youths in such an environment. Effective drug abuse prevention programming for many of these students is imperative to help them channel back into mainstream society.

Continuation high school youth must want to cope differently; they need reasons to change their behaviour that they 'own' within their belief systems, and goals for which they might strive. In addition, perceived obstacles to reaching those goals should be acknowledged, and means to surmount those obstacles should be suggested. **Project Towards No Drug Abuse (TND)** involved use of an empirical curriculum development process, in which consumer demand is a primary criterion of lesson selection, to develop a drug abuse prevention programme that is tailored to continuation high school youth. Consumer demand considers the motivations and preferences of the consumer. By considering specific motivations of continuation high school youth, perhaps optimal programming may be developed (Sussman 2001a).

Project TND programme development results and curriculum content

Research while developing the TND programme indicated that generic comprehensive social influences lessons are less likely to be effective for use with the present high-risk population (Sussman 1996). For example, while continuation high school students acknowledge the operation of social influence in facilitating their drug use behaviour, they tend to endorse as more important other prevention instruction. In particular, they endorse as relevant to them instruction in alternatives to drug use and drug counselling, lessons with chemical dependency recovery themes, lessons which impart physical consequences information, or lessons which impart life skills. In addition, they react negatively to refusal assertion training and practice. To meet the needs of these youth, lesson material was developed which can motivate students against drug use and justify to students why it is in their interests to learn new skills (Sussman 1996; Sussman *et al.* 1998a).

The final nine-lesson curriculum for implementation in the first main prevention trial of Project TND was shown to exert preventive effects on alcohol and hard drug use. Alcohol use was reduced at higher levels by approximately 30 per cent, whereas hard drug use was reduced by approximately 50 per cent across levels of baseline use. Also, another trial with a twelve-lesson version of the TND curriculum is showing extension of effects among continuation high school youth to marijuana and cigarette smoking (Sussman *et al.*, under review b). Further, the alcohol and hard drug use preventive results were replicated in a comprehensive high school setting (Dent *et al.*, in press). Thus, Project TND has achieved significant one-year effects on both alcohol use and hard drug use when administered at continuation (alternative) or comprehensive (regular) high schools.

Project TND lesson contents
Lessons in the first trial were taught across three weeks, in blocks of three per week. The first lesson attempts to elicit cooperation, and instructs young people in communication and listening skills, to assist in learning of subsequent information. The second lesson attempts to motivate students to listen further by discussion of stereotype information (for example that others believe all continuation high school students are drug abusers) and facilitating their own rebellion against such stereotyping (Fishkin *et al.* 1993). Finally, the

third lesson provides information regarding myths that continuation high school students themselves hold about drug use (Sussman *et al.* 1996a; Ames *et al.* 1999).

The second week shifts into instruction in chemical dependency (fourth lesson), perspective taking regarding those affected by one's drug use (talk show – fifth lesson) and learning how to change behaviours to fulfil one's life goals (health as a value and stress coping – sixth lesson: see for example Wills 1986). Students are taught that consequences of drug use tend to accumulate over time, that they really do value their own physical health to be able to achieve their life goals, and that they can learn healthful means of coping (for example Weinstein 1982; Sussman 1996; Sussman *et al.* 1996a).

Finally, the third week material presents information on increasing self-control to better acquire environmental resources (seventh lesson). In addition, the third week material helps the student see that, since they desire to be a moderate type of person, drug use does not fit into their plans (eighth lesson – attitudinal perspective theory: Upshaw and Ostrom 1984). Finally, the last lesson encourages a decision and a commitment regarding drug use. In summary, the first week stimulates learning, the second week teaches consequences of chemical dependency and coping alternatives, and the third week encourages additional development of skills and motivation in the direction of becoming more moderate in behaviour and attitudes.

A model of drug abuse prevention is implicit in the curriculum. It might be referred to as a motivation-skills-decision model. Students' motivations are harnessed against drug abuse (through correction of cognitive misperceptions), students are provided with skills to change, and they make a decision. This model integrates ideas by Levanthal and Keeshan (1993) on motivation with Eggert *et al.* (1994) on skills training and decision-making. A motivation-skills-decision model may help optimize effects of preventing drug abuse among high-risk young people. Students' *motivations* are harnessed against drug abuse. They learn that

- they don't have to yield to stereotypes of others and use drugs
- they can place partly formed specific self-attitude ratings within a more general self-rating as a moderate
- their health should be valued as a means to achieving life goals.

Students are also provided with *skills to change*, including

- effective listening skills
- effective communication skills
- self-control skills.

Finally, they learn to make a *decision* about their behaviour after being provided with information, including

- maladaptive myths that people hold about drug use
- the insidious nature of life consequences of drug abuse

Table 8.1 What contents should compose universal, selective and indicated prevention programmes?

Substantive component	Universal	Selective	Indicated
Facilitator–student trust-building	X	X	X
Drug use consequences information	X	X	X
Listening and communication skills	X	X	X
Decision-making	X	X	X
Socratic dialogue	X	X	X
General assertiveness skills	X	X	X
Community support	X	X	x
Activism skills	X	x	x
Public commitment	X	0	0
Refusal assertion skills	x	0	0
Prevalence overestimates reduction	X	x	0
Normative restructuring	X	x	0
Social influences awareness	X	X	0
Cognitive and behavioural coping	x	X	X
Self-control	x	X	X
High-risk situations information	x	x	x
Perspective-taking	0	X	x
Motivation material	0	X	X
Mood management	0	X	X
Dealing with withdrawal	0	x	X
'Recovery' material (for example myths)	0	x	X
Harm reduction	0	0	x
Alternative medicine-oriented	0	0	x

Notes: X = very important; x = may be useful; 0 = probably not important
For additional reading see Sussman *et al.* 1995a, 1998a

- the effects of drug abuse on others
- means to integrate all previous information by use of a decision-making process.

This model may be a prototype of indicated prevention programming (Sussman *et al.* 1998a). It would appear that different types of programming are needed for older, high-risk youth other than comprehensive social influences programming.

Summary

Project TND added three additional lessons in later research. One and a half additional lessons focus on marijuana use. This material attempts to provide an understanding of how marijuana can create 'negative thought loops' – that is, a reversal of cause and effect. Marijuana use may be thought to be the solution to negative thinking, whereas it actually is the cause (for example through bypassing corrective emotional processing: Sussman *et al.* 1996a). A second lesson focused on cigarette smoking cessation. The purpose of this lesson was to emphasize the dangers of smoking and to provide material on how to quit smoking. The other new material expanded on the self-control lesson in the earlier Project TND programme. The current lesson involved additional practice of self-control skills. In addition, conflict situations are introduced and an emphasis on anger control is provided. As the result of adding this new material, the programme has now achieved an effect on four drugs at a one-year follow-up (Sussman *et al.*, under review a).

Universal programming involves comprehensive social influence lessons, as administered to young teenagers. Selective programming may apply, perhaps, to older, higher risk youth in general population settings, such as regular high school, and could involve a motivation-skills-decision-making programme integrated with social influences features. Indeed, use could be made of the wider school setting to pressure for more conservative behaviour. Finally, indicated drug abuse prevention programming involves a motivation-skills-decision-making only, as applied to young people in alternative settings. These three types of programming all show promise to prevent escalation in drug use before complete cessation programming becomes necessary (see Table 8.1 for contents of universal, selective and indicated programming that are likely to be effective). On the other hand, some cigarette smoking cessation material was added into the later TND programme. Approximately 45 per cent of continuation high school youth are daily smokers. Regarding this drug, maybe they needed cessation programming to have an impact on them. Possibly, we need to think about the option of integrating both prevention and cessation material together for higher-risk populations. There may be a different mix of such material that is needed for different populations, depending on the problem behaviour. The next chapter will discuss cessation programming in detail.

9

Drug abuse cessation programmes and relapse prevention

While considered cost-effective (Fountain 1995; Hubbard 1995; Hubbard *et al.* 1997; NIDA 1999b), treatment paradigms for the cessation of drug abuse and maintenance of habit change generally are successful for only a minority of persons who go through them (Powell *et al.* 1993). This current status of treatment may be due in part to the fact that although the physical components of an addiction are easily disrupted (for example withdrawal), other factors contributing to the maintenance of drug use behaviour continue to challenge practitioners and researchers. Programme attrition continues to present serious challenges to treatment effectiveness (Leshner 1997). In addition, relapse rates continue to be very high (Carroll 1989; Marlatt 1990; Sussman *et al.* 1996c). Given a first cessation attempt after treatment, approximately 80 per cent of individuals relapse. Considering multiple attempts to quit using (relevant to tobacco, alcohol, heroin and marijuana use), up to only 40 per cent are abstinent or non-problematic users after ten years (Littrell 1991). Pharmacological efforts have been undertaken as a harm reduction strategy among those who seem unable to quit drug use. For example, methadone maintenance appears to benefit approximately 50 per cent of heroin addicts (Bell *et al.* 1999). However, these treatments do not provide a solution for maintenance of habit change. Available treatments certainly save the lives of some drug abusers, but not most of them.

It also appears that most treatment for drug abuse around the world is provided to males (65–99 per cent: 65 per cent in Central America; 76 per cent in western Europe; 90 per cent in Mexico; 96 per cent in East Asia; 99 per cent in South Asia: US DHHS 1998). Also, a majority of persons treated for drug abuse fall into an age range of 20–34 years old (15–24 years old may be a more accurate range in Mexico). Thus, available treatments tend to focus on young males. These same treatments are not often used with younger or older persons or with females. Thus, it is difficult to ascertain the overall success of treatment programmes. Maybe these current treatments are in need of revision to be more applicable for young males; we are not sure what works for others.

This chapter focuses on components of drug abuse cessation, including how individuals reach treatment programmes, stages of recovery, motivation to change, setting treatment goals, significant treatment programmes, treatment techniques and **aftercare**. Each of these components continues to be refined and may lead to more effective programming in the future. These components of drug abuse cessation are depicted in Figure 9.1 as a flow chart. We begin with an overview of treatment programmes.

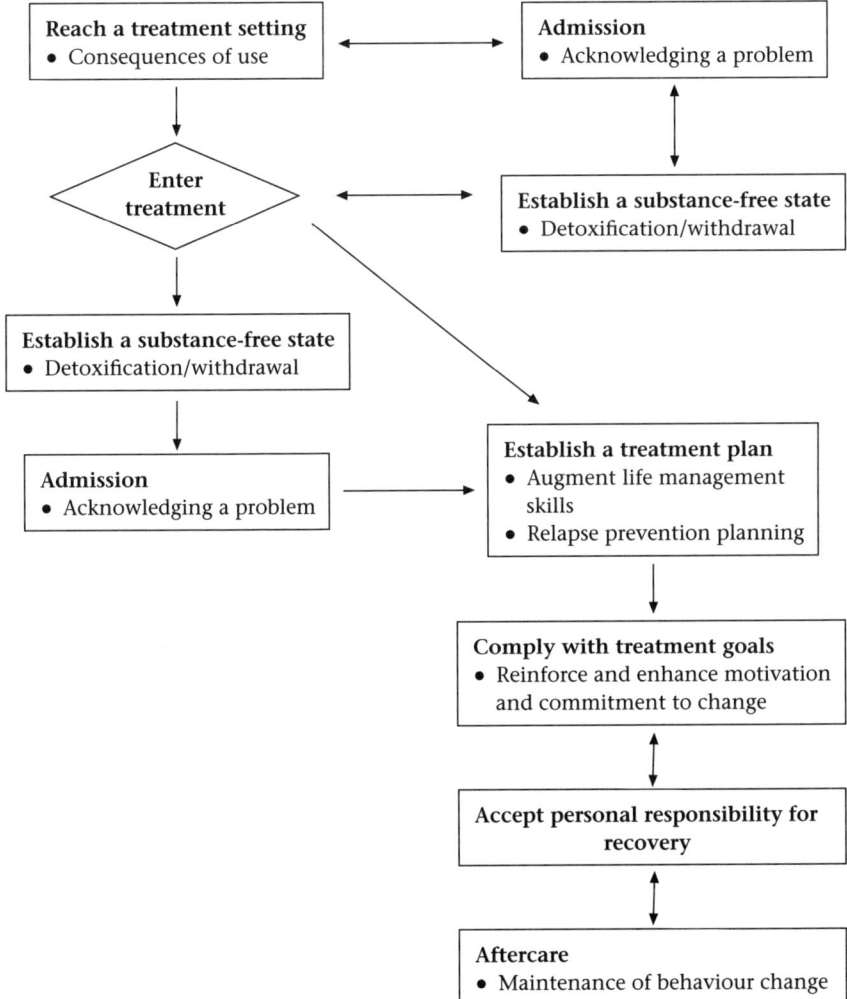

Figure 9.1 A treatment process model
For additional reading see: Marlatt and Gordon 1985; NIDA 1999b

Overview of treatment programmes

Although there is evidence that individuals do recover from substance abuse without formal treatment programmes, many substance abusers have difficulty changing their behaviour without first learning effective coping strategies and obtaining supportive social networks (that is how to deal with problems without drinking or using to excess). Effective coping may be learned through informal channels, or may be learned in treatment programmes. Comprehensive drug abuse treatment programmes generally incorporate stabilization, early recovery and middle-to-late recovery phases (for example Gorski and Miller 1984; Milam and Ketcham 1983). During stabilization, goals include initial detoxification or withdrawal, assessment of co-morbid psychological problems, medical care for health-related problems and nutritional status assessment. Early recovery typically includes treatment planning for the change of long-term behaviour, involving use of cognitive-behavioural therapies, skills training, counselling and rehabilitative therapies. Middle-to-late recovery typically includes instruction in relapse prevention and provision of aftercare programmes.

Programmes are tailored to a variety of populations (for example children, adults, individuals and groups) and utilize a variety of treatment agents (for example medical doctors, psychologists, social workers, nurses or recovering addicts). Programmes are provided in a variety of settings (for example hospitals, **outpatient clinics**, prisons, inpatient or residential programmes) and utilize a variety of treatment models (for example AA, NA, milieu, cognitive-behavioural or behavioural). Additionally, treatment programmes frequently include additional strategies for family systems (including parenting classes), AIDS education and awareness, nutritional education and strategies to improve retention and compliance with treatment. Since treatment techniques utilized in programmes affect compliance, compliance-gaining strategies should be integrated into treatment planning. In general, compliance to treatment regimens is around 50 per cent and varies with the treatment population, how people interpret their addictions, what roles they assume, who they talk to and what they say about their addictions, and the complexity of treatment regimen (Epstein and Cluss 1984). The more motivated or functional the treatment population is, the more the population views itself as an active consumer, the greater the belief is in potential change, the greater the social support received is for change, and the simpler the treatment regimen is, the greater is the compliance with treatment. With all these variations in populations, treatment agents, settings and strategies in mind, let us first look at the beginning of treatment: different ways the drug abuser may reach a treatment situation.

Reaching a treatment setting

How do individuals actually reach treatment settings and enter treatment programmes? Cessation of drug abuse appears to be linked to *consequences of use*. For example, people may experience legal consequences such as being arrested resulting in court mandated treatment (which may keep people in treatment longer, with potentially better outcomes: Fletcher *et al.* 1997). Or, people may experience social consequences, such as family or interpersonal conflict related to use, and they may be persuaded to go to treatment. Or, people may be behind on credits at school, be in trouble at work, or have lost their jobs, homes, cars and friends, and acknowledge the need for treatment. After many years of engaging in drug abuse, people may find themselves in public shelter situations that offer treatment that they are now willing to accept. Many scenarios are possible, but most are linked to negative consequences of use. At some or various points, as the consequences accumulate, the drug abuser seeks assistance, or is asked or ordered to seek assistance.

School settings
In the school setting, a youth who abuses drugs is likely to fall behind in class work or fail to show up for class (truancy). This young person might have been caught stealing other students' property, might show mood swings, might appear in class smelling of alcohol or appear unkempt, might appear pale and tired, and might have been involved in verbal or physical disputes with other students while acting 'strangely'.

Student assistance generally is available first through a contact with someone at the school, perhaps a teacher, the security guard, other students or the school nurse. Typically, there may be around five hours of in-service training for staff and peer counsellors regarding conceptions of addiction, how to recognize drug problems and referral skills. Peer counsellors may lead education groups, which teach coping skills and values development. Peer support groups may also be available for youths who are struggling to get and stay sober. Usually these groups also provide referral information and take a twelve-step group support model. Finally, sometimes a resource library and peer advising are available (Bosworth 1996).

The work-site
Approximately 40 per cent of drug abusers have a problem with absenteeism from their job, and 40 per cent arrive late at work on a regular basis. At least 30 per cent make mistakes on the job. Also, 25 per cent have problems with the boss, 25 per cent have problems completing work and 10 per cent suffer on-the-job injuries. Those employees most likely to work while using drugs are males under 30 years old, who are unhappy about their jobs and who socialize frequently with co-workers away from the place of employment after hours (Hollinger 1988). Co-workers who do not abuse drugs are affected by their peers' drug abuse. They report relatively low work identity when they experience high use among their co-workers (Bennett and Lehman 1996).

Since the late 1940s, businesses and government agencies have developed various policies to deal with employee drug abuse. **Employee assistance programmes (EAPs)** began with the notion of motivating employees to improve their performance rather than risk losing their jobs; using these programmes, companies could also attempt to contain rising health costs and reduce corporate losses. Most of these policies support a treatment orientation (that is to deal with the drug problem when it has got out of hand). Such programmes tend to be offered in organizations that include relatively older workers. Involvement in an EAP is generally intended to be separate from personnel records, and participation is not intended to affect job ratings. EAP components may include

- educational and counselling programmes, including crisis counselling
- supervisory training in confronting troubled employees
- drug testing and other diagnostic screening services
- referral services.

(Bennett and Lehman 1996)

In addition, informal networks of recovering professionals and skilled labour groups have developed and formed self-help and activism groups. Future programming should consider carefully the organizational culture of the workplace and the local community that interacts with the workplace. Increasing cooperation within the organizational hierarchy and networking with local resources may improve the efficacy of EPAs (Centers for Substance Abuse Prevention (CSAP) 1992).

Medical hospital

Several drug-related disorders involve placement in a hospital (recall Table 1.1). The medical patient needs to be treated, of course, for their medical condition. A variety of conditions may be treated. While the patient is at the hospital, they will be discouraged from drinking any alcohol or using any drugs other than those prescribed for the medical condition. This is a situation in which the patient may experience withdrawal symptoms. The patient may become irritable and depressed while in this situation. It is possible that the patient may 'sneak' some drug use while at the hospital, or complain of pain to obtain drugs, or simply brave it out. A physician may ask the patient if they have been drinking, smoking, and so on, either as part of a health status assessment, in reaction to the qualities of the disorder reported, the sight of apparent withdrawal symptoms, or evidence obtained through biological data collection. The patient may deny ('lie about') having a problem. Alternatively, the patient is away from drug-related cues, and illness may motivate the patient to change and seek treatment. Health assistance may include admonitions to quit drug use, group self-help meetings on the unit, bedside counselling, and administration of self-help materials (for example Stevens *et al.* 2000, regarding cigarette smoking cessation).

Prison

Approximately 20 per cent of prison inmates report heavy drinking every day for one year before entering prison; 75 per cent report drug-related problems at prison intake and the same percentage report having used drugs or having been drunk on the day they did the crime for which they were incarcerated (Lightfoot 1993). Upon discharge from a prison, an ex-convict generally has no job or money, weakened family ties and little social support. Without sufficient support and monitoring, it is likely that the individual will revolve back into prison 'on the heels' of drug use.

Treatment options include helping to increase inmate motivation for change, providing education regarding awareness of effects of substance abuse, and teaching skills such as self-control, as well as general social skills to help inmates learn how to avoid setting themselves up for drug use again. Skills need to be taught relevant to employment and leisure situations, and should include pre-release planning. Finally, relapse management might be taught. Training for inmates requires relatively intense, long periods (up to one year) to elicit an effect, since many in this population are removed from mainstream society (Lightfoot 1993).

Residential facilities

This setting involves a myriad of placements for disabled, homeless and elderly people. Although there is variation across **residential facilities**, the statistics that apply to individuals in some facilities are frightening. For example, in nursing homes, 20–50 per cent of elderly residents have alcohol-related problems. Also, there is a tendency for medication to be used as a means of chemical restraint, particularly at nursing homes (Mansdorf *et al.* 1999). Many individuals who might otherwise be homeless reside in public residential facilities, such as homeless shelters and psychiatric hospitals. Perhaps 50 per cent are considered dually diagnosed (that is they are drug abusers and have some psychiatric impairment). Physicians ought to scrutinize medications being administered to residents, and provide education to staff regarding the potential for drug abuse among the tenants. The nursing staff should be involved in inpatient education regarding drug abuse and drug screening, and help to coordinate care that might counteract drug use as a means of spending one's time. More of a reliance on behavioural interventions (for example contingency management), in addition to medication, should be considered as means of curtailing disruptive behaviour. The resident should also be assessed for potential independent living. If possible, relapse prevention and job or leisure training skills should be offered.

Family home

Traditional schools of thought tend to view family members of drug abusers as functioning in a dysfunctional system (for example V.E. Johnson 1980). Empirical data indicate that families of alcohol/drug abusers show lower levels of cohesion, expressiveness, independence, intellectual orientation (including problem-solving skill) and active-recreational orientation, and higher levels of conflict (for example hostile communication), than do non-drug-abusing families. However, these conditions simply relate to existence in a dysfunctional family, across a variety of disorders, not necessarily the use of drugs *per se* (Sher 1993).

The empirical literature also suggests that spouses of drug abusers have more psychological problems than do spouses of non-abusers. They tend to be either depressed and anxious, or psychopathic. They may dominate the relationship if their drug-abusing spouse is relatively socially incompetent. They are relatively likely to have come from families containing other drug abusers. Children of drug abusers tend to exhibit lower achievement behaviour, more behavioural problems and lower self-esteem. There is some tendency to grow up to become drug abusers themselves; although these types of children also are more likely to grow up and avoid drug use more strongly than others. There is little support for the concept of different family roles (for example the 'hero' or 'scapegoat'), although responsibilities for home tasks do tend to shift to the non-abusers.

Families of binge users tend to function more poorly than families of steady, functional users. Cohesive and affectionate families have better effects on the drug-abusing member's behaviour than disengaged and hostile families. Family members do not tend to decompensate (get worse, themselves) when the drug abuser quits using (Gordon and Barrett 1993).

Traditional treatment for the family, aside from confronting the abusers, would be to avoid **enabling** (that is acting in ways that support continued drug use, such as 'cleaning up' the consequences produced by the drug abusers). The family would let the drug abusers 'hit bottom' (that is reach a low point in their using careers in which they are finally honestly receptive to assistance), seek treatment or support separately from the drug abusers, and do so with emotional detachment. However, empirical research suggests that treatment is likely to be more successful in keeping the family together when both the abusers and other family members are seen together, rather than when they are separated. Also, for the drug use to stop, the drug use behaviour should be a focus of the treatment (Littrell 1991).

Family assistance programmes definitely should instruct the family regarding the parameters of addiction. All family members might do well to receive some sort of counselling. They may need to be separated from the drug abusers if the drug abusers need to go through a detoxification programme, or desire an inpatient stay. After a month or so, regular family treatment sessions are recommended. Key prevention and treatment characteristics include instruction in family skills training, potentially through in-home support, and family therapy to improve family communication, decrease conflict and improve parenting (O'Farrell and Fals-Stewart 2000).

Stages of recovery

When individuals enter a treatment setting, they may or may not be under the influence of a drug. If they are under the influence, they should initially be relieved of symptoms of distress and discomfort related to withdrawal.

Once a drug-free state has been established, the 'real' recovery work begins. Individuals presenting for treatment at inpatient facilities seemingly progress through various stages of recovery.

Johnson's stages of recovery

Vernon E. Johnson (1980) proposes that individuals progress through the following stages of recovery (based on a disease model of alcoholism): *admission, compliance, acceptance* and *surrender*. The first stage of *admission* occurs when individuals enter treatment settings and accept or admit that they have a drug abuse problem. This stage reinforces the disease concept of addiction. A disease perspective recognizes that individuals presenting for treatment are not responsible for their disease, but they are responsible for the process of recovery (Marlatt and Gordon 1985; Zweben 1993).

The second phase of recovery is *compliance*. Compliance involves a change in an individual's attitude from resisting to complying with treatment. *Resistance* is an individual's unwillingness to change or participate in their treatment, and can be problematic.

The third stage of recovery, *acceptance*, involves personal responsibility for recovery. This occurs when the individuals gain some insight into the severity of their problems. Gratitude may replace feelings of alienation from others. There exists an increase of self-awareness and self-acceptance, and congruency in indivduals' verbalizations, affect and body language.

The fourth stage of recovery, *surrender*, is signalled by an 'appropriate display of caution about the future' and the realization that aftercare is necessary for the continued maintenance of change. At this time, individuals may need the support of groups, such as Alcoholics Anonymous and Narcotics Anonymous, to help them cope with future difficulties. At this stage of recovery, individuals are ready for outpatient programmes.

Gorski and Miller's model of recovery

Gorski and Miller's **developmental model of recovery** (Gorski and Miller 1984, 1986) established a series of developmental periods and goals for each period. These periods are:

1 the *pretreatment period* or recognition of the addiction
2 the *stabilization period*, which involves crisis management or recovery from acute withdrawal and severe symptoms of post-acute withdrawal
3 the *early recovery period*, or acceptance and non-chemical coping
4 the *middle recovery*, at which time balanced living becomes a goal
5 the *late recovery*, which involves personality changes
6 *maintenance*, which entails a significant period of growth and development.

Recovery is a developmental process that varies from individual to individual, progressing in stages, and relapse is always a possibility. The phenomenon of post-acute withdrawal (PAW) (Gorski and Miller 1984, 1986) refers to the period of up to approximately eighteen months following acute withdrawal from drug use. Post-acute withdrawal is a biopsychosocial syndrome involving the occurrence of a variety of symptoms as a result of abstinence from drugs (for example psychosocial stress of coping with life drug-free). Post-acute withdrawal may be affected by chronic stress, personality factors (for example depression, sensation seeking and obsessive-compulsive disorders) and triggering events. Symptoms of PAW include

- the inability to think clearly
- emotional over-reactivity, numbness or artificial affect
- memory impairment or problems
- stress sensitivity
- sleep disturbances
- physical coordination problems

The danger of PAW is that the unbalanced experiences may lead to early relapse.

Motivation in cessation

Motivation is an essential component of drug use cessation and the maintenance of behaviour change. Motivation varies between individuals, and may fluctuate within an individual at any given time during an effort to stop using drugs, and during the maintenance of change. The willingness and ability to overcome unpleasant affect to achieve subsequent improved physical and emotional well-being is an important milestone. Several definitions of the concept of motivation for change have been proposed. Motivation may be a function of goals (*direction*) or tendencies to act (*energy*) (Bindra and Stewart 1966). The motivational source may be extrapersonal or intrapersonal. Others view motivation as an intrapersonal *state of readiness* to change (for example Prochaska and DiClemente 1982; DiClemente *et al.* 1991; Miller and Rollnick 1991). Conceptually, definitions of motivation all describe awareness of discrepancies between possible, desired goals and current states. This section of the chapter will examine briefly several models of motivation that have been used to advance drug abuse cessation (also see Nezami *et al.* 2001).

Direction-energy model
The direction-energy model (Young 1936; Bindra and Stewart 1978; Miller and Rollnick 1991; Emmons *et al.* 1995; Sussman 1996) was mentioned in Chapter 8 as one of the components of Project Towards No Drug Abuse, an indicated drug abuse prevention programme. This motivation model addresses the need to consider two components of motivation – a goal and the energy to reach the goal. A desire for self-image change, curiosity and a desire for mood enhancement guide the goal component of motivation. The

amount of energy invested in behaviour change is guided by perceiving a match between one's response repertoire with the demands of reaching the goal. In addition, the amount of energy invested in change is guided by one's embeddedness in a lifestyle about which a comfortable end state is perceived to be reached, and social or intrapersonal pressure to change (for example fear: Sutton and Eiser 1984).

Transtheoretical model

The transtheorectical model (Prochaska and DiClemente 1983; Prochaska *et al.* 1985, 1990; DiClemente *et al.* 1991) consists of a series of stages of change with early stages involving establishing a commitment to a goal, and later stages providing the energy to complete the goal. According to this model, an individual's *state of readiness* for change can be conceptualized as their motivation for change. This model includes five stages. The first is *precontemplation*, which is marked by a lack of interest in change. The second is *contemplation*, or the realization of a problem, the evaluation of the consequences of the person's present behaviour, and consideration of behaviour change. The third stage is *preparation*, occurring when individuals are motivated to make behavioural changes; individuals focus on actions that will bring about behaviour change. The fourth stage is *action*, or the actual quit attempt and willingness to stay abstinent through withdrawal symptoms. The final stage is *maintenance*, which reflects individuals' efforts to avoid relapse and solidify changes made.

Motivational interviewing

Motivational Interviewing (Miller and Rollnick 1991) is based on principles of cognitive therapy, Carl Rogers' client-centred approach, and the transtheoretical model. It involves a series of procedures for therapists to help clients clarify goals and follow through with their efforts to change behaviour. Motivation is conceptualized as the probability that a person will enter into, continue and adhere to a specific change strategy (Council of Philosophical Studies 1981). Motivation for change fluctuates over time, and *addressing this ambivalence* is considered a key for facilitating behavioural change. Motivational interviewing involves eight strategies to motivate behaviour change. One is *giving advice*, which entails problem identification, clarification of the need for change, and specific change encouraged. A second is *removing impediments to change* through identification, effective problem solving and cognitive restructuring. A third is *providing choices*. A fourth is *decreasing desirability (of not changing)* by promoting benefits of behaviour change. A fifth is providing *empathy*, which is marked by 'warmth, respect, caring, and understanding'. A sixth is *providing accurate feedback* of one's behaviour and outcomes to aid in altering or modifying risky behaviours. A seventh is *clarifying goals* by confronting the individual about discrepancies between future goals and present situation. Finally, an eighth is *supporting the development of self-efficacy (active helping)*.

Intrinsic-extrinsic motivation model

The Intrinsic-extrinsic motivation model proposes that goals are more likely to be obtained if the individual identifies with the desirability of obtaining that goal, as opposed to reaching the goal for some other reward (Curry *et al.* 1990). Different strategies, including motivational interviewing and proximal goal setting, have been shown to enhance intrinsic motivation (Manderlink and Harackiewicz 1984). Several theories of behaviour change emphasize intrinsic motivation, for example health belief model (Becker 1974) and protection motivation theory (R. Rogers 1975). Other theories focus on social/environmental elements (extrinsic rewards) that facilitate or motivate change (for example social learning theory: Rotter 1954), while others combine personal (intrinsic) and social (extrinsic) aspects as influencing motivation for behaviour change (for example theory of reasoned action: Fishbein and Ajzen 1975). There is an indication that extrinsic motivation will work as well as intrinsic motivation as long as behaviour is performance-dependent (see Nezami *et al.* 2001).

Self-regulation models of motivation

Self-regulation models of motivation propose that someone is motivated to achieve an optimal state or system balance; that awareness of lack of balance will lead to efforts to restore balance. Physiological mechanisms and self-initiated behaviour are pursued to reach homeostasis or an ideal state (Sommers 1972). In other words, individuals seek to reach a desirable subjective state (for example level of arousal: O'Connor 1989), level of coping or store of psychosocial assets (Ockene *et al.* 1981; Ho 1992; Leventhal *et al.* 1992), or physiological homeostasis (Sommers 1972).

Self-efficacy theory

Self-efficacy theory proposes that individuals will change if they are confident that they can do what is expected to achieve a possible outcome. Bandura (1977) suggested that self-efficacy is a common denominator in predicting behavioural change. Relevant to cessation of drug use, self-efficacy theory infers, in part, that cessation attempts depend on individuals' belief in their ability to abstain under a variety of high-risk situations. Self-efficacy includes magnitude (that is individuals' perception of their best performance), strength (that is the confidence in the perception of their strengths) and generality (that is the extent to which self-efficacy experiences are generalizable). The expectation of personal efficacy will enhance pursuit of coping behaviours that lead to drug use behavioural change and maintenance of change.

Treatment goals

Typically, the main goal of treatment programmes for drug abuse is to help drug abusers abstain from any drug use, with the exception of caffeine and cigarettes. In some programmes, or in some cases, the goal might be to provide regulatory controls over the drug use (for example to facilitate moderate or **controlled use** over alcohol). The secondary goal of most treatment programmes is to reinforce the maintenance of behaviour change through skills programming or continued support. Cigarette smoking in treatment programmes, however, often is accepted, is used as a shared activity among persons in recovery, and is cited with some fond reminiscing in recovery literature (for example Alcoholics Anonymous 1976). Nicotine dependence has been viewed as different from other dependencies, since the consequences are less immediately severe. Frequently, addicts in treatment programmes are encouraged to quit another drug first before attempting to quit smoking to avoid relapse (Hurt *et al.* 1993). However, 30 to 40 per cent of chemical dependency patients desire to quit tobacco concurrently with their drug of choice (main drug(s) abused). Cessation of tobacco use may actually reduce exposure to relapse cues, help cessation, and prevent relapse from others' drugs (Hurt *et al.* 1993; Sussman 2001b). The recovery movement more recently has been promoting the aspiration that drug abusers in recovery quit smoking while quitting other drugs.

The next two subsections of this chapter consider abstinence versus controlled use as treatment goals. Some drug abusers may desire to control their use rather than quit. Other drug abusers may desire to quit, but are having trouble quitting, and desire at least to minimize consequences of their behaviour (harm reduction).

Cessation versus controlled use

Treatment strategies aimed at reducing harmful drug and alcohol consumption may include both abstinence oriented and moderation goals. Among twelve-step models, total abstinence is deemed necessary to recover from an addiction; total abstinence is defined as no use of alcohol and any other mood-altering drugs, with the exception of cigarettes or caffeine. Many drug abusers abuse alcohol in addition to other drugs; but some do not have a history of alcohol abuse. In general, though, abusers of drugs other than alcohol ('drug addicts') believe that use of alcohol quickly disinhibits the drinker and reduces the probability of effective coping in high-risk situations. A lapse may then be inevitable if the individual values immediate gratification and loses perspective of long-term goals (Zweben 1993). Thus, alcohol use is not viewed as a safe alternative among drug addicts.

Among those who accept the disease model of addictive behaviours, there is no controlled drinking or use. Indeed, for many individuals total abstinence is necessary; any use at all results in out-of-control use and negative consequences. However 'the disease model produces a dichotomous restriction on the possible range of treatment outcomes: one is either abstinence (exerting control) or relapse (losing control)' (Marlatt and Gordon 1985: 7). For those who accept the concept that addictive behaviours are overlearned habits that are modifiable, controlled use is a feasible treatment outcome.

Strategies aimed at moderation of consumption (that is controlled drinking) may benefit some individuals, but in order to justify the superiority of controlled use over abstinence among individuals, extensive assessment of the population must be made. The ability to maintain controlled use of alcohol varies among individuals (the **continuum notion**) and may not be a viable or reliable option for most individuals abusing other drugs. On the other hand, controlled drinking or use as a goal may at least bring individuals into treatment sooner. Those who fail at controlled use then may be willing to consider abstinence as a goal. In fact, the abstinence rate among those who choose controlled drinking as a treatment goal is about the same as those who choose abstinence as a goal (Galaif and Sussman 1995).

Those few who become controlled drinkers tend previously to have been lighter drinkers, have suffered fewer legal and social consequences, may report having been less likely to experience gross behavioural changes when drinking, and have been abstinent a few years before drinking again. They tend to drink one to four drinks on social occasions, only occasionally. Interestingly, it appears that problem drinkers who receive treatment are twice as likely to become abstinent, but are half as likely to become controlled drinkers, than those who do not receive treatment, one year later (Peele 1998). Possibly, this could reflect a social bias in which problem drinkers in recovery come to believe in an abstinence violation effect (Marlatt and Gordon 1985). In other words, if they ever drink alcohol, they may feel that they 'lost the game' and that they might as well give up and drink regularly again. For information on current popular moderation-allowable programmes, please see

- Addiction Alternatives: www.addictionalternatives.com
- DrinkWise: www.med.umich.edu/drinkwise/
- moderation management: www.moderation.org

Harm reduction model
Quitting drug use is relatively difficult for many people, relapse rates are disconcerting, and many individuals have a long history of drug reinforcing behaviour that requires commitment to long-term change goals that cannot be established overnight. The concept of *harm reduction* as a drug abuse control policy has been a recent focus of attention. Harm reduction is an educational approach that is more respectful of responsible decision-making processes and which emphasizes the need to understand and appreciate existing individual control mechanisms (Erickson 1995). It has been used to protect drug addicts from many life-threatening consequences and to help them quit use in small steps.

A principal feature of harm reduction is the acceptance that some drug users cannot be expected to cease their drug use immediately. The idea of harm reduction is to ameliorate adverse consequences of drug use and reduce the risk of harm associated with addictive behaviours (Marlatt *et al.* 1993; Duncan *et al.* 1994; Pentz *et al.* 1997). Harm reduction focuses on short-term goals that are accessible and achievable (Single 1995). A harm reduction approach goal might be to gradually guide individuals away from engaging in problem behaviours, as well as to reduce the risks associated with involvement in the behaviours (Marlatt *et al.* 1993). Alternative behaviours may be seen as less immediately harmful and a step in the direction of decreased long-term risk. For example, tobacco use might be considered a substitute behaviour for another problem behaviour, such as heroin addiction. Although tobacco use is associated with numerous negative health outcomes, the consequences may be perceived as less immediately severe than the consequences of use of other drugs (Hurt *et al.* 1993).

Harm reduction programmes began in the United Kingdom for drug abusers who were being prescribed heroin and cocaine for maintenance of their habits. The Netherlands subsequently adopted a policy in which drug addicts and users were viewed as normal citizens and not as criminals or dependent persons (Roberts and Marlatt 1999). Currently, many harm reduction strategies for drug abuse have been implemented in various countries. These strategies include needle exchange programmes to decrease the risk of contracting blood diseases (for example HIV, hepatitis C) transmitted by sharing needles, legal needle sales, and methadone maintenance and detoxification programmes. These strategies also include designated driver programmes for drunk drivers, detoxification programmes for drug addicts where they can legally obtain a daily dose under the care of a physician to help minimize physical withdrawal, and pharmacological adjuncts for drug use. Other potentially beneficial harm reduction tactics, used in various private community clinics or 'street settings', include the instruction in safe methods of inhalant huffing, instruction in methods of safe sex, the distribution of condoms and the use of marijuana as a maintenance drug for other drugs (see Pentz *et al.* 1997; see also www.harmreduction.org).

Treatment programmes

Twelve-step recovery model

Twelve-step programmes such as Alcoholics Anonymous (AA) and Narcotics Anonymous (NA) provide the basic philosophy of change for many inpatient and outpatient alcohol and drug abuse treatment facilities in the United States in particular, but also worldwide. More importantly, these programmes are probably the main sources of social support for the maintenance of habit change. AA and NA are abstinence oriented, multidimensional, non-profit, humanistic, voluntary, supportive, self-help fellowships for individuals for whom drug use has become problematic. Bill Wilson and Dr Robert Smith, both self-proclaimed alcoholics, founded Alcoholics Anonymous in 1935. AA has become one of the most widely disseminated self-help treatment groups, where membership is estimated at well over 2 million. AA begat numerous other twelve-step programmes, over 100 of them now, that are based on the structure and principles of AA (for example NA – Narcotics Anonymous, MA – Marijuana Anonymous, CA – Cocaine Anonymous, and so on). All of the twelve-step sobriety-based programmes are based on a disease model of addiction and require complete abstinence from all drugs except cigarettes and coffee. (There also exists a Nicotine Anonymous fellowship: www.nicotine-anonymous.org). The only requirement for membership is a desire to stop using. The twelve-step programme model is self-supporting, does not accept outside contributions, and has no opinion on outside issues.

The essential component of these twelve-step programmes is that drug abusers help one another to stay sober. These programmes are built on the principle that a recovering alcoholic or addict can altruistically and effectively help a fellow sufferer to gain or maintain sobriety. Members openly talk about their struggles and successes and develop problem-solving skills, as well as friendships with others, comforted in the knowledge that they are not alone in their plight (Yoder 1990).

Drug addiction and alcoholism are believed to be allergies, manifested by a baseline subjective sense of restlessness, irritability, and discontent ('r.i.d.'), along with implicit cognitive processes that place alcohol or drug use as a desired behavioural option in high-risk situations (Alcoholics Anonymous 1976; Narcotics Anonymous 1988; Marijuana Anonymous 1995). The alcoholic or drug addict, when sober, may feel quite uncomfortable within their skin, and can 'fall' victim to their 'alcoholic/addict voice'. Self-statements such as 'I won't use cocaine as long as this terrible event doesn't happen, but it happened', 'I could smoke marijuana safely under a certain condition; this is it', or automatic thoughts of 'It would be nice to have a drink' may suddenly pop to mind as individuals pass by a club or experience emotional turmoil. When the alcohol or other drug is imbibed, many times without much forethought, there may be a great calming effect, perhaps subjective alterations in sensory perceptions, and perhaps a greater subjective sense that their role in the world is quite different from what it was before drinking or using. However, at the same time, there may be a loss of control over the amount used, generally after using for a brief period of hours or days, and loss of behavioural control exhibited while drunk or high.

An important adjunct to the programme is self-selecting a sponsor who provides support and helps to guide the individual in the programme. The Twelve Traditions outline AA's basic premises about the organization, such as ensuring members' anonymity, and protecting the privacy and integrity of the organization and the sobriety of its members (Yoder 1990). The Twelve Steps provide an internal process of change through which members break through the denial that may accompany the addiction, admit their powerlessness over alcohol or other drugs and learn to make lifelong changes in daily living (Spiegel and Mulder 1986). By following the twelve-steps, members learn to trust a 'higher power' as a means to obtaining a daily reprieve from urges or thoughts of using drugs (for example Chappel 1992).

Anonymity is an essential component of twelve-step programmes, affirming the concept – principles *before personalities*. The anonymity of membership creates an atmosphere of intimacy, trust and support. Members maintain personal anonymity at the level of the press, radio and films. The twelve-step programme is not connected with political, religious or law enforcement groups. Individuals of all ages, races, sexual identity and religion or lack of religion may join the programme. However, an attitude of indifference or intolerance towards spiritual principles may defeat a person's recovery. Honesty, open-mindedness and willingness are essential components of the recovery process.

The twelve-steps as a programme of recovery are as follows:

1 We admitted that we were powerless over our addiction, that our lives had become unmanageable.
2 We came to believe that a power greater than ourselves could restore us to sanity.
3 We made a decision to turn our will and our lives over to the care of God, as we understood Him.
4 We made a searching and fearless moral inventory of ourselves.
5 We admitted to God, to ourselves, and to another human being the exact nature of our wrongs.
6 We were entirely ready to have God remove all these defects of character.
7 We humbly asked Him to remove our shortcomings.
8 We made a list of all persons we had harmed and became willing to make amends to them all.
9 We made direct amends to such people wherever possible, except when to do so would injure them or others.
10 We continued to take personal inventory and when we were wrong promptly admitted it.
11 We sought through prayer and meditation to improve our conscious contact with God as we understood Him, praying only for knowledge of His will for us and the power to carry that out.
12 Having had a spiritual awakening as a result of these steps, we tried to carry this message to addicts (alcoholics), and to practise these principles in all our affairs (see also www.alcoholics-anonymous.org or www.na.org).

Support for and criticisms of twelve-step programmes

There has been much anecdotal support of AA, in particular, but very little controlled research. Research determining AA's effectiveness is scanty and difficult to achieve, mostly because of the enforced anonymity of its members, even though AA supports the value of scientific inquiry. Empirical support for the efficacy of AA is often based solely on the number of individuals who participate in AA, or on the testimony of individual members. However, some empirical outcome research does exist. Some studies have examined AA's effectiveness using correlational data. Correlational studies illustrate a favourable relationship between AA participation and sobriety. Studies of attrition in AA and experimental studies generally fail to support AA's efficacy over other treatments (see Galaif and Sussman 1995).

Recent work suggests that AA, cognitive behavioural treatment, and motivational interviewing approaches are about equal in effectiveness for the treatment of alcoholism (Project MATCH: Connors 1998). Likewise, an alternative medicine approach (for example, meditation, relaxation) has been found to be as effective at a twelve-month follow-up as a brief coping skills approach for the treatment of cocaine abuse (Rohsenow *et al.* 2000). Looking at these findings another way, AA or other 'spiritual' approaches appear to do no worse than other approaches.

Another major criticism is that some researchers and practitioners may think of twelve-step programmes as cult-like organizations (Bufe 1991). Some critics believe that twelve-step programmes encourage dependence upon the programme itself, openly discourage scepticism, and may lead to a lack of involvement in other social organizations and resentment towards those not involved in the programmes. Also, the programmes have been criticized as becoming a substitute of one addiction for another. Furthermore, some members actively promote the idea that twelve-step programmes are the only 'road' to recovery. Those who do not readily embrace twelve-step concepts may be made to feel unwelcome at meetings (Bufe 1991). Moreover, those who do not remain in twelve-step programmes may be blamed for their 'character defects' or their lack of desire to stop drinking or using, instead of being sympathized with or being viewed as individuals pursuing other avenues of gaining sobriety (Trimpey 1989, 1996).

However, there is no named leader, no hierarchical, authoritarian structure within the organization, and all groups are autonomous. Twelve-step programmes do not exploit members financially, nor do they become actively involved in the political arena, exemplary of cults. They do not go to any lengths to retain members, nor are they supposed to recruit newcomers actively, or provide closed, all-encompassing environments exclusively for members; rather, twelve-step programmes provide an open environment for anyone who wants to stop drinking or using. Thus, twelve-step programmes are not cults, although they appear to have some cult-like qualities, as do many fellowships.

The cure for the 'disease': on spirituality

Twelve-step programmes strongly espouse the notion that spiritual experiences are the means to arrest the diseases of alcoholism and drug addiction. Programme literature asserts that these diseases are not only physical, mental and emotional diseases, but also diseases of the spirit (for example Alcoholics Anonymous 1976). The topic of **spirituality** as applied to human affairs has a very long history. Perhaps the main influence in the twentieth century has been the work of William James. James ([1902] 1958) argued that the basis of personal religious experience is derived from two considerations: first, that there is something wrong with the human condition as it 'naturally stands', and second, that people are remedied through connection with higher powers. James' work heavily influenced the thinking of the pioneers of Alcoholics Anonymous. AA suggested that belief in a higher power, and attempts to conform one's behaviour with that of this higher power, would lead one to recovery from alcoholism. Wellness advocates, in turn, were strongly influenced by Alcoholics Anonymous, and contemporary weight-watching groups, and espoused theories such as salutogenesis (belief in and comfort from holding a personal construct of life: Antonovsky 1984). The wellness research and recovery movements are inextricably related. Arguably, conscientiousness (thinking of others) and experiential peace (or lack of negative affectivity) may be the two main components of spirituality, which are attained through a change in beliefs and engagement in spiritual-related activities (Sussman *et al.* 1997b).

Who do twelve-step programmes help?
These programmes help those who actively participate in the programmes, and who become stable members. These programmes seem to attract certain types of individuals. Stable members tend to be middle class, male, gregarious (comfortable in social contexts), comfortable with high self-disclosure, and single or estranged from their family. Also, stable members tend to have familial problems, feel anxious and lonely, are older and less educated, embrace a disease model, report more drug-related symptoms prior to treatment, and are more religious than non-members or those who drop out of these programmes.

Coping programmes as alternatives to a disease model

Many drug abusers (alcoholics and addicts) may best regain control of their lives through a programme that does not require moral betterment or belief in a higher power to gain sobriety. Some individuals do not want to feel powerless or dependent upon others, or to attend meetings for the rest of their lives. Thus, there is a need for alternative programmes in the treatment of drug abuse. Other self-help treatment alternatives to AA include Rational Recovery, SMART Recovery and Secular Organizations for Sobriety, which are discussed in this section.

Rational Recovery (RR), established in 1985 by Jack Trimpey, a recovered alcoholic, was originally based on the principles of rational emotive therapy. It is considered to be a non-traditional cognitive-oriented programme of self-empowered recovery from substance dependency. Although RR makes no demands on the participant, the individual should have the internal motivation and desire to maintain sobriety (abstinence from alcohol or other drugs).

It advocates that individuals learn to abstain from drugs through many means, such as adhering to rational thought (Trimpey 1989, 1996). Individuals learn that their use of a drug is an irrational decision. RR is a programme in which the individual comes to terms with the issues of addiction and recovery and problem solves that there is no place for alcohol or other drugs in their lives.

Unlike AA, this programme separates spirituality from sobriety. Meeting attendance has been recommended between six months to one year, not lifelong; in recent times meetings are even discouraged because of the side-effects of group experience. Anecdotally, it appears that affiliation of RR members with each other and the organization is much longer. Moreover, the focus is on self-affirmation through taking responsibility for one's actions. This approach identifies several specific irrational beliefs that perpetuate the addictive behaviour and then offers a means to change ones' emotions and behaviours. A key component is 'The Big Plan' or a commitment never to drink again. RR is focused on the here-and-now and attempts to prevent relapses as well as enhance self-esteem and personal empowerment. Individuals gain insight into how self-defeating beliefs encourage drinking behaviour, as directed by one's BEAST, one's primitive brain operations. Individuals learn to replace these thoughts with rational ones that are opposed to drinking or using (Trimpey 1989, 1996). They feel empowered when they rationally choose not to drink or use again (their 'rational' brain defeats their 'irrational', 'primitive' brain). Relapse prevention involves the use of problem-solving strategies, which could be used in high-risk situations – those in which the individual might be tempted to drink or use. In summary, RR is a learning process based on rational self-empowerment, where the person beats the addiction and gains self-esteem in the process (see also www.rational.org).

Self-Management and Recovery Training (SMART Recovery) sponsors about 250 weekly support groups in North America for individuals who desire to abstain from any type of addictive behaviour. Support groups are run by individuals who have had difficulties with drugs and by individuals who have not had any personal struggles with drugs but who have received sufficient training. SMART Recovery argues that addictive behaviour is problematic because it interferes with other activities – and causes harm. SMART Recovery views addictive behaviours as learned habits that have become extreme, and that the same learning contingencies apply to both substance and process addictions. Habit change is viewed as a psychological problem. The SMART programme is cognitive-behavioural in orientation (Hovarth 1999). Its Four Point Programme involves enhancing and maintaining motivation (for example considering the costs and benefits of using and quitting, increasing self-awareness), coping with urges (not acting on temptation, developing alternative behaviours), solving other problems (for example identifying and resolving conflict) and balancing momentary and enduring satisfactions (see www.smartrecovery.org).

Secular Organizations for Sobriety/Save Our Selves (SOS) was formed in 1986 as a non-spiritual programme specifically for those alcoholics or addicts who were uncomfortable with the spiritual nature of twelve-step programmes (see www.secularhumanism.org/sos/index.htm). As a secular approach to recovery, abstinence and sobriety are both prioritized as separate issues from all other issues in people's lives, including religion and spirituality. This non-religious programme encourages self-empowerment, self-determination, self-affirmation and free thought. It is believed that sobriety can be successfully achieved through personal responsibility and self reliance (Christopher 1988). There are even self-help books for persons to quit drinking and drug use, that reflect a general philosophy of self-reliance (for example Dorsman 1991).

SOS is a non-profit national organization of autonomous, non-professional groups dedicated solely to helping individuals achieve and maintain abstinence. The only demand of SOS is that participants are sincere about wanting sobriety, the major goal of this programme. Like twelve-step programmes, this organization does not endorse any unrelated matters or become involved in any outside controversy. However, SOS does directly encourage the scientific study of drug abuse and it does not limit its beliefs to one theory of addiction. Members share experiences, information, strength and encouragement in a friendly, honest, supportive and anonymous atmosphere. Each group is self-supported, using only members' contributions. SOS also publishes an eight-page quarterly newsletter offering items of interest to recovering persons, professionals and families of alcoholics and addicts.

Cognitive-behavioural residential programmes

Cognitive-behavioural residential programmes consist of 24-hour supervised treatment. These residential treatment programmes are frequently based on the principles of Narcotics or Alcoholics Anonymous but they include a variety of methods to eliminate chemical dependency through continuous exposure to structured cognitive behavioural programming. They include both behavioural tasks to modify habits as well as cognitive restructuring. The objectives of these programmes include the elimination of dependency on all drugs (except nicotine and caffeine). They also include development of self-awareness and self-worth; the practice of self-discipline; identification and clarification of problems that may threaten sobriety, and problem-solving techniques; the enhancement of physical and psychological well-being; and the enhancement of coping mechanisms and alternative solutions to self-destructive behaviours. These programmes also assist in establishing or enhancing social support and healthy familial and interpersonal relationships through counselling and educational classes, and milieu therapy. In addition, many of these programmes provide relapse prevention programming, assist in determining vocational aptitude and educational needs through skills development, assist in establishing realistic personal goals, and enhance the utilization and access to community resources. Treatment contracts in these programmes tend to vary in length of stay (that is some are 30 days, some 90, some 4–6 months, etc.; see also NIDA 1999b; Etheridge *et al.* 1997). High alcohol and drug involvement and cognitively impaired individuals benefit more by inpatient stays, with any type of treatment orientation, than those who are relatively low in alcohol or drug involvement or not cognitively impaired (Rychtarik *et al.* 2000).

Outpatient clinics

Outpatient services are appropriate for individuals who have a diagnosis of substance abuse but do not require treatment in residential facilities, partial hospitalization or inpatient settings. Outpatient services can provide weekly groups and personal counselling sessions, and case management, designed to assist those who are abstinent and adjusting to the community. In addition, problem-solving, reality therapy and several cognitive-behavioural approaches may be taught (Etheridge *et al.* 1997). Outpatient clinics and self-help programmes require self-regulation, commitment to abstinence and a high level of motivation. They may be best tailored to individuals who have completed residential treatment and have acquired necessary coping skills and commitment to sobriety so as to be able to live as sober outpatients. Outpatient services may be most appropriate when an individual's environmental support systems (for example family and those with whom the individual lives) and clinical indicators do not impact negatively on the treatment process or reduce the likelihood of success. Outpatient treatment is counterindicated if the individual is suicidal, assaultive or demonstrating any thought disorder or other concomitant emotional/psychological/behavioural crises; and when the individual reports difficulties maintaining sobriety without 24-hour supervised treatment. For those persons who receive outpatient services, a combination of twelve-step programming with weekly outpatient treatment (for example counselling) has been shown to result in higher abstinence rates than use of only one modality or neither modality. Thus, more intensive treatment for outpatients tends to lead to better results (Mathias 1999).

Treatment techniques

Behavioural and cognitive-behavioural approaches

Behavioural approaches focus on observable antecedents and consequences of a behaviour without acknowledging cognitive mediation of behaviour. Behaviour modification techniques consist of a variety of behaviour-rewarding shaping experiences in an attempt to attain and maintain change. Cognitive-behavioural approaches include modification of the behaviour and cognition, and assert that cognitive structures and processes (thinking) are events that may precipitate or maintain the behaviour (Kadden 1999). Behavioural and cognitive-behavioural approaches seek at least three goals.

First, they desire to decrease or increase the frequencies of certain behaviours (that is decrease the frequency of behaviours compatible with drug use and increase the frequency of behaviours incompatible with drug use). Second, they desire to shape new adaptive behaviours (for example social skills development). Finally, they desire to modify cognition appropriately (that is decrease the frequency of cognition compatible with drug use and increase the frequency of cognition incompatible with drug use). Changing behaviour patterns or frequency can occur by using a variety of methods, including systematic desensitization, aversive conditioning, cue exposure, flooding, token systems, environmental shifts, stimulus control and **contracting** (see Gottman and Leiblum 1974 for details). Training new behaviours can be accomplished using shaping, modelling or observational learning, role playing and assertiveness training. Finally, modifying one's thinking or inner speech can be accomplished through use of strategies, including self-instructional training and cognitive restructuring (Meichenbaum 1977). Other strategies used to modify one's thinking include self-verbalizations, positive affirmations, thought stopping, rehearsal and imaging (for example Meichenbaum 1977).

Social skills training

An integral component of cognitive-behavioural programmes implemented throughout treatment is social skills training. Social skills training may include self-control skills (showing restraint under simulated high-risk conditions; urge control), shaping of good listening or conversational skill (for example through direct instruction, role-play instruction or by example) and stimulus control approaches (learning how to remove oneself from drug cues, avoidance or escape behaviour learning). Social skills training involves the receipt of reinforcement based on the performance of specified behaviours in interpersonal situations. Because a lack of social skills may influence drug use (for example the inability to refuse drugs, involvement in drug-related activities), social skills training often involves assertiveness training. Methods of assertiveness training vary, but in general, assertiveness focuses on enhancing appropriate expression of feelings and personal rights, and skills training in refusal of unreasonable requests of others. Role playing is a primary vehicle for social skills training. Often modelling of assertive behaviour, behavioural rehearsal, practice, performance and immediate feedback, and reinforcement components are included in the development of role-playing skills (Sussman *et al.* 1995a).

One example of social skills training is instruction in drug refusal. Drug refusal involves training individuals that they need to be able to refuse drugs and that it takes skills to do so. Individuals brainstorm situations in which they have to refuse drugs, as well as ways in which individuals offer or pressure one to use. For example drinkers might ask, 'How come you're not drinking? What's the matter – you're too good to drink with us?' Recognition of risk situations helps the individual learn to resist social pressures.

Individual goals may be established, such as feeling comfortable with refusal assertion, and reinforcing personal commitment to abstain, and a list of refusal techniques may be generated (Marlatt and Gordon 1985). Role playing is a technique used to provide opportunities to practise refusal methods in a non-threatening environment in which mistakes do not lead to relapse.

Contracting

Contracting is a method of formalizing or reinforcing individuals' commitment to change, and is helpful when individuals express ambivalence about change or have been unable to maintain abstinence or control their behaviours. Contracting can include contingencies describing penalties for violation of the contract, such as paying a fine in the event of a lapse or relapse. This approach may work while the contract is in operation. For example, contracting between members of a couple in which one member is alcoholic has shown some promise (behavioural couples therapy (BCT): O'Farrell and Fals-Stewart 2000). However, the use of external restraints or penalties can backfire. For example, when a relapse contract expires or the contingencies lose their incentive appeal, an individual may drink or use other drugs again (Marlatt and Gordon 1985).

Who should be the treatment agent (former drug abusers or professionals)?

Twelve-step programmes accept the therapeutic value of one drug abuse victim helping another; that one 'alcoholic' or 'addict' can best understand and help another alcoholic or addict. An integral aspect of many inpatient treatment programmes based on the principles of NA or AA is the employment of certified chemical dependency counsellors with personal histories of drug abuse and familiarity with the standards and values of the drug culture. These individuals function as role models that, by example, demonstrate the contrasting drug lifestyle with more prosocial lifestyle changes. The belief is that the sooner drug abusers face their problems within society and in everyday living, the faster they become acceptable, responsible and productive members of society. Ex-abusers treating current abusers lend credibility to treatment programmes and insight into the culture. Also, many professional non-drug abusing ('normies') treatment agents often are provided with minimal training in chemical dependency while in professional school.

There are, however, aspects of treatment that ex-drug abuser counsellors may not be able to address thoroughly or acknowledge as attributable to causes other than the 'addiction disease'. It is helpful to employ the support of professional personnel who might be better equipped to deal with issues of co-morbidity (for example, clinical depression, post-traumatic stress disorder, eating disorders, bipolar disorder) and are able to teach social skills training and provide other therapeutic services (for example see Horvath 1999 or www.smartrecovery.org).

Relapse prevention

Treatment of addictive behaviours often involves relapse prevention. Relapse refers to the use of a drug after a period of abstinence. Recurrence of use can vary from a single event (slip or lapse) to a time-limited episode or a binge, to a full-blown return to the frequency and pattern of use prior to abstinence (relapse) (Marlatt and Gordon 1985). The concept of a relapse can also refer to a chain of events preceding the recurrence of the drug use behaviour (the relapse situation). Relapse appears to be linked to factors such as *failure to avoid drug use settings* (for example social pressure), *failure to maintain effective coping mechanisms* in high-risk situations (that is self-efficacy when exposure to drugs cannot be prevented) and *drug cravings or intrusive thoughts about using drugs*. Background factors found frequently to influence relapse include negative affective states such as anger, sadness, boredom, anxiety, depression, guilt, apprehension and loneliness; interpersonal problems and conflict; and social pressures or inappropriate social support networks (Marlatt and Gordon 1985; Daley and Salloum 1999).

Gorski and Miller (1984, 1986) developed a list of relapse phases and warning signs based on analyses of histories of relapse-prone individuals committed to maintaining sobriety, but who were unable to stay sober, and returned to compulsive use. The relapse process entails several sequential phases. First, individuals may experience *internal changes* in thinking, feelings and behaviour. They may not feel they are balanced. Next, they may engage in *denial* – individuals may stop being honest with others about their thoughts and feelings. Next, these individuals may engage in *avoidance and defensiveness*. Individuals might begin avoiding others or any situation that might force them to be honest about changes in thoughts, feelings and behaviours. Soon individuals may experience *crisis building* – problems in sobriety that they do not understand. Soon these individuals may feel a sense of *immobilization*, of being trapped while problems seem unmanageable. Soon individuals may begin to experience *confusion and overreaction* – the individuals have difficulty thinking clearly and managing feelings and emotions. Next, they may experience *depression*. In other words, they may come to believe that life is not worth living and lack the desire to take action. At this point, *behavioural loss of control* begins. These individuals can no longer control their thoughts, feelings and behaviours and they may experience feelings of helplessness. Also there comes *recognition of loss of control*. Individuals realize that their life has become unmanageable. Next, individuals may experience a sense of *option reduction*. They may feel trapped and unable to manage their lives; they may believe self-medication with drugs or alcohol is their only way out. At this point comes the final phase of *alcohol and drug use*. Individuals return to using, they try to control their use and they lose control. (For an in-depth review of warning signs see Gorski and Miller 1984, 1986.)

Although it is possible that behavioural interventions with external controls during early recovery may help individuals achieve abstinence following a lapse or relapse, ultimately individuals need to establish control and self-regulatory mechanisms to maintain abstinence. Some externally controlled behavioural interventions that might benefit the return to abstinence following a relapse include urine testing, the use of antagonist drugs (such as naltrexone or antabuse), regulatory controls of finances (for example turning moneys over to family members) and structuring individuals' time (Zweben 1993). However, maintaining perceived self-control or self-efficacy and being able to exert effective coping skills when confronted with high-risk situations is essential to preventing relapse. If individuals do not effectively cope in response to high-risk stimuli, then self-efficacy (that is the perceived ability to cope when confronted with obstacles) may decrease and threaten ones' ability to resist relapsing. Regardless of measurement of coping skill level, individuals who do experience greater increases in self-efficacy while in treatment have been shown to exhibit higher abstinence rates at follow-up (L. Miller 1991).

Marlatt's relapse prevention model

Marlatt (1985: 3) conceptualizes relapse prevention as a 'self-management program designed to enhance the maintenance stage of the habit-change process'. The objective is to enhance individuals' ability to anticipate and cope with the problem of relapse. Relapse prevention is a *self-control programme that combines behavioural skills training, cognitive interventions and lifestyle change procedures and is based on the principles of social-learning theory.* The goals of the programme for relapse prevention are: first, to anticipate and prevent the occurrence of a relapse after the initiation of a habit change attempt, and second, to help someone recover from a 'slip' or lapse before it escalates into a full-blown relapse. Relapse prevention can be applied towards the effective maintenance of abstinence regardless of the methods used to initiate abstinence (for example attending AA meetings, aversion therapy).

For the purpose of general lifestyle change the relapse prevention programme can be used to facilitate changes in personal habits and daily activities to minimize the risk of physical disease and psychological stress, and to achieve a balanced lifestyle. The relapse prevention model proposes that individuals are not considered responsible for the development of their problem lifestyles but they are able to compensate for their difficulties in treatment by *assuming responsibility* for changing their behaviour. As individuals undergo a process of reconditioning, cognitive restructuring and the acquisition of various skills, they begin to accept greater responsibility for behaviour change (Marlatt and Gordon 1985). Individuals acquire new skills and learn new coping strategies through involvement in *self-management* of relapse prevention. Additionally, individuals are actively involved in the learning of mental processes including *awareness* of high-risk stimuli (vigilance) and *responsible decision-making*.

Aftercare

It is beneficial to engage individuals in some form of aftercare treatment upon completion of a programme of behaviour change. Aftercare is encouraged to enhance treatment efforts, monitor changes being made in independent living and ensure delivery of helpful, ongoing services, such as individual counselling, group sessions, crisis intervention, environmental advocacy and social support. It is an essential component of the treatment process. Although many individuals are able to obtain the skills necessary to maintain abstinence, the rehearsal of these skills during residential treatment and the maintenance and generalization of these skills to other environments and social settings is crucial to lifestyle changes. Aftercare of some kind may be the most important element in the maintenance of cessation (for example Sussman *et al.* 1986).

Summary

Treatment programmes can be effective in reducing the incidence of future negative consequences of drug abuse. A very important prerequisite for effective treatment is that individuals want to solve their drug abuse problems, are willing to work hard and will honestly comply with a treatment plan. However, it is unclear at this time whether or not any treatment is superior to any other over substantial periods of time (Vaillant 1983; Peele and Brodsky 1991). Given the current state of knowledge, political bickering among different treatment camps probably is counterproductive. Stopping problematic drug use should supersede *how* individuals accomplish such goals. Perhaps individuals should be able to select treatments from a menu based on their willingness to comply with that treatment they will receive.

The literature does provide compelling evidence that some type of *long-term treatment*, formal or informal, is necessary to treat problem drug use effectively. Indeed, it appears that organizations providing long-term supportive treatment can minimize relapse while increasing sobriety maintenance (for example Sussman *et al.* 1986; Fletcher *et al.* 1997). Also, in order to minimize relapse and disrupt the course of addictive behaviours, continuous exposure to alternative reinforcing behaviours (that is rewarding health behaviours) is recommended, implemented in conjunction with traditional treatment and relapse prevention programmes. Involvement in healthy hobbies, engaging in regular exercise and development of healthy relationships are very helpful to the development of a balanced lifestyle. Finally, we note that many individuals recover from substance abuse problems spontaneously without formal treatment programmes. The evaluation of factors that contribute to spontaneous recovery may help provide insight into the interplay of factors affecting formal interventions, real-life events and lifestyle changes (Blomqvist 1996).

Future considerations in the drug abuse arena

We have now presented several chapters on the delineation, aetiology, prevention and cessation of drug abuse. Numerous issues were discussed and some answers were provided. Now what? What should we be thinking of for the future of drug abuse research and practice? This chapter addresses this question and suggests possible future research directions.

What is drug abuse?

First, we emphasize the importance of clarifying terms and remaining open to new ideas to permit learning from each other. While speaking with some people about drug abuse, they commented, 'Well, finally we all agree that drug abuse is a disease.' In response, we questioned whether these individuals wanted to know our opinions about the subject, to which they responded that they were not sure they did but to go ahead. We commented that our opinions depend on their definition of a disease. To that response, these individuals did not wish to discuss the issue further. Does this example sound familiar?

It is our goal to increase our understanding of drug abuse. Unfortunately, there are many political misgivings such that open communication is difficult. Some of these misgivings are due to the allocation of moneys – those individuals whose theoretical stance on drug abuse commands the most respect also may control use of government and private funds. Use of certain terms over others may lead to receipt of more insurance coverage as well (Quintero and Nichter 1996). Conversely, people who control the flow of money may also control the ideas propagated. Hence, the flow of funds and the power of lobbyists and decision-makers can limit the study of drug use and abuse.

Additionally, some misgivings pertain to fragility of personal construct systems. Some individuals may feel that they remain drug-free because they firmly 'believe' in something. In discussions with 'non-believers', their belief system can be challenged. They are forced to think through their assumptions. Who wants to have their conceptual world attacked? They may resent and resist any challenges regarding their perspective on drug use and abuse. Alternatively, they may simply not process contrary information (Stacy and Ames 2001). Hence, nothing is learned.

Finally, some misgivings pertain to uniformity of treatment. Many people want to believe that one kind of treatment works for everyone. If one kind of treatment works for everyone, one may deduce that one aetiology or one conceptual framework of drug use and abuse applies to everyone. Do we know that? What has been written in this text thus far would suggest that no one simple framework is applicable to all drug users and abusers. It may follow that no one treatment works for everyone.

So, we repeat the question – what is drug abuse? The best answer we can provide at this time is that 'drug abuse is what drug misuse does'. Drug abuse means consequences. People get hurt. To stop drug abuse is to stop the consequences of drug use – physical, social, emotional, legal, functional and environmental.

Is drug abuse a disease? It appears to be a recurrent condition. Individuals who appear to suffer from it used to love it, then hate it, and cannot stop it. If that is good enough to define it as a disease, then okay. If one demands to know the mediation of drug abuse (for example the social or biological bases of substance abuse) before accepting a disease notion, then it does not yet qualify as a disease construct. Also, if one considers sudden onset a criterion of a disease, then it is only a disease for a minority of drug abusers. If one tends to view bad habits as a reflection of lack of alternative reinforcement and a poorly developed personality, then arguably it is not a disease, but rather an abuse of normal wiring. We would posit that drug abuse is a disease as extrinsically defined. We believe that people do not generally choose to suffer consequences of drug use – that an involuntary component is operative – and that social support, information, skills and hard work are required to conquer drug abuse. It generally is not the purposeful act of amoral wrongdoers.

Is drug abuse the same as other maladaptive habits, such as gambling or sex addiction? In other words, are compulsive behaviours and drug intake one of the same constellation of problem behaviours with some underlying common aetiologic source (for example such as a biochemical imbalance that demands means to provide a sense of calm)? If these behaviours have similar underpinnings, then why do some individuals become compulsive only about certain behaviours and not others? Some pathological gamblers do not have drinking problems. Many people do not become addicted to soccer, and so on. Arguably some addictions involve engaging in behaviour repeatedly to obtain a 'high' feeling (that is the behaviour affects endogenous neurotransmitters), whereas other addictions involve intake of drugs to induce a similar 'high' feeling. Future work is needed to further our understanding of the involuntary component of health behaviour disorders. Possibly, some of this work will be enter the realm of philosophy, while other work will be in the public health arena, as researchers continue to clarify what is and is not a 'disease' versus a 'disorder'. We can all agree that if a 'disease' label 'didn't do anything', it probably would not be used.

Assessment of drug abuse

Certainly, with moderate error of measurement, we can detect the prevalence of drugs in an individual's system. We can also observe drug-related behaviours and accidents. Of course, when the definition of drug abuse is not clear, its measurement will be even less so. As more work is completed to define the parameters of drug abuse, we can develop more accurate measures. Currently, the primary measure of drug abuse is a DSM-IV type interview, in which the clinician decides whether or not individuals suffer legal consequences, engage in dangerous activities, do not meet major role obligations, and suffer social consequences. Certainly, suffering legal consequences of drug use and engaging in dangerous activities while using are easy to measure. But, when do we decide that an individual *really* has failed to meet major role obligations and when does someone *really* suffer social consequences of drug abuse? If an individual does not have a job, and they are part of a subgroup within which a large minority does not work, what are the main obligations that remain? Certainly, if someone does not put on new clothes while using drugs, and remains in one location for a long period, isolated from other people, one might suggest that this person – whose body smells poorly and is doing little else – is a drug abuser. (This assumes that one controls for other potential diagnoses, such as depression.) But where is the dividing line? After all, the DSM-IV criteria consist of combinations of binary responses. The problem here may be trying to assess a quantitative phenomenon (that 'drug abuse continuum') as if it were qualitative. Possibly, the Alcohol Use Inventory and related measures provide a better means of understanding the dimensionality of drug abuse. Further investigation into, and development of, more multidimensional assessment tools is needed.

Also, identification of those at high risk for drug abuse – through assessment of non-drug use behaviour – needs investigation if targeted programming is to be implemented. To date, genetic research has not been too helpful in this regard, aside from revealing that a percentage of sons or brothers of male alcoholics are at risk for drug abuse. There is some suggestion of EEG or Chromosome 1 abnormalities among those at risk for alcoholism (Reich 2000). Observations of emotional lability and hostility may also be important predictors (Shedler and Block 1990). However, how do we identify these characteristics from an idiographic perspective?

Biochemical validation and assessment is not without its drawbacks in terms of protection of confidentiality, possibilities of false-positive and false-negative results, as well as imperfect measurement. Thus, not only do we question the validity of various assessment tools, but also we question the ethics and reliability of these tools. For the time being, the more ways drug abuse is defined and the more measures used, while protecting human subjects, the better. Presently, individuals responsible for assessment tend to use multiple measures and multiple sources of information. They also frequently err on the side of caution. Of course, caution can swing two ways – protection of individual privacy (do not diagnose too quickly) versus protection of society (diagnose readily to prevent social problems). Somewhere out there is a true covariance matrix that contains the *real* drug abuse label.

Aetiology of drug abuse

What do we know? Drug abuse appears to be determined by a combination of risk factors that appear to differ for different individuals. These factors include both intrapersonal (genetics, personality, cognition, emotion) and extrapersonal (sociocultural, environmental) factors. How these factors combine to determine drug abuse subtypes is not clear. We may speculate that the greater the number of 'risk' predictors that are operative, the greater will be the likelihood of drug abuse occurring, and the greater will be the drug abuse problem when it does occur (for example high levels of use, high impairment). Also, we may conjecture that combinations from both intrapersonal and extrapersonal domains lead to greater drug abuse impairment. We believe that dopamine metabolism is related to drug abuse. Dopamine is a brain neurotransmitter with defined endpoints that has been found to increase in activity as a function of drug use. However, recent work suggests that dopamine may be more important for novelty seeking than for the maintenance of pleasure (Garris *et al.* 1999). Serotonin, a neurotransmitter associated with mood, anxiety and dream-states, may be more strongly related to the maintenance of pleasure. This is about all we can say right now. Over the next 100 years, we shall be able to combine psychosocial and genetics research better to predict drug abuse and other disorders, and perhaps this work will disclose variable 'toxic combos' that will help identify at-risk individuals and help tailor prevention and treatment efforts based on need. One thing is clear – drug use serves a purpose for the users – generally to feel better about themselves and the world in which they live. They change their experience of themselves and others by ingesting a drug. There is nothing wrong with wanting to feel better or different, is there?

Maybe there is something wrong with using drugs grossly to change perceptions of one's self and others. We might take the stance that using drugs rob us of opportunities to self-actualize or attain our goals. We might also argue that drug use deters our ability really to experience the world, and to experience the range of human emotion and cognition that is unique to human beings, and unique to each individual. Maybe there are phenomenological milestones we either pass or do not pass, and that drug use bombards that process. In any case, if drug use causes undeniable and unavoidable negative consequences, it is best to avoid drug use. To try to prevent the onset of drug use or the onset of drug abuse, and the cessation of drug abuse, prevention and cessation programming are needed.

Prevention and cessation

The more treatment options available for the potential drug abuser, the better. Programmes delivered through the media, worksite and recreational institutions, and at home, and at different points in the life span, can be provided. These programmes are most beneficial when an individual is developmentally able to learn the material, and when the programme material is meaningful and relevant to the individual's lifestyle. It is not clear that such programming needs to be provided over the full life span. However, certainly teaching children how to bond with institutions and family is an important early preventive function. Also, affect management seems to be an important skill to instruct across the life span. During adolescence, social influence counteraction is important. If the person continues to use drugs, then motivation, skills and decision-making appear to be the key words of successful prevention. At some point, for some individuals, detoxification is needed and cessation programming has to be provided along with relapse management. At this point, an alternative non-drug-use lifestyle needs to be offered.

Prevention is not just for children. Adults and elderly people can begin to develop drug abuse problems as they move away from family in early adulthood or retire in later adulthood. Certainly, means to warn those who engage in self-defeating behaviour, and means to connect them with prosocial outlets, should be entertained for people of all ages.

What sort of treatment is needed? Is twelve-step programming the way to go in terms of drug abuse treatment? It is a way to heal and it appears to be a beneficial structure for recovery because it involves giving up trying to control drug use. 'Twelve-steppers' accept that use means more consequences. These programmes emphasize learning from others, working towards improving coping and maladaptive behaviours, making amends for past wrongs, and working towards achieving a balance in life as well as service work to others. However, twelve-step programming is not the only way available and many people do not recover through this means. Certainly much wisdom can be derived at a twelve-step meeting; however, participants are likely to be bombarded with references to religious terminology. Sometimes excessive dependence on others results. Doubters, who do not have any other place to go, may be treated unfairly or ignored by those in twelve-step groups. Most people recover without outside treatment, through whatever 'non-specific' means are at their disposal. More self-help recovery modalities are needed, as are various types of secular social support programmes.

Of course, much work is needed to know why a treatment is successful. Is it the content of the treatment? Is it because a charismatic person tells one not to use drugs? Is it related to the interactive process that goes on between 'treater' and 'treatee', or 'treatee' with 'treatee'? Is it related to having a safe haven to go to? The answers to these questions are not known. One answer seems to be that continued treatment, for many years – anything that is ongoing – seems to provide a means for one to remain abstinent. Eventually drug use may become more and more of a choice. If the person does not choose to use drugs, and it may not be a difficult choice to make; the person will remain sober. Of course, with accessibility to drugs and old memories of reinforcing effects, anything is possible.

Integrating prevention and cessation

One interesting treatment option is to consider the potential importance of combining prevention with cessation programming for treatees at all levels of drug use. The drawback of sole use of a prevention orientation would be if some people thought that it was 'too late' for them to benefit from such material. The drawback of sole use of a cessation orientation would be if some people thought that they would not have to quit unless they began to suffer withdrawal symptoms or severe negative consequences (Pentz *et al.* 1989a). Integrating prevention with cessation information would help minimize these potential difficulties. Prevention material could be used to assist non-users and light users, and suggest cessation as a last resort, rather than as an attractive option.

Several drug use education activities have been implemented across adult and adolescent prevention and cessation contexts. For example, teaching assertiveness, dealing with direct social pressure to use drugs, learning awareness of and countering subtle advertising and peer modelling influences, and making a commitment not to use drugs are provided in both types of programming. It also is the case that some knowledge and skill domains generally taught only in cessation programming not only are applicable to regular drug users, or their support persons, but also to anyone who is at risk for future drug addiction. For example, one component of cessation programming typically emphasizes 'cues' or 'triggers' for relapse, based on the well-established link between situational-cues and addiction processes (for example Marlatt and Gordon 1985). In adolescence, relapse cues (for example presence of others who use drugs) are likely to pervade certain social settings (for example Sussman *et al.* 1998b, 2000a). Programming is needed to link acquired knowledge and skills to these potential 'high-risk' situations, so that programme contents can become accessible enough from memory to effectively counter pressures to use fostered by these settings (Stacy and Ames 2001). This is consistent with memory accessibility models of health behaviour (Stacy 1995). Cessation-oriented components can be integrated with prevention into a more comprehensive approach. To maximize the chances of success of such a programme, programme development testing is needed to develop and integrate prevention and cessation activities (Sussman 2001a).

Other programming needs

Three other arenas of programming should be considered: ethnic-specific work, implicit processing approaches, and dissemination work. A great deal of current research is focused on developing culturally sensitive programming tailored to maximize impact on ethnic minorities. **Cultural sensitivity** refers to an awareness of and accommodation to the lifestyle of an identifiable group of people (for example Amuleru-Marshall 1991; Sussman *et al.* 1995c). In certain sub-populations in most countries of the world, clear cultural distinctions exist which include use of a different language and adoption of cultural traditions obviously related to past residence in a different country or region, or with events that have severed a group from its earlier cultures. These cultural variations might need to be considered when developing new programming, particularly cessation programming. Programme information should be taught in several languages, or be provided in verbal form (for example on tapes, in-person). Sensitivity to cultural norms should be considered when providing drug abuse treatment. For example, learning how to cope effectively with racial prejudice and enriching opportunity for pro-social modelling experiences in the purview of hypersegregated locations are relatively important for treatments among African Americans (Sussman *et al.* 1995c).

Research also now is beginning on implicit processing approaches to prevention and cessation (for an implicit cognition theory (ICT) prevention approach, see Stacy and Ames 2001). Information processing approaches assume there are many cognitive processes involved in behaviour change, and most of these processes are not necessarily measurable by self-reports on typical reflective questionnaire measures of beliefs, attitudes and other correlates or predictors of drug use. Some of the fundamental variables in information processing approaches include attentional focus, context, compatibility in cognitive processing, memory encoding, elaboration, and storage, memory association and memory retrieval or activation. An information processing perspective, with a focus on the dynamic and highly conditional nature of human cognition and memory, can provide a fresh approach to prevention and cessation efforts. New interventions may include components such as elaborative processing, for example, to aid in 'hard wiring' or increasing the accessibility of healthy memory associations (for example tying the concept of sobriety to individuals' own high-risk cues). Newly learned programme materials are unlikely to influence behaviour unless the material becomes part of what is activated in memory when behavioural decisions are being made.

Finally, much needs to be learned regarding the **diffusion** of effective programming, built on a strong empirical foundation. Diffusion is defined as the spread of new knowledge, usually referred to as an innovation, to a defined population over time through specific channels. Innovations are ideas, practices or objects that are perceived as new by units of adoption (E. Rogers 1983). The diffusion of innovative programmes is characterized as a four-stage process (E. Rogers 1983). The first stage is dissemination, in which treaters are made aware of successful programmes and are encouraged to adopt them. The second stage is adoption, in which treaters make a commitment to initiate a programme. The third stage, implementation, occurs when treaters deliver the programme. The final stage is maintenance, in which treaters are encouraged to continue use of the programme. Even after a programme is deemed successful, a community still may not own or adopt it. Institutionalization of a programme into a system is requisite, with supervisor oversight and encouragement, not necessarily intensive training.

The drug abuse arena can benefit from a science of programme development that permits evaluation of programme components, as they are being developed (Sussman *et al.* 1996b; Sussman 2001a). Practitioners and researchers should join together to provide integrative means of developing programmes. There needs to be more research regarding the modalities of effective programming, the potential breadth of effective programming (co-morbidity issues), and the specificity of programming needed for different groups.

Summary

We hope that this text has helped to educate the reader about the various issues permeating the arena of drug abuse, including many social psychological topics. The issues or questions discussed in this chapter are summarized in Table 10.1. There may be many more fundamental questions to be answered. Given our limited knowledge at this time, we can at least suggest that drug abusers consider using antidepressant medications to feel better, and minimize any harm and risk of disruption to self and others in the community. Many drug abusers need to learn how to live one day at a time, and chunk life hurdles into manageable pieces. Drug abusers might want to utilize any social support networks available, and the wisdom of mentors who can teach them to cope effectively with unpredictable life events that might threaten their sobriety. Drug abusers need to 'hang in there' for the long run – endure the challenge of sobriety. Living may be scary, breathing may hurt, but it does get easier – and life is a trip.

Table 10.1 Summary of remaining issues

General issues pertaining to drug abuse
- There is a need to try to clarify or integrate drug category systems.
- More work is needed to clarify what is and is not a 'disease' (that is the involuntary component) versus a 'disorder', as this pertains to drug abuse
- Are compulsive behaviours and drug abuse among the same constellation of problem behaviours with some underlying common aetiologic source?

Assessment issues
- Further work is needed to clarify drug abuse criteria. For example, when has someone failed to meet major role obligations? When has someone *really* suffered drug use social consequences?
- More work is needed to establish the qualitative and quantitative dimensions of drug abuse.
- Development of more multidimensional assessment tools is needed.
- Further work is needed to identify individuals at high risk for drug abuse through assessment of non-drug use behaviour, if targeted programming is to be implemented.
- Continued work is needed in providing valid and reliable biochemical assessment tools and the ethical protection of possible drug users.

Aetiologic issues
- How do combinations of risk and protective factors differ for different individuals?
- How do factors combine to determine drug abuse subtypes? What variable 'toxic combos' exist and can help in identifying at-risk individuals?
- Psychosocial and genetics arenas of drug abuse research might be investigated together.

Prevention and cessation issues
- More treatment options are needed.
- More work is needed to understand what elements of treatment modalities work for whom.
- More work is needed in the evaluation of factors leading to self-initiated cessation.
- More comprehensive approaches are needed. For example, programme development to integrate prevention and cessation activities together may be important.
- Programming is needed to link acquired knowledge and skills to 'high-risk' situations.
- Further work in the substantive arenas of culturally sensitive programming, implicit processing approaches and dissemination is needed.
- Institutionalization of programmes into natural systems is needed.
- A science and practice of programme development is needed that permits evaluation of programme methods as they are developed.
- More research is needed regarding the effective modalities, breadth and population targets of programming (for example co-morbidity issues).

For additonal reading see Quintero and Nichter 1996; Sussman 2001a

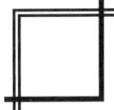

Glossary

Abstinence: the act of refraining from the use of the substance or substances on which a person has become psychologically or physically dependent.

Abstinence syndrome: withdrawal symptoms: consists of adjustment in physical functioning and behaviour attributed in part to overactivity of the nervous system; experienced when physically dependent persons cease their drug use.

Addict: an individual who abuses drug(s) of choice including drugs other than or in addition to alcohol.

Addiction: the physical and psychological craving for a substance and related behaviour that continues even after it causes an individual physical, psychological, legal or social harm. The process of addiction is viewed by some as progressive and chronic.

Addiction concern: a person's recognition that they may have a drug problem in the present or in the future.

Addictive process: a compulsive problem behaviour.

Aetiology: cause(s) or causal history of disease.

Affective states: a term used interchangeably to describe various states of feeling, mood or emotion.

Aftercare: delivery of ongoing services upon completion of an initial programme, such as individual counselling, group sessions, crisis intervention, environmental advocacy and social support; an essential component of the treatment process.

Alcohol: legal depressant; chemicals containing hydroxyl derivatives of hydrocarbons, one of which is ethanol, found in alcoholic beverages.

Alcoholics Anonymous (AA): a voluntary, anonymous self-help organization of individuals who have recognized their chemical dependence on alcohol and are committed to living a life of abstinence. Abstinence is achieved by a twelve-step programme and members of AA support each other by sharing their own struggles, experiences and hopes.

Amphetamines: central nervous system stimulants, for example dexedrine, benzedrine and methedrine.

Amyl nitrite: a vasodilator administered by inhalation; used recreationally due to its ability to induce euphoria.

Anabolic-androgenic steroids: approximately eighteen different substances; exert their effects by overwhelming the hypothalamic-pituitary hormonal system; create abnormally high testosterone levels and lead to increased muscle mass and aggression.

Anaesthetics: substances that induce anaesthesia or the partial or complete loss of sensation and loss of consciousness, for example nitrous oxide, 'laughing gas'.

Analgesics: any substance used to relieve or minimize pain, such as opioids.

Anorexia nervosa: an eating disorder characterized by (1) a refusal or inability to maintain a minimally normal weight for age and height, leading to maintenance of body weight 15 per cent below expected, (2) an intense fear of gaining weight or becoming fat, (3) a significant disturbance in body image (always seeing oneself as fat), and (4) in females, at least three consecutive missed menstrual cycles that should otherwise be expected to occur.

Antecedents: precursors of a behaviour of interest.

Anti-convulsants: drugs that block epileptic convulsions; these drugs are classified as depressants, for example barbiturates.

Antihistamines: substances that block the effects of the allergy chemical, histamine, such as doxylamine succinate, which is found in Formula 44 and Nyquil.

Anxiolytics: drugs that relieve anxiety; sometimes classified as depressants.

Assessment: measurement of an individual's involvement with drugs of abuse, psychological and medical status, psychosocial functioning, social supports, attitudes towards drug use and motivation for initial abstinence.

Attitude(s): consciously held belief(s) or opinion(s) or positive/negative evaluations (cognitive component), emotional tone or feeling towards an object (affective component) and/or ways of behaving that follow from or are consistent with the cognitive or affective components (behavioural component).

Barbiturates: sedative-hypnotic drugs derived from barbituric acid; share a six-member ring chemical structure; anti-convulsant, sometimes classified as depressants.

Behaviour therapy: a type of psychotherapy that focuses on the modification of manifested behaviour, and changing maladaptive patterns of behaviour through processes of extinction and inhibition, and positive and negative reinforcement or punishment. Cognitive behaviour therapy also considers cognitive or affective mediating mechanisms of behaviour change in therapy.

Benzodiazapines: anti-anxiety drugs; minor tranquillizers used in treating anxiety and tension, such as Valium or Librium.

Binge behaviour: periodic pattern of addictive behaviour; alternating periods of abstinence and typically out-of-control behaviour. Regarding alcohol, sometimes defined as having more than five drinks in one sitting, but fewer than five sittings within a thirty-day period (*National Household Survey* data definition).

Biochemical validation: chemical testing to detect drug use; corroborative method of assessment since response demand problems can render self-reports invalid; plays an important role in the assessment and treatment of individuals with drug use disorders.

Biopsychosocial model: models grouping risk factors according to biological, psychological and social categories.

Bulimia nervosa: process addiction characterized by repeated episodes of eating followed by self-induced vomiting.

Butyl nitrite: room odorizer that has been misused as an inhalant.

Caffeine: central nervous system stimulant, derived from the fruit of the Coffea arabica plant.

Cannabis: marijuana or any product derived from the hemp plant; second largest drug creating treatment demand in America and Europe, third largest problem drug in Asia.

Cessation: discontinuing a behaviour.

Clinical interviewing: in-clinic, detailed, primarily verbally obtained assessments regarding an individual's involvement with drugs and related information.

Cocaine: central nervous system stimulant; derived from leaves of the coca plant.

Codeine: natural narcotic closely related to morphine; an opiate.

Cognition: activities or processes of thinking, conceiving, reasoning and so on; any class of mental processes.

Cognitive-behavioural residential programmes: residential treatment programmes designed to modify behavioural habits and restructure cognitions.

Co-morbidity: the presence of a substance abuse or chemical dependency diagnosis with a coexisting psychiatric disorder, such as depression. Also referred to as a dual diagnosis.

Comprehensive social influences programming: type of drug abuse prevention programming; key features involve creating an awareness of social influences and teaching social skills to counteract these influences.

Compulsive problem behaviours: repetitive, irrational behaviour motivated by factors compelling a person to act against their own wishes; often to relieve negative effect.

Compulsive shopping: process addiction characterized by excessive buying behaviour leading to unsecured debt; not recognized as an official mental disorder by the DSM-IV, though one out of every twelve residents of the United States is overwhelmed by debt; associated with its own twelve-step programme.

Continuum notion: loss of control as a result of drug use may fall on a quantitative continuum. In other words, different drug abusers may differ to the degree to which they tend to lose control. Treatment matching may need to consider this notion.

Contracting: method of formalizing or reinforcing individuals' commitment to change. Involves signing an agreement between two or more people to carry out a plan, with built-in consequences.

Controlled use: treatment goal of moderation as opposed to abstinence. Applied primarily towards alcohol use.

Correlate: variable that tends to co-occur with, varies with, or is associated with the behaviour of interest in a way that is not expected simply on the basis of chance.

Craving: urges and obsessions that drug abusers may experience regarding obtaining and using a drug.

Cue: 'trigger' for relapse according to various theories of drug abuse (generally visual or other sensory stimuli).

Cultural influences: cultural precursors of behaviour, including life habits and rituals that are important and meaningful to a definable group (often based on geographics), normative structures and expectations (cultural morality) and beliefs and attitudes associated with group life habits and norms.

Cultural sensitivity: an awareness of and accommodation to the lifestyle of an identifiable group of people.

Demographic influences: characteristics of a population such as socio-economic status, gender, age, living situation and ethnicity which influence an individual's behaviour.

Denial: not to admit, to oneself or others, to having a substance abuse problem.

Depressants: substances whose effects slow down central nervous system function, tranquillizes an individual or produces sleep, for example sedatives for relaxation, hypnotics to induce sleep, anxiolytic to reduce anxiety and anti-convulsants such as barbiturates.

Designer drugs: substances popular in public circles which may not yet be classified according to established drug use classification categories, such as GHB.

Developmental model of recovery: outlines a series of developmental periods and goals for each period that attempt to support a quest towards permanent sobriety.

Differential socialization: development of beliefs, intentions, expectations, perceptions and modelling of social behaviours that may be influential in experimental drug use. 'Differential' implies socialization away from the mainstream, or on different lifestyle trajectories.

Diffusion: a four-stage process that describes the spread of new innovations (for example successful drug treatment programmes) to a community. *Dissemination* involves making providers aware of an effective programme. *Adoption* involves the agreement to use the effective programme. *Implementation* involves actual community delivery of the programme. *Maintenance* pertains to continuing to deliver the programme on an ongoing basis.

Disease *intentional (rule-based definition):* outcome condition that involves impairment of bodily functions, resulting from exposure to a living or non-living object, that is mediated by some causal mechanism. *Extensional (listing-type) definition:* outcome condition (for example drug abuse) that shares similarities with other outcome conditions (for example cardiovascular disease), such that it is consensually considered to be a member of the set 'disease'.

Distal structures: believed to be indirectly related to problem-prone behaviour, whereas proximal structures are directly related.

Dopamine: a type of central nervous system neurotransmitter thought to be of primary importance in drug abuse and novelty seeking; affects multiple aspects of addictive behaviours including arousal, reward and motivation; dopaminergic activity is associated with pleasure, and increased dopamine transmission appears to reinforce the repetition of behaviours.

Drug processing: four-step process by which drugs enter and leave the body, including administration, distribution, action and elimination.

Drug-related stimuli: cues that signal one to use drugs; 'triggers' such as drug paraphernalia.

Drug testing: chemical assays (that is analysis of a chemical substance) used to detect drug use in bodily fluids.

Drug use history: information regarding an individual's duration, frequency (latency), pattern and consequences of different types of drug use; also information regarding prior involvement in drug treatment programmes, psychiatric facilities, participation in self-help groups or public sanctions (for example court, prison); helps uncover level of addiction, occurrence of other compulsive behaviours and psychiatric difficulties, and motivation to stop using.

DSM-IV: *Diagnostic and Statistical Manual of Mental Disorders* (4th edn) of the American Psychiatric Association; widely used in establishing whether or not an individual has a drug abuse disorder; contains specific criteria sets for substance abuse, dependence, intoxication and withdrawal applicable across different classes of drugs.

Dual diagnosis: see *co-morbidity.*

Dysregulation: abnormal or impaired functioning, regulation, or adjustment of the amount, rate or degree of what is expected to be typical or normal (for example dysregulation of the opoid system implies abnormal functioning of the opoid system).

Ecstasy (MDMA): one type of designer drug; synthesized in 1914 as an appetite suppressant; exerts an amphetamine-like reaction.

Employee assistance programmes (EAPs): policies and programming developed by employers to deal with employee drug abuse; involvement kept separate from personnel records, and participation is not intended to affect job ratings.

Enabling: acting in ways that support continued drug use, such as 'cleaning up' the consequences produced by drug abusers.

Environmental influences: influence of an individual's physical surroundings, including geographical location, dwelling contexts and changes occurring in these contexts (for example disorganization, modernization).

Ephedrine: stimulant contained in Vicks Inhaler or Sudafed.

Epidemiology: the study of the incidence and prevalence of disease.

Ethnicity: national or racial characteristics of a group of people.

Extensional definition: listing-type definitional framework; see *Disease*.

Extrapersonal factors: characteristics external to the individual influencing drug use, such as interactions with others.

Family assistance programmes: treatment to assist families to deal with drug abuse in the family; key prevention and treatment characteristics include instruction in family skills training, potentially through in-home support, and family therapy to improve family communication, decrease conflict and improve parenting.

Flushing response: alcohol sensitivity reaction related to differences in alcohol metabolizing enzymes; the skin appears flushed.

Functional meaning: understanding drug use by discovering what using drugs 'means' to individuals.

Gateway drugs: types of drugs that people first start experimenting with, that predict or may facilitate use of other often 'harder' drugs (for example heavy caffeine use among children may predict experimentation with amphetamines later on in life).

Genetic heritability: genetic predisposition, in-born, for example, to enjoy and abuse drugs.

Hallucinogens: recognized drug use classification; sensory changes experienced as visual illusions and hallucinations, alteration of perceptual experience of external stimuli and thoughts; can involve paranoia; for example PCP, LSD.

Harm reduction: minimizing the consequences of substance abuse behaviour; educational approach that emphasizes responsible decision-making and the need to consider existing individual control mechanisms; goal is to protect drug addicts from many life-threatening consequences and to help them quit drug use in small steps.

Hashish: see *marijuana*.

Hedonic treadmill: an explanation of drug use; based on an ancient Roman ideal, the notion of endless, uncontrolled pursuit of pleasure-related goals.

Heroin: semi-synthetic narcotic made by treating morphine with acetic anhydride; opiate.

Hit bottom: to reach a low point in one's using career such that one is receptive to assistance, may seek treatment or support.

Hypnotics: sedatives; often prescribed to induce sleep; classified as depressants.

Impulsivity: personality trait: lack of behavioural inhibition.

Informational social influence: one of two main types of pressure that the peer group exerts on its members; described as wanting members of the group to share similar attitudes about the frequencies of various behaviours and their social meanings. See also *normative social influence*.

Inhalants: volatile substances that induce drug-like effects when inhaled; can be classified as depressants but administration (sniffed or huffed) is quite different from other depressants; intoxication includes euphoria, headaches, dizziness, nausea and fainting, for example amyl nitrite.

Integrated theory: the combination of single-factor models to provide more comprehensive explanations of the development of drug use and abuse.

Intentional definition: rule-based definitional framework; see *Disease.*

Interaction effects: the ways in which the body will process ingestion of more than one drug at a time.

International Classification of Diseases (ICD-9): the World Health Organization's disease classification scheme (now updated to ICD-10). Its drug classifications are similar to the DSM-IV scheme.

Intoxication: inebriation; drunkenness; a temporary state resulting from excessive consumption of mood-altering substances.

Intrapersonal factors: characteristics internal to the individual influencing drug use such as genetics.

Julien biomedical-type scheme: scheme for classifying drugs of abuse, based on biological effects (for example neurotransmitter, hormonal).

Just Say No Campaign: example of a drug abuse prevention media campaign popular in the 1970s and 1980s that utilized a simplistic, though widespread, approach to refusal assertion training; probably ineffective.

Ketamine (Special K): one type of designer drug; an anaesthetic approved for human use since 1970; can produce dream-like states, hallucinations, delirium, impaired motor functions, depression and potentially fatal respiratory problems.

Life Process Model: proposes that addiction stems from non-drug-related life problems and can be outgrown through treatment (for example instruction in coping strategies and social skills), as applied to any compulsive problem behaviour.

Loss of control: implies inability to predict and control when one will engage in an addictive behaviour, when the behaviour will stop, or what will be the course and consequences of the behaviour.

Lysergic acid diethylamide (LSD): synthetic psychedelic derived from ergot fungus; hallucinogen.

MDMA: see *ecstasy.*

Marijuana: parts of the cannabis plant (flowers, leaves, stems) that produce physical or psychic changes. 'Hashish' is differentiated from marijuana in that it is extracted from cannabis resins.

Media influences: extrapersonal factors affecting drug use; portrayals in the media (for example television, magazines, cinema) that glamorize drug use and may influence fluctuations in use.

Mental status examination: means of gathering psychological and behavioural data; assesses health status and suggests other assessments to determine whether a diagnosis of psychiatric disease is warranted; includes the assessment of appearance, attitude and behaviour, speech, mood and affect, thought and language, perceptions and cognitive functioning, insight and judgement.

Meperdine: Demerol, a pure agonist opioid analgesic.

Mescaline: psychoactive ingredient of peyote cactus; hallucinogen (catecholamine-like phenylalkylamine).

Metabolite: a breakdown product of a chemical compound, such as a metabolite of a drug.

Methamphetamine: synthetic stimulant (methedrine; known as 'speed' or 'meth').

Methaqualone: synthetic depressant (known as 'Quaalude').

Morphine: a naturally occurring opiate derived from opium; used medically as an analgesic.

Motivation: a classical definition pertains to energy and direction aspects of goal attainment.

Motivational interviewing: series of procedures for therapists to use to help clients clarify goals, surmount ambivalent attitudes, and follow through with their efforts to change behaviour.

Narcotics Anonymous (NA): like Alcoholics Anonymous, a voluntary, anonymous self-help organization of individuals who have recognized their chemical dependence and are committed to living a life of abstinence.

Negative consequences (of drug use): accumulation of negative outcomes as a result of using drugs; may be medical/physical (for example alcoholic liver disease, psychosis), social (for example rejection), legal (for example arrest for driving under the influence), emotional (for example truncated development), physically/environmentally hazardous (for example accidents, overdoses, fires), involve role failure (for example poor grades or work performance), or be socio-economic (for example debt, loss of job), as examples.

Neurobiological processes: processes involving the physiology of the brain.

Neurotransmitter: endogenous chemical substance (for example acetylcholine, dopamine, serotonin) that transmits nerve impulses across a synapse.

Nicotine: behavioural stimulant found in tobacco.

Normative social influence: one of two main types of pressure that the peer group exerts on its members; described as wanting members to act consistently with the group to gain or maintain acceptance of other group members. See also *informational social influence*.

Opiates: narcotic analgesics derived from the opium poppy or made synthetically to have the same drug action; includes some twenty alkaloids that act on opioid receptors; for example morphine, codeine, thebaine (all of natural origin); heroin, hydrocodone, hydromorphine, oxycodone (all semi-synthetic); and meperdine, fentanyl and pentazocine (all synthetic). Intoxication includes slurred speech, analgesia, slowed respiration, drowsiness, euphoria and possibly itching.

Opioid receptors: molecular structure or site on the surface or interior of a neuron cell that binds with opioid substances. These receptors function naturally for endorphins (endogenous opiates) but will also take up other exogenous opiates (both natural and synthetic).

Opium: an addictive narcotic extracted from seed capsules of the opium poppy; main source of non-synthetic narcotics.

Outpatient clinics: clinics providing treatment services to individuals not living on the premises; most appropriate for individuals who have completed residential treatment or otherwise have acquired the necessary coping skills and commitment to sobriety for sober living in the absence of 24-hour supervision.

Pathological gambling: compulsive problem behaviour characterized by a loss of control over gambling behaviour and automatic responses to environmental events; tending to lead to negative consequences such as debt; perhaps serving underlying sensation seeking or self-medication functions.

Peer pressure/influence: social pressure/influence exerted on an individual by those of the same age, or by those with whom the individual has frequent contact, to conform to group norms.

Personality: the complex of all the attributes – behavioural, temperamental, emotional and mental – that characterize a unique individual; intrapersonal risk factor for drug abuse (for example sensation seeking).

Phencyclidine (PCP): originally developed as an animal anaesthetic and tranquillizer but no longer used as such. Categorized by American Psychiatric Association and others as a drug of abuse; effects are both depressant and hallucinogen-like; involves intense analgesia, delirium, stimulant and depressant actions, staggering gait and slurred speech. It can also produce catatonia, paranoia, flushing, coma, violent behaviour and memory loss.

Physiological susceptibility: genetic make-up and neurobiological processes which contribute to individual differences in drug use.

Positive reinforcement: an event or reward that follows drug use (for example feelings of euphoria) and increases the likelihood that the behaviour will be repeated.

Post-synaptic neurotransmitter supersensitivity: often experienced as a reaction to termination of drug use; the post-synaptic sites 'crave' the neurotransmitter now missing in sufficient quantities. Neurochemical reactions may exert effects opposite of that achieved by the drug.

Predictors of drug use: factors leading to drug use such as demographics, genetics.

Prevention: to keep drug (ab)use from happening; primary prevention (before the problem behaviour starts), secondary prevention (before the disease starts) and tertiary prevention (before death is likely) are terms used to describe levels of an intervention in public health. Prevention may also be designated as universal (designed to affect the general population), selective (designed to affect subgroups at elevated risk for developing a problem) or indicated (designed to affect high-risk subgroups already identified as having some detectable signs or symptoms of a developing problem).

Prevention programming: drug use education programmes that focus on the antecedents of the behaviour (that is drug abuse) and on anticipating and preventing future negative consequences.

Problem behaviours: behaviours correlated with drug abuse and each other that cause someone difficulties, that may violate societal norms or that are unhealthy such as crime, violence and poor diet.

Process addictions: actions, as opposed to substances, that expose one to mood-altering events on which one becomes dependent (for example gambling, workaholism, excessive exercise, sex, spending or television watching). Distinguished from substance addictions by a more indirect manipulation of pleasure through situational and physical activity manipulations (that is where substance addictions involve direct manipulation of pleasure through use of products that are taken into the body).

Programme: a course of instruction, which may include a curriculum (a set of instructional/educational materials), other materials (for example videos, pamphlets, workbooks) and training materials (guides to instruction).

Project Towards No Drug Abuse (TND): effective drug abuse prevention programme that is tailored to older, higher risk youth.

Prospective studies: studies in which a group of individuals is measured on characteristics (for example drug use) over multiple time points; also called longitudinal studies.

Protective factors: factors that reduce the risk of substance abuse and promote positive development, such as cooperativeness, social competence, attachment to parents, lack of drug availability.

Proximal structures: directly predictive of problem-prone behaviour (for example behavioural intentions), whereas distal structures are indirectly related.

Psychosocial functioning: terms used to described one's functioning in which both psychological and social factors are influential.

Psychostimulants: chemical structures that accelerate central nervous system function, for example cocaine, amphetamines, nicotine, caffeine (also stimulants).

Psychotic symptoms: any of numerous symptoms including delusions, hallucinations, dramatically inappropriate mood and markedly incoherent speech; symptoms that may be induced through the use or abuse of various substances, for example paranoid ideation as a result of use of crack cocaine.

Rational Recovery (RR): non-traditional cognitive-oriented programme of self-empowered recovery from substance dependency; treatment alternative to Alcoholics or Narcotics Anonymous. For example, it is based on confronting and defeating one's primitive, pleasure-seeking brain.

Recovery: developmental process varying from individual to individual through which someone discontinues drug use and learns to maintain a sober lifestyle.

Recovery movement: treatment programmes based on the twelve-step recovery approach, such as Alcoholics Anonymous and Narcotics Anonymous. More broadly, seeks to reduce stigma associated with having a history of substance abuse.

Refusal assertion training: instruction in how to refuse requests, often involving behavioural demonstration, modelling, rehearsal, performance, feedback and practice components.

Relapse: significant use of a drug after a period of abstinence; losing control. Sometimes differentiated from one instance of using again (a 'slip' or 'lapse').

Relapse prevention: a self-control programme combining behavioural skills training, cognitive interventions and lifestyle change procedures; based on the principles of social learning theory.

Residential facilities: facilities (for example hospitals, clinics) designed to provide treatment services to individuals living on the premises.

Reverse tolerance: an individual's increased reactivity to the effects of using a drug, often after some period of non-use, which may be due to previous conditioning to the drug (for example use in specific settings) and/or alteration in neurotransmission function related to previous use of the drug.

Risk factors: factors that contribute to the initiation and continuation of drug use, such as genetic predisposition, aggression, poor social and coping skills, poverty.

School-based drug abuse prevention programming: prevention education delivered in classrooms; school-based primary prevention programming has been found to be effective for up to six years post-programme delivery.

Secular Organizations for Sobriety/Save Our Selves (SOS): non-profit, non-spiritual national organization of autonomous, non-professional groups dedicated solely to helping individuals achieve and maintain abstinence; designed specifically for those alcoholics or addicts who are uncomfortable with the spiritual nature of twelve-step programmes.

Sedative-hypnotics: category of depressants, often used for relaxation, such as Placydil, Doriden.

Self-efficacy not to use drugs: the extent of someone's belief in their ability to abstain from drinking or using drugs under a variety of high-risk situations; includes magnitude (that is an individual's perception of their best performance), strength (that is the confidence in the perception of one's strengths) and generality (that is the extent to which self-efficacy experiences are generalizable). High self-efficacy will enhance pursuit of coping behaviours that lead to prevention, cessation and recovery.

Self-Management and Recovery Training (SMART Recovery): argues that addictive behaviour is problematic because it interferes with other activities – and causes harm; cognitive-behavioural in orientation. An alternative programme of recovery besides twelve-step groups or Rational Recovery.

Self-medication: use of drugs as a means of controlling unpleasant feelings.

Sensation seeking: a personality trait defined by the seeking of varied, novel, complex and intense sensations and experiences, and the willingness to take physical, social, legal and financial risks for the sake of such experiences.

Serotonin: neurotransmitter involved in sleep, depression and memory; may be more strongly related to the maintenance of pleasure than dopamine; regulation of the serotonergic system may be altered by drug use.

Sobriety: abstinent and/or balanced lifestyle.

Social influences: characteristics of people in one's social environment that influence one's social perceptions or behaviour.

Social psychology: the branch of human psychology that deals with the behaviour of groups and the influence of groups on the individual.

Social skills training: educational strategies in which individuals are taught how to become more socially competent (for example listening, conversation and assertiveness skills).

Social support: the assistance that people in social networks give each other (social networks are the connections among individuals, such as between friends or colleagues). There are various types/processes of social support individuals can offer each other: companionship, instrumental, conformity, informational, as examples.

Socio-economic influences: influences pertaining to an individual's or group's financial or educational situation or background.

Spirituality: cognitive, emotional or behavioural involvement in religious or other activities involving notions of higher powers; cornerstone of AA philosophy and teaching; conscientiousness (thinking of others) and experiential peace (lack of negative affectivity) may be the two main components of spiritual experience.

Stage modelling: theories based on the fact that different predictors may operate at different points in the history of individuals' drug use, and that drug use behaviour and consequences may be qualitatively different at these different points, suggesting the operation of stages in the progression of drug abuse.

Stereotyping: fixed, simplistic overgeneralizations about a group of people.

Structured Clinical Interview for the DSM-IV (SCID): a diagnostic interview used to assess any number of DSM-IV diagnoses, including substance abuse and dependence disorders.

Substance abuse: recent drug use which results in a failure to fulfil life roles, engaging in use that presents a physical danger, use that causes legal consequences, or use that results in social rejection.

Substance addictions: addiction to any mood-altering products, including drugs and food.

Substance dependence: a more severe disorder than a diagnosis of substance abuse; diagnosed if three or more of seven criteria outlined in the DSM-IV are met. The seven criteria include (1) tolerance, (2) withdrawal, (3) consumption of larger amounts or for a longer duration than intended, (4) a persistent desire or unsuccessful efforts to cut down or control use, (5) excessive time spent on activities involving drugs, (6) social, occupational or recreational activities are reduced or abandoned due to use, and (7) despite knowledge of persistent or recurrent physical or psychological problems, one continues to use.

Sussman/Ames scheme: one of several drug classification schemes, which places an emphasis on behavioural effects.

Tailor: to adapt to a special need, population, or purpose (for example tailoring programmes to specific populations entails age-appropriate content and skill level).

Thebaine: opiate of natural origin; chemically similar to morphine and codeine with stimulant effects.

Tobacco: leaves of the tobacco plant prepared for smoking, chewing or sniffing.

Tolerance: an individual's reduced sensitivity resulting in the need for increased dosage to achieve desired effects; reduction in the pharmacological response to a drug by continued intake of the same dose.

Toluene: an inhalant; a solvent used in adhesives such as airplane glue, aerosols such as spray paint, and commercial solvents such as paint thinner. A benzene ring with the addition of a methyl group.

Toxicology: the study of the characteristics and effects of drug poisoning, including intoxication.

Tranquillizers: a generic label used for several classes of drugs characterized by one or more of the following properties: sedative, muscle relaxant, anti-convulsive, anti-anxiety, such as Valium, Librium, Tranxene, Rohypnol.

Treatment: procedure intended to cure or lesson the severity of a disease or other abnormal condition.

Triadic influence theory: theory designed to integrate fourteen multivariate theories of teenage experimental drug use; involves three domains (interpersonal, attitudinal/cultural and intrapersonal) with variables of differing 'distances' from drug use behaviour (ultimate, distal and proximal).

Tripartite conceptual framework: developed by Goldstein (1985, 1998) to examine drug-related violence; consists of the psychopharmacological model, the economically compulsive model and a systemic model.

Victimization: physical harm, threats of physical harm, harm to property, or mental/emotional harm, suffered by an individual.

Web of causation: in the present context, reference to the fact that it is not clear whether various factors precede, or are the result of, drug use.

Withdrawal: the experience of changes in physical functioning and behaviour due in part to overactivity of the nervous system after cessation of drug use by a physically dependent individual.

Workaholism: process addiction characterized by excessive involvement in work, which interferes with other life domains.

World Health Organization (WHO): an agency of the United Nations whose aim is to promote the highest possible level of health for people of all nationalities.

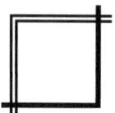

Bibliography

Adams, E.H., Gfoerer, J.C. and Rouse, B.A. (1989) Epidemiology of substance abuse including alcohol and cigarette smoking, *Annual New York Academy of Science*, 562: 14–20.

Akers, R.L., Krohn, M.D., Lanza-Kaduce, L. and Radosevich, M. (1979) Social learning and deviant behavior: a specific test of a general theory, *American Sociological Review*, 44: 636–55.

Alcoholics Anonymous (1976) *Alcoholics Anonymous*, 3rd edn. New York City: Alcoholics Anonymous World Services.

Almog, Y.J., Anglin, M.D. and Fisher, D.G. (1993) Alcohol and heroin use patterns of narcotics addicts: gender and ethnic differences, *American Journal of Drug and Alcohol Abuse*, 19: 291–38.

American Psychiatric Association (APA) (1994) *Diagnostic and Statistical Manual of Mental Disorders*, 4th edn (DSM-IV). Washington, DC: APA.

Ames, S.L. and Stacy, A.W. (1998) Implicit cognition in the prediction of substance use among drug offenders, *Psychology of Addictive Behaviors*, 12(4): 272–81.

Ames, S.L., Sussman, S. and Dent, C.W. (1999) Pro-drug use myths and competing constructs in the prediction of substance use among youth at continuation high schools: a one-year prospective study, *Personality and Individual Differences*, 26: 987–1003.

Ames, S.L., Zogg, J.B. and Stacy, A.W. (under review) Implicit cognition, sensation seeking, marijuana use, and driving behavior among drug offenders, *Experimental and Clinical Psychopharmacology*.

Amuleru-Marshall, O. (1991) Culturally-appropriate refinements in AIDS prevention among African-Americans. Unpublished manuscript.

Annis, H.M. (1982) *Inventory of Drinking Situations*. Toronto: Addiction Research Foundation.

Annis, H.M. (1984) A basic follow-up package, in F.B. Glaser, H.A. Skinner, S. Pearlman *et al.* (eds) *A System of Health Care Delivery*, vol. 3. Toronto: Addiction Research Foundation.

Annis, H.M. and Graham, J.M. (1992) *Inventory of Drug Taking Situations User's Guide*. Toronto: Addiction Research Foundation of Ontario.

Annis, H.M., Graham, J.M. and Davis, C.S. (1987) *Inventory of Drinking Situations (IDS) User's Guide*. Toronto: Addiction Research Foundation of Ontario.

Antonovsky, A. (1984) The sense of coherence as a determinant of health, in J.D. Matarazzo, S.M. Weiss, J.A. Herd, N.E. Miller and S.M. Weiss (eds) *Behavioral Health: A Handbook of Health Enhancement and Disease Prevention*. New York: Wiley.

Bandura, A. (1977) *Social Learning Theory*. Englewood Cliffs, NJ: Prentice Hall.

Bandura, A. (1986) *Social Foundations of Thought and Action: A Social Cognitive Theory*. Englewood Cliffs, NJ: Prentice Hall.

Barbor, T.F. (1994) Overview: demography, epidemiology, and psychopharmacology – making sense of the connections, *Addiction*, 89: 1391–6.

Barnes, G.M. and Welte, J.W. (1986) Patterns and predictors of alcohol use among 7–12th grade students in New York State, *Journal of Studies on Alcohol*, 47: 53–62.

Baumgartner, W.A., Hill, V.A. and Blahd, W.H. (1989) Hair analysis for drugs of abuse, *Journal of Forensic Sciences*, 34: 1433–53.

Becker, M.H. (ed.) (1974) *The Health Belief Model and Personal Health Behavior*. Thorofare, NJ: Charles B. Slack.

Bell, C.S. and Battjes, R. (eds) (1985) *Prevention Research: Deterring Drug Abuse among Children and Adolescents*, NIDA Research Monograph 63. Rockville, MD: National Institute on Drug Abuse.

Bell, J., Sarfraz, A., Fischer, B., Kapczinski, F. and Lima, M. (1999) Substance user drug substitutions and chemotherapy. Paper presented to the Towards the Year 2000 Meeting, Jerusalem, Israel, 18–22 July.

Bennett, J.B. and Lehman, W.E.K. (1996) Employee attitude crystallization and substance use policy: test of a classification scheme, *Journal of Drug Issues*, 26: 831–65.

Bindra, D. and Stewart, J. (eds) (1966) Introduction, in *Motivation*. Baltimore, MD: Penguin.

Blomqvist, J. (1996) Paths to recovery from substance misuse: change of lifestyle and the role of treatment, *Substance Use and Misuse*, 31(13): 1807–52.

Blum, K., Cull, J.G., Braverman, E.R., Chen, T.J. and Comings, D.E. (1997) Reward deficiency syndrome: neurobiological and genetic aspects, in E.P. Noble and K. Blum (eds) *Handbook of Psychiatric Genetics*. Boca Raton, FL: CRC Press.

Bosworth, K. (1996) Definition of SAP, *Teacher Talk*, 3, 15 pages (http://education.indiana.edu/cas/tt/v3i3/sapdef.html)

Botvin, G.J., Baker, E., Dusenbury, L., Botvin, E.M. and Diaz, T. (1995) Long-term follow-up results of a randomized drug abuse prevention trial in a white middle-class population, *Journal of the American Medical Association*, 273: 1106–12.

Bozwarth, M.A. (1994) Opiate reinforcement processes: re-assembling multiple mechanisms, *Addiction*, 89: 1425–34.

Brooner, R.K., King, V.L., Kidorf, M. and Bigelow, G.E. (1997) Psychiatric and substance use comorbidity among treatment-seeking opioid abusers, *Archives of General Psychiatry*, 54: 71–80.

Brown, S.A., Goldman, M.S., Inn, A. and Anderson, L.R. (1980) Expectations of reinforcement from alcohol: their domain and relation to drinking patterns, *Journal of Consulting and Clinical Psychology*, 48: 419–26.

Brown, S.A., Christiansen, B.A. and Goldman, M.S. (1987) The alcohol expectancy questionnaire: an instrument for the assessment of adolescent and adult alcohol expectancies, *Journal of Studies on Alcohol*, 48(5): 483–91.

Brownell, K.D. and Wadden, T.A. (1992) Etiology and treatment of obesity: understanding a serious prevalent, and refractory disorder, *Journal of Consulting and Clinical Psychology*, 4: 505–17.

Brust, J.C.M. (1999) Substance abuse, neurobiology, and ideology, *Archives of Neurology*, 56(12): 1528–31.

Bry, B.H., McKeon, P. and Pandina, R.J. (1982) Extent of drug use as a function of number or risk factors, *Journal of Abnormal Psychology*, 91: 273–9.

Bufe, C. (1991) *Alcoholics Anonymous: Cult or Cure?* San Francisco, CA: See Sharp Press.

Burke, H. and Markus, R. (1977) MacAndrew MMPI Alcoholism Scale: alcoholism and drug addiction, *Journal of Psychology*, 96: 141–8.

Burke, R. (2000) Workaholism in organizations: psychological and physical well-being consequences, *Stress Medicine*, 16: 11–16.

Butcher, J.N. and Owen, P.L. (1978) Objective personality inventories: recent research and some contemporary issues, in B.B. Wolman (ed.) *Clinical Diagnosis of Mental Disorders: A Handbook*. New York: Plenum.

Carnes, P.J. (1996) Addiction or compulsion: politics or illness, *Sexual Addiction and Compulsivity*, 3: 127–50.

Carroll, C.R. (1989) *Drugs in Modern Society*, 2nd edn. Dubuque, IA: W.M.C. Brown.

Centers for Substance Abuse Prevention (CSAP) (1992) *ATOD Resource Guide: Employee Assistance Programs*. Rockville, MD: National Clearinghouse for Alcohol and Drug Information (#MS439: www.health.org/pubs/resguide/eap.htm), May.

Chaloupka, F.J. and Grossman, M. (1996) Price, tobacco control policies and smoking among young adults, *Journal of Health Economics*, 16(3): 359–73.

Chasnoff, I.J. (1991) Drugs, alcohol, pregnancy and the neonate: pay now or pay later, *Journal of the American Medical Association*, 266: 1567–8.

Chappel, J.N. (1992) Effective use of Alcoholics Anonymous and Narcotics Anonymous in treating patients, *Psychiatric Annals*, 22: 409–18.

Chou, C.P., Montgomery, S., Pentz, M.A. *et al.* (1998) Effects of a community-based prevention program on decreasing drug use in high-risk adolescents, *American Journal of Public Health*, 88: 944–8.

Christopher, J. (1988) *How to Stay Sober: Recovery without Religion*. New York: Prometheus.

Cloninger, C.R. (1994) Temperament and personality, *Current Opinion in Neurobiology*, 4: 266–73.

Cloninger, C.R., Sigvardsoon, S. and Bohman, M. (1988) Childhood personality predicts alcohol abuse in young adults, *Alcoholism*, 12: 494–503.

Cloninger, C.R., Svrakic, D.M. and Przybeck, T.R. (1993) A psychobiological model of temperament and character, *Archives of General Psychiatry*, 50: 975–90.

Clopton, J.R. (1978) Alcoholism and the MMPI: a review, *Journal of Studies on Alcohol*, 39: 1540–58.

Clopton, J.R., Weiner, R.H. and Davis, H.G. (1980) Use of the MMPI in identification of alcoholic psychiatric patients, *Journal of Consulting and Clinical Psychology*, 48: 416–17.

Connors, G.J. (1998) Overview of Project MATCH, *The Addictions Newsletter*, 5: 4–5.

Cooney, N.L., Gillespie, R.A., Baker, L.H. and Kaplan, R.F. (1987) Cognitive changes after alcohol cue exposure, *Journal of Consulting and Clinical Psychology*, 55: 150–5.

Cooney, N.L., Kadden, R.M., Litt, M.D. and Getter, H. (1991) Matching alcoholics to coping skills or interactional therapies: two-year follow-up results, *Journal of Consulting and Clinical Psychology*, 59: 598–601.

Cooper, D.A. (2000) *Future Synthetic Drugs of Abuse*. McLean, VA: US Drug Enforcement Administration.

Council of Philosophical Studies (1981) *Psychology and the Philosophy of Mind in the Philosophy Curriculum*. San Francisco, CA: San Francisco State University.

Cunningham, J.A., Sobell, L.S. and Sobell, M.B. (1996) Are disease and other conceptions of alcohol abuse related to beliefs about outcome and recovery? *Journal of Applied Social Psychology*, 26: 773–80.

Curry, S., Wagner, E.H. and Grothaus, L.C. (1990) Intrinsic and extrinsic motivation for smoking cessation, *Journal of Consulting and Clinical Psychology*, 58: 310–16.

Daley, D.C. and Salloum, I. (1999) Relapse prevention, in P.J. Ott, R.E. Tarter and R.T. Ammerman (eds) *Sourcebook on Substance Abuse, Etiology, Epidemiology, Assessment, and Treatment*. Boston, MA: Allyn and Bacon.

Davison, G.C. and Neale, J.M. (1990) *Abnormal Psychology*. New York: Wiley.

De Leon, G., DiClemente, C.C., Gorski, T. and Marlatt, G.A. (1994) Recovery stage theory in chemical dependency: current paradigms, issues, and findings. Symposium presented at the 102nd Annual Convention of the American Psychological Association, Los Angeles, August.

DeMoor, C., Johnston, D.A., Werden, D.L. *et al.* (1994) Patterns and correlates of smoking and smokeless tobacco use among continuation high school students, *Addictive Behaviors*, 19: 175–84.

Dent, C.W., Sussman, S. and Stacy, A.W. (2001) Drug abuse prevention among youth at comprehensive high schools, *Preventive Medicine*, 32: 514–20.

Deykin, E.Y., Levy, J.C. and Wells, V. (1987) Adolescent depression, alcohol, and drug abuse, *American Journal of Public Health*, 77: 178–82.

Diaz-Guerrero, R. (1984) Behavioural health across cultures, in J.D. Matarazzo, S.M. Weiss, J.A. Herd, N.E. Miller and Stephen M. Weiss (eds) *Behavioral Health: A Handbook of Health Enhancement and Disease Prevention*. New York: Wiley.

DiChiara, G. (1998) A motivational learning hypothesis of the role of mesolimbic dopamine in compulsive drug use, *Journal of Psychopharmacology*, 12(1): 54–67.

DiClemente, C.C., Prochaska, J.O., Fairhurst, S.K. *et al.* (1991) The process of smoking cessation: an analysis of precontemplation, contemplation, and preparation stages of change, *Journal of Consulting and Clinical Psychology*, 59: 295–304.

DiClemente, C., Carbonari, J., Montgomery, R. and Hughes, S. (1994) The Alcohol Abstinence Self-Efficacy Scale, *Journal of Studies on Alcohol*, 85: 141–8.

Doherty, K.T. and Szalay, L.B. (1996) Statistical risk versus psychological vulnerability: why are men at greater risk for substance abuse than women? *Journal of Alcohol and Drug Education*, 42(1): 57–77.

Donaldson, S.I. (1995) Peer influence on adolescent drug use: a perspective from the trenches of experimental evaluation research, *American Psychologist*, 50: 801–2.

Donaldson, S.I., Graham, J.W. and Hansen, W.B. (1994) Testing the generalizability of intervening mechanism theories: understanding the effects of adolescent drug use prevention interventions, *Journal of Behavioral Medicine*, 17: 195–216.

Donovan, J.E. and Jessor, R. (1985) Structure of problem behavior in adolescence and young adulthood, *Journal of Consulting and Clinical Psychology*, 53: 890–904.

Donovan, J.E., Jessor, R. and Costa, F.M. (1993) Structure of health-enhancing behavior in adolescence: a latent-variable approach, *Journal of Health and Social Behavior*, 34: 346–62.

Dorsman, J. (1991) *How to Quit Drinking without AA: A Complete Self-help Guide*. Newark, DE: New Dawn.

Duncan, D.F., Nicholson, T., Clifford, P., Hawkins, W. and Petosa, R. (1994) Harm reduction: an emerging new paradigm for drug education, *Journal of Drug Education*, 24: 281–90.

Dunn, M.E. and Goldman, M.S. (1996) Empirical modeling of an alcohol expectancy memory network in elementary school children as a function of grade, *Experimental and Clinical Psychopharmacology*, 4(2): 209–17.

Earleywine, M. (1994) Cognitive bias covaries with alcohol consumption, *Addictive Behaviors*, 19(5): 539–44.

Earleywine, M. and Finn, P.R. (1991) Sensation seeking explains the relation between behavioral disinhibition and alcohol consumption, *Addictive Behaviors*, 16: 123–8.

Earleywine, M. and Martin, C.S. (1993) Anticipated stimulant and sedative effects of alcohol vary with dosage and limb of the blood alcohol curve, *Alcoholism: Clinical and Experimental Research*, 17(1): 135–9.

Eggert, L.L., Thompson, E.A., Herting, J.R., Nicholas, L.J. and Dicker, B.G. (1994) Preventing adolescent drug abuse and high school dropout through an intensive school-based social network development program, *American Journal of Health Promotion*, 8: 202–15.

Elder, J.P. and Stern, R.A. (1986) The ABCs of adolescent smoking prevention: an environment and skills model, *Health Education Quarterly*, 13: 181–91.

Ellickson, P.L. and Bell, R.M. (1990) Drug prevention in junior high: a multi-site longitudinal test, *Science*, 247: 1299–305.

Emmons, K., Glasgow, R.E., Marcus, B., Rakowski, W. and Curry, S.J. (1995) Motivation for change across behavioral risk factors: conceptual and clinical advances. Symposium presented at the Sixteenth Annual Scientific Sessions of the Society of Behavioural Medicine, San Diego, CA, 22–25 March.

Epstein, L.H. and Cluss, P.A. (1984) A behavioral medicine perspective on adherence to long-term medical regimens, *Journal of Consulting and Clinical Psychology*, 50: 950–71.

Erickson, P.G. (1995) Harm reduction: what it is and is not, *Drug and Alcohol Review*, 14: 283–5.

Etheridge, R.M., Hubbard, R.L., Anderson, J., Craddock, S.G. and Flynn, P.M. (1997) Treatment structure and program services in the drug abuse treatment outcome study (DATOS), *Psychology of Addictive Behaviors*, 11: 244–60.

Ewing, J.A. (1984) Detecting alcohol: the CAGE questionnaire, *Journal of the American Medical Association*, 252: 1905–7.

Faber, R.J. and O'Guinn, T.C. (1992) A clinical screener for compulsive buying, *Journal of Consumer Research*, 19: 459–69.

First, M.B., Spitzer, R.L., Gibbon, R.L. and Williams, J.B.W. (1995) *Structured Clinical Interview for DSM-IV Axis I Disorders*. Washington, DC: American Psychiatric Association Press.

Fishbein, M. and Ajzen, I. (1975) *Belief, Attitude, Intention, and Behavior: An Introduction to Theory and Research*. Reading, MA: Addison-Wesley.

Fishkin, S.A., Sussman, S., Stacy, A.W. *et al.* (1993) Ingroup versus outgroup perceptions of the characteristics of high-risk youth: negative stereotyping, *Journal of Applied Social Psychology*, 23: 1051–68.

Flay, B.R. (1985) Psychosocial approaches to smoking prevention: a review of findings, *Health Psychology*, 4: 449–88.

Flay, B.R., d'Avernas, J.R., Best, J.A., Kersell, M.W. and Ryan, K.B. (1983) Cigarette smoking: why young people do it and ways of preventing it, in P. McGrath and P. Firestone (eds) *Pediatric and Adolescent Behavioral Medicine*. New York: Springer-Verlag.

Fletcher, B.W., Tims, F.M. and Brown, B.S. (1997) Drug Abuse Treatment Outcome Study (DATOS): treatment evaluation research in the United States, *Psychology of Addictive Behaviors*, 11: 216–29.

Fountain, D. (1995) Cost-effectiveness of substance abuse treatment. Paper presented at the Third Annual Conference on Psychopathology, Psychopharmacology, Substance Abuse and Culture, Los Angeles, October.

Friedman, A. and Utada, A. (1989) A method for diagnosing and planning the treatment of adolescent drug abusers (the Adolescent Drug Abuse Diagnosis instrument), *Journal of Drug Education*, 19: 285–312.

Fromme, K., Stroot, E. and Kaplan, D. (1993) Comprehensive effects of alcohol: development and psychometric assessment of a new expectancy questionnaire, *Psychological Assessment*, 5: 19–26.

Fromme, K., Katz, E.C. and Rivet, K. (1997) Outcome expectancies and risk-taking behavior, *Cognitive Therapy and Research*, 21(4): 421–42.

Galaif, E. and Sussman, S. (1995) For whom does Alcoholics Anonymous work? *International Journal of the Addictions*, 30: 161–84.

Galaif, E.R., Chou, C.P., Sussman, S. and Dent, C.W. (1998) Depression, suicidal ideation, and substance use among continuation high school students, *Journal of Youth and Adolescence*, 27(3): 275–99.

Garris, P., Kilpatrick, M.R., Bunin, M. *et al.* (1999) Dissociation of dopamine release in the nucleus accumbens from intracranial self-stimulation, *Nature*, 398: 67–9.

Glynn, T.J. (1989) Essential elements of school-based smoking prevention programs, *Journal of School Health*, 59: 181–8.

Goldberger, B.A. and Cone, E.J. (1994) Confirmatory tests for drugs in the workplace by gas chromatography-mass spectrometry, *Journal of Chromatography*, 674: 73–86.

Goldberger, B.A. and Jenkins, A.J. (1999) Drug toxicology, in P.J. Ott, R.E. Tarter and R.T. Ammerman (eds) *Sourcebook on Substance Abuse: Etiology, Epidemiology, Assessment, and Treatment.* Boston, MA: Allyn and Bacon.

Goldman, M.S., Brown, S.A., Christiansen, B.A. and Smith, G.T. (1991) Alcoholism and memory: broadening the scope of alcohol expectancy research, *Psychological Bulletin*, 110: 137–46.

Goldstein, P.J. (1985) The drugs/violence nexus: a tripartite conceptual framework, *Journal of Drug Issues*, 15: 493–506.

Goldstein, P.J. (1998) Drugs, violence, and federal funding: a research odyssey, *Substance Use and Misuse*, special issue on research careers in unraveling the drug-crime nexus in the United States, 33: 1915–36.

Gordon, R. (1987) An operational classification of disease prevention, in J.A. Steinberg and M.M. Silverman (eds) *Preventing Mental Disorders.* Rockville, MD: DHHS.

Gordon, J.R. and Barrett, K. (1993) The codependency movement: issues of context and differentiation, in J.S. Baer, G.A. Marlatt and R.J. McMahon (eds) *Addictive Behaviors across the Life Span.* Newbury Park, CA: Sage.

Gorski, T.T. (1989) The CENAPS model of relapse prevention planning, *Journal of Chemical Dependency Treatment*, 2: 153–69.

Gorski, T.T. and Miller, M. (1984) *The Phases and Warning Signs of Relapse.* Independence, MO: Independence Press.

Gorski, T.T. and Miller, M. (1986) *Staying Sober: A Guide for Relapse Prevention.* Independence, MO: Independence Press.

Gottman, J.M. and Leiblum, S.R. (1974) *How to do Psychotherapy and How to Evaluate it: A Manual for Beginners.* New York: Holt, Rinehart and Winston.

Graham, J.W., Johnson, C.A., Hansen, W.B., Flay, B.R. and Gee, M. (1990) Drug use prevention programs, gender, and ethnicity: evaluation of three seventh-grade Project SMART cohorts, *Preventive Medicine*, 19: 305–13.

Grant, B.F. (1994) ICD-10 harmful use of alcohol and the alcohol dependence syndrome: prevalence and implications, *Addiction*, 88: 413–20.

Gray, J.A. (1990) Brain systems that mediate both emotion and cognition, *Cognition and Emotion*, 4: 269–88.

Griffiths, M. (1997) Exercise addition: a case study, *Addiction Research*, 5: 161–8.

Hanley, A. and Wilhelm, M.S. (1992) Compulsive buying: an exploration into self-esteem and money attitudes, *Journal of Economic Psychology*, 13: 5–18.

Hansen, W.B. (1992) School-based substance abuse prevention: a review of the state of the art in curriculum, 1980–1990, *Health Education Research: Theory and Practice*, 7: 403–30.

Hansen, W.B. and Graham, J.W. (1991) Preventing alcohol, marijuana, and cigarette use among adolescents: peer pressure and resistance training versus establishing conservative norms, *Preventive Medicine*, 20: 414–30.

Hansen, W.B., Johnson, C.A., Flay, B.R., Graham, J.W. and Sobel, J. (1988) Affective and social influences approaches to the prevention of multiple substance abuse among seventh grade students: results from Project SMART, *Preventive Medicine*, 17: 135–54.

Harrell, T., Honaker, L. and Davis, E. (1991) Cognitive and behavioral dimension of dysfunction in alcohol and polydrug abusers, *Journal of Substance Abuse*, 3: 415–26.

Hathaway, S.R. and McKinley, J.C. (1943) *The Minnesota Multiphasic Personality Inventory*, revised edition. Minneapolis, MN: University of Minnesota Press.

Hawkins, J.D., Catalano, R.F. and Miller, J.Y. (1992) Risk and protective factors for alcohol and other drug problems in adolescence and early adulthood: implications for substance abuse prevention, *Psychological Bulletin*, 112: 64–105.

Hays, R., Stacy, A.W. and DiMatteo, M.R. (1987) Problem behavior theory and adolescent alcohol use, *Addictive Behaviors*, 12: 189–93.

Heath, D.B. (1999) Culture, in P.J. Ott, R.E. Tarter and R.T. Ammerman (eds) *Sourcebook on Substance Abuse, Etiology, Epidemiology, Assessment, and Treatment*. Needham Heights, MA: Allyn and Bacon.

Hegerl, U., Lipperheide, K., Juckel, G., Schmidt, L.G. and Rommelspacher, H. (1995) Antisocial tendencies and cortical sensory-evoked responses in alcoholism, *Alcoholism: Clinical and Experimental Research*, 19(1): 31–5.

Hendricks, C.M., Echols, D. and Nelson, G.D. (1989) The impact of a preschool health curriculum on children's health knowledge, *Journal of School Health*, 59(9): 389–95.

Henry, B., Feehan, M., McGee, R. *et al.* (1993) The importance of conduct problems and depressive symptoms in predicting adolescent substance use, *Journal of Abnormal Child Psychology*, 21: 469–80.

Hershow, R.C., Riester, K.A., Lew, J. *et al.* (1997) Increased vertical transmission of human immunodeficiency virus from hepatitis C virus-coinfected mothers: Women and Infants Transmission Study, *Journal of Infectious Diseases*, 176: 414–20.

Hill, A.B. and Paynter, S. (1992) Alcohol dependence and semantic priming of alcohol related words, *Personality and Individual Differences*, 13(6): 745–50.

Hill, S.Y. (1982) Biological consequences of alcoholism and alcohol-related problems among women, in National Institute on Alcohol Abuse and Alcoholism, *Special Populations Issues: Alcohol and Health Monograph no. 4*. Washington, DC: US Government Printing Office.

Hill, S.Y. (1984) Vulnerability to the biomedical consequences of alcoholism and alcohol-related problems among women, in S.C. Wilsnack and L.J. Beckman (eds) *Alcohol Problems in Women: Antecedents, Consequences and Interventions*. New York: Guilford Press.

Ho, R. (1992) Cigarette health warnings: the effects of perceived severity, expectancy of occurrence, and self-efficacy on intentions to give up smoking, *Australian Psychologist*, 27: 109–13.

Hollinger, R.C. (1988) Working under the influence (WUI): correlates of employees' use of alcohol and other drugs, *Journal of Applied Behavioral Science*, 24: 439–54.

Horn, J.L., Wanberg, K.H. and Foster, F.M. (1990) *Guide to the Alcohol Use Inventory (AUI)*. Minneapolis, MN: National Computer Systems.

Hovarth, A.T. (1999) *Sex, Drugs, Gambling and Chocolate: A Workbook for Overcoming Addictions*. San Luis Obispo, CA: Impact.

Hubbard, R. (1995) Drug treatment works: an update from the drug abuse treatment outcome study. Paper presented at the Third Annual Conference on Psychopathology, Psychopharmacology, Substance Abuse and Culture, Los Angeles, October.

Hubbard, R.L., Craddock, S.G., Flynn, P.M., Anderson, J. and Etheridge, R.M. (1997) Overview of 1-year follow-up outcomes in the Drug Abuse Treatment Outcome Study (DATOS), *Psychology of Addictive Behaviors*, 11: 261–78.

Hurt, R.D., Eberman, K.M., Slade, J. and Karan, L. (1993) Treating nicotine addiction in patients with other addictive disorders, in C.T. Orleans and J. Slade (eds) *Nicotine Addiction: Principles and Management*. New York: Oxford University Press.

Institute on Alcoholic Studies (1995) Factsheet: www.ias.org.uk/factsheets/crime.htm

Irons, R. and Schneider, J.P. (1997) When is domestic violence a hidden face of addiction? *Journal of Psychoactive Drugs*, 29: 337–51.

James, W. (1958) *The Varieties of Religious Experience*. New York: Mentor Books (original lectures were given in 1902).

Jellinek, E.M. (1952) Phases of alcohol addiction, *Quarterly Journal of Studies on Alcohol*, 13: 673–84.

Jessor, R. (1984) Adolescent development and behavioral health, in J.D. Matarazzo, S.M. Weiss, J.A. Herd, N.E. Miller and S.M. Weiss (eds) *Behavioral Health: A Handbook of Health Enhancement and Disease Prevention*. New York: Wiley.

Jessor, R. (1987) Problem-behavior theory, psychosocial development, and adolescent problem drinking, *British Journal of Addictions*, 82: 331–42.

Jessor, R. and Jessor, S. (1977) *Problem Behavior and Psychosocial Development: A Longitudinal Study of Youth*. New York: Academic Press.

Johnson, C.A., Pentz, M.A., Weber, M.D. *et al.* (1990) Relative effectiveness of comprehensive community programming for drug abuse prevention with high-risk and low-risk adolescents, *Journal of Consulting and Clinical Psychology*, 58: 447–56.

Johnson, C.A., MacKinnon, D.P. and Pentz, M.A. (1996) Breadth of program and outcome effectiveness in drug abuse prevention, *American Behavioral Scientist*, 39: 884–96.

Johnson, V. and Pandina, R.J. (2001) Choosing assessment studies to clarify theory-based program ideas, in S. Sussman (ed.) *Handbook of Programme Development for Health Behavior Research and Practice*. Thousand Oaks, CA: Sage.

Johnson, V.E. (1980) *I'll Quit Tomorrow: A Practical Guide to Alcoholism Treatment*. San Francisco, CA: Harper and Row.

Johnston, L.D., O'Malley, P.M. and Bachman, J.G. (1999) *National Survey Results on Drug Use from the Monitoring the Future Study, 1975–1998*, vols 1 and 2. Rockville, MD: US DHHS (NIH Publication nos. 99-4660 and 99-4661).

Johnstone, B.M. (1994) Sociodemographic, environmental, and cultural influences on adolescent drinking behavior, in National Institute on Alcohol Abuse and Alcoholism (NIAAA) *The Development of Alcohol Problems: Exploring the Biopsychosocial Matrix of Risk*, Research Monograph 26. Rockville, MD: US DHHS.

Jonas, J.M., Gold, M.S., Sweeney, D. and Pottash, A.L. (1987) Eating disorders and cocaine abuse: a survey of 259 cocaine abusers, *Journal of Clinical Psychiatry*, 48: 47–50.

Julien, R.M. (1998) *A Primer of Drug Action.* New York: W.H. Freeman.

Kadden, R.M. (1999) Cognitive behavior therapy, in P.J. Ott, R.E. Tarter and R.T. Ammerman (eds) *Sourcebook on Substance Abuse: Etiology, Epidemiology, Assessment, and Treatment.* Boston, MA: Allyn and Bacon.

Kandel, D.B. and Andrews, K. (1987) Processes of adolescent socialization by parents and peers, *International Journal of the Addictions*, 22, 319–42.

Kandel, D.B., Yamaguchi, K. and Chen, K. (1992) Stages of progression in drug involvement from adolescence to adulthood: further evidence for the gateway theory, *Journal of Studies on Alcohol*, 53: 447–57.

Kapur, B.M. (1993) Drug-testing methods and clinical interpretations of test results, *Bulletin on Narcotics*, 45: 115–54.

Kauhanen, J., Kaplan, G.A., Goldberg, D.E., Salonen, R. and Salonen, J.T. (1999) Pattern of alcohol drinking and progression of atherosclerosis, *Arteriosclerosis, Thrombosis and Vascular Biology*, 19: 3001–6.

Kendler, K.S. and Prescott, C.A. (1998) Cannabis use, abuse, and dependence in a population-based sample of female twins, *American Journal of Psychiatry*, 155: 1016–22.

Kerr, J.K., Skok, R.L. and McLaughlin, T.F. (1991) Characteristics common to females who exhibit anorexic or bulimic behavior: a review of current literature, *Journal of Clinical Psychology*, 47: 846–53.

Khantzian, E.J. (1985) The self-medication hypothesis of addictive disorders: focus on heroin and cocaine dependence, *American Journal of Psychiatry*, 142: 1259–64.

Kranzler, H.R. and Anton, R.A. (1994) Implications of recent neuropsychopharmacologic research for understanding the etiology and development of alcholism, *Journal of Consulting and Clinical Psychology*, 62(6): 1116–26.

Kuhar, M.J., Ritz, M.C. and Boja, J.W. (1991) The dopamine hypothesis of the reinforcing properties of cocaine, *Trends in Neurosciences*, 14: 299–302.

Kunst-Wilson, W.R. and Zajonc, R.B. (1980) Affective discrimination of stimuli that cannot be recognized, *Science*, 207(4430): 557–8.

Kushner, M.G. and Sher, K.J. (1993) Comorbidity of alcohol and anxiety disorders among students: effects of gender and family history of alcoholism, *Addictive Behaviors*, 18: 543–52.

Leigh, B.C. (1989) In search of the seven dwarves: issues of measurement and meaning in alcohol expectancy research, *Psychological Bulletin*, 105: 361–73.

Leigh, B.C. and Schafer, J.C. (1993) Heavy drinking occasions and the occurrence of sexual activity, *Psychology of Addictive Behaviors*, 7: 197–200.

Leigh, B.C. and Stacy, A.W. (1991) On the scope of alcohol expectancy research: remaining issues of measurement and meaning, *Psychological Bulletin*, 110(1): 147–54.

Leigh, B.C. and Stacy, A.W. (1993) Alcohol outcome expectancies: scale construction and predictive utility in higher order confirmatory models, *Psychological Assessment*, 5: 216–29.

Leshner, A.I. (1997) Introduction to the special issue: the National Institute on Drug Abuse's (NIDA's) Drug Abuse Treatment Outcome Study (DATOS), *Psychology of Addictive Behaviors*, 11: 211–15.

Leventhal, H. and. Cleary, P. (1980) The smoking problem: a review of research and theory in behavioral risk modification, *Psychological Bulletin*, 88: 370–405.

Leventhal, H. and Keeshan, P. (1993) Promoting healthy alternatives to substance abuse, in S.G. Millstein, A.C. Peterson and E.O. Nightingale (eds) *Promoting the Health of Adolescents: New Directions for the Twenty-first Century*. New York: Oxford University Press.

Leventhal, H., Diefenbach, M. and Leventhal, E.A. (1992) Illness cognition: using common sense to understand treatment adherence and affect cognition interactions, *Cognitive Therapy and Research*, 16: 143–63.

Li, T.K., Lumeng, L. and Doolittle, D.P. (1993) Selective breeding for alcohol preference and associated responses, *Behavior Genetics*, 23: 163–70.

Li, T.K., Beard, J.D., Orr, W.E. *et al.*, (1998) Gender and ethnic differences in alcohol metabolism, *Alcohol Clinical Experimental Research*, 22(3): 771–2.

Lightfoot, L.O. (1993) The Offender Substance Abuse Pre-release Programme: an empirically based model of treatment for offenders, in J.S. Baer, G.A. Marlatt and R.J. McMahon (eds) *Addictive Behaviors across the Lifespan*. Newbury Park, CA: Sage.

Littrell, J. (1991) *Understanding and Treating Alcoholism: An Empirically Based Clinician's Handbook for the Treatment of Alcoholism*. Hillsdale, NJ: Erlbaum.

Luepker, R.V., Pechacek, T.F., Murray, D.M. *et al.* (1981) Saliva thiocyanate: A chemical indicator of cigarette smoking in adolescents, *American Journal of Public Health*, 71: 1320–4.

MacAndrew, C. (1965) The differentiation of male alcoholic outpatients from non-alcoholic psychiatric patients by means of the MMPI, *Quarterly Journal of Studies on Alcohol*, 26: 238–46.

MacAndrew, C. (1989) Factors associated with the problem-engendering use of substances by young men, *Journal of Studies on Alcohol*, 50: 552–6.

McCourt, W.F., Williams, A.F. and Schneider, L. (1971) Incidence of alcoholism in a state mental hospital population, *Quarterly Journal of Studies on Alcohol*, 32(4, pt A): 1085–8.

McGuire, W.J. (1964) Inducing resistance to persuasion, in L. Berkowitz (ed.) *Advances in Experimental Social Psychology*, volume 1. New York: Academic Press.

MacKinnon, D.P., Johnson, C.A., Pentz, M.A., Dwyer, D.P. and Hansen, W.B. (1991) Mediating mechanisms in a school-based drug prevention program: first year effects of the Midwestern Prevention Project, *Health Psychology*, 10: 164–72.

McLellan, A.T., Luborsky, L., Woody, G.E. and O'Brien, C.P. (1980) An improved diagnostic evaluation instrument for substance abuse patients, *Journal of Nervous and Mental Disease*, 168: 26–33.

McLellan, A.T., Luborsky, L., Cacciola, J. *et al.* (1985) New data from the Addiction Severity Index: reliability and validity in three centers, *Journal of Nervous and Mental Disease*, 173: 412–28.

Malin, H., Coakley, J. and Kaelber, C. (1982) An epidemiologic perspective on alcohol use and abuse in the United States, in National Institute on Alcohol Abuse and Alcoholism, *Alcohol Consumption and Related Problems*. Rockville, MD: National Institute on Alcohol Abuse and Alcoholism.

Manderlink, G. and Harackiewicz, J.M. (1984) Proximal versus distal goal setting and intrinsic motivation, *Journal of Personality and Social Psychology*, 47: 918–28.

Mansdorf, I.J., Calapai, P., Caselli, L., Burnstein, Y. and Dimant, J. (1999) Reducing psychotropic medication usage in nursing home residents: the effects of behaviourally oriented psychotherapy, *The Behavior Therapist*, 22, 21–3: 39.

Marijuana Anonymous (1995) *Life with Hope*, 1st edn. Van Nuys, CA: Marijuana Anonymous World Services.

Marlatt, G.A. (1985) Relapse prevention: theoretical rationale and overview of the model, in G.A. Marlatt and J.R. Gordon (eds) *Relapse Prevention: Maintenance Strategies in Addictive Behavior Change*. New York: Guilford Press.

Marlatt, G.A. (1990) Cue exposure and relapse prevention in the treatment of addictive behaviors, *Addictive Behaviors*, 15: 395–9.

Marlatt, G.A. and Gordon, J.R. (1985) *Relapse Prevention: Maintenance Strategies in Addictive Behavior Change*. New York: Guilford Press.

Marlatt, G.A., Somers, J.M. and Tapert, S.F. (1993) Harm reduction: applications to alcohol abuse problems, in L.S. Onken, J.D. Blaine and J.J. Boren (eds) *Behavioral Treatments for Drug Abuse and Dependence*. Bethesda, MD: National Institute on Drug Abuse.

Mathias, R. (1999) Adding more counseling sessions and 12-step programs can boost drug abuse treatment effectiveness, *NIDA Notes*, 14: 6–7.

Meichenbaum, D. (1977) *Cognitive Behavior Modification: An Integrative Approach*. New York: Plenum.

Melis, M.R. and Argiolas, A. (1995) Dopamine and sexual behavior, *Neuroscience and Biobehavioral Reviews*, 19: 19–38.

Meyers, K., McLellan, A.T., Jaeger, J.L. and Pettinati, H.M. (1995) The development of the Comprehensive Addiction Severity Index for adolescents (CASI-A), *Journal of Substance Abuse Treatment*, 12: 181–93.

Miele, G.M., Carpenter, K.M., Cockerham, M.S. *et al.* (2000) Substance Dependence Severity Scale (SDSS): reliability and validity of a clinician-administered interview for DSM-IV substance use disorders, *Drug and Alcohol Dependence*, 59: 63–75.

Milam, J.R. and Ketcham, K. (1983) *Under the Influence*. New York: Bantam.

Miller, L. (1991) Predicting relapse and recovery in alcoholism and addiction: neuropsychology, personality and cognitive style, *Journal of Substance Abuse Treatment*, 8: 277–91.

Miller, W.R. (1992) Building bridges over troubled waters: a response to 'alcoholism, politics, and bureaucracy: the consensus against controlled-drinking therapy in America', *Addictive Behaviors*, 17: 79–81.

Miller, W.R. and Marlatt, G.A. (1984) *Comprehensive Drinker Profile (Manual)*. Odessa, FL: Psychological Assessment Resources.

Miller, W.R. and Rollnick, S. (1991) *Motivational Interviewing: Preparing People to Change Addictive Behavior*. New York: Guilford Press.

Miller, W.R., Leckman, A.L., Delaney, H.D. and Tinkcom, M. (1992) Long-term followup of behavioral self-control training, *Journal of Studies on Alcohol*, 53: 249–61.

Mitchell, J.E., Specker, S. and Edmonson, K. (1997) Management of substance abuse and dependence, in P.E. Garfinkel and D.M. Garner (eds) *Handbook of Treatment for Eating Disorders*, 2nd edn. New York: Guilford Press.

Montague, P.R., Dayan, P. and Sejnowski, T.J. (1996) A framework for mesencephalic dopamine systems based on predictive Hebbian learning, *Journal of Neuroscience*, 16: 1936–47.

Mundis, J. (1986) A way back from debt: Debtors Anonymous, *The New York Times Magazine*, 5 January.

Narcotics Anonymous (1988) *Narcotics Anonymous*, 5th edn. Van Nuys, CA: Narcotics Anonymous World Services.

National Institute on Drug Abuse (NIDA) (1999a) Club drugs, *Community Drug Alert Bulletin*, December, NIH Publication no. 00-4723. Bethesda, MD: US DHHS.

National Institute on Drug Abuse (NIDA) (1999b) *Principles of Drug Addiction Treatment: A Research-Based Guide*, NIH Publication no. 99-4180. Bethesda, MD: US DHHS.

Newcomb, M.D. and Bentler, P.M. (1988) *Consequences of Adolescent Drug Use*. Newbury Park, CA: Sage.

Newcomb, M.D. and Bentler, P.M. (1989) Substance use and abuse among children and teenagers, *American Psychologist*, 44: 242–8.

Newcomb, M. and Earlywine, M. (1996) Intrapersonal contributors to drug use: the willing host, *American Behavioural Scientist*, 39: 823–37.

Newcomb, M.D. and Felix-Ortiz, M. (1992) Multiple Protective and Risk Factors for drug use and abuse: cross-sectional and prospective findings, *Journal of Personality and Social Psychology*, 63(2): 280–96.

Newcomb, M.D. and McGee, L. (1991) Influences of sensation seeking on general deviance and specific problem behaviors from adolescence to young adulthood, *Journal of Personality and Social Psychology*, 61: 614–28.

Nezami, E., Sussman, S. and Pentz, M.A. (2001) Motivation in tobacco use cessation research, *Substance Use and Misuse*.

Niaura, R.S., Rohsenow, D.J., Binkoff, J.A. *et al.* (1988) Relevance of cue reactivity to understanding alcohol and smoking relapse, *Journal of Abnormal Psychology*, 97(2): 133–52.

Ockene, J.K., Nutall, R., Benfari, R.C., Hurwitz, I. and Ockene, I.S. (1981) A psychosocial model of smoking cessation and maintenance of cessation, *Preventive Medicine*, 10: 623–38.

O'Connor, K. (1989) A motor psychophysiological model of smoking and personality, *Personality and Individual Differences*, 10: 889–901.

O'Farrell, T.J. and Fals-Stewart, W. (2000) Behavioural couples therapy for alcoholism and drug abuse, *Behavior Therapist*, 23: 49–54, 70.

Olson, G.A., Olson, R.D. and Kastin, A.J. (1992) Endogenous opiates: 1991, *Peptides*, 13: 1247–87.

Orpinas, P.K., Basen-Engquist, K., Grunbaum, J. and Parcel, G.S. (1995) The co-morbidity of violence-related behaviors with health-risk behaviors in a population of high school students, *Journal of Adolescent Health*, 16: 216–25.

Peele, S. (1998) Ten radical things NIAAA research shows about alcoholism, *Addictions Newsletter*, 5(6–7): 2020–2.

Peele, S. and Brodsky, A. (1991) *The Truth about Addiction and Recovery*. New York: Simon and Schuster.

Pentz, M.A., Brannon, B.R., Charlin, V.L. *et al.* (1989a) The power of policy: relationship of school smoking policy to adolescent smoking, *American Journal of Public Health*, 79: 857–63.

Pentz, M.A., Dwyer, J.H., MacKinnon, D., Flay, B.R., Hansen, W.B., Wang, E.Y.I. and Johnson, C.A. (1989b) A multi-community trial for primary prevention of adolescent drug abuse: effects on drug use prevalence, *Journal of the American Medical Association*, 262: 3259–66.

Pentz, M.A., Bonnie, R.J. and Shopland, D.R. (1996) Integrating supply and demand reduction strategies for drug abuse prevention, *American Behavioral Scientist*, 39: 897–910.

Pentz, M.A., Sussman, S. and Newman, T. (1997) The conflict between least harm and no-use tobacco policy for youth: ethical and policy implications, *Addiction*, 92(9): 1165–73.

Petraitis, J., Flay, B.R. and Miller, T.Q. (1995) Reviewing theories of adolescent substance use: organizing the pieces in the puzzle, *Psychological Bulletin*, 117: 67–86.

Pfaus, J.G., Damsma, G., Wenkstern, D. and Fibiger, H.C. (1995) Sexual activity increases dopamine transmission in the nucleus accumbens and striatum of female rats, *Brain Research*, 693: 21–30.

Phillips, A.G. (1984) Brain reward circuitry: a case for separate systems, *Brain Research Bulletin*, 12: 195–201.

Pickering, H. and Stimson, G.V. (1994) Prevalence and demographic factors of stimulant use, *Addiction*, 89: 1385–9.

Polich, J.M., Armor, D.J. and Braiker, H.B. (1981) *The Course of Alcoholism: Four Years after Treatment*. New York: Wiley.

Powell, J., Dawe, S., Richards, D. *et al.* (1993) Can opiate addicts tell us about their relapse risk? *Addictive Behaviors*, 18(4): 473–90.

Prochaska, J.O. and DiClemente, C.C. (1982) Transtheoretical therapy: toward a more integrative model of change, *Psychotherapy: Theory, Research and Practice*, 19: 275–88.

Prochaska, J.O. and DiClemente, C.C. (1983) Stages and processes of self-change of smoking: toward an integrative model of change, *Journal of Consulting and Clinical Psychology*, 51: 390–5.

Prochaska, J.O., DiClemente, C.C., Velicer, W.F., Ginpil, S. and Norcross, J.C. (1985) Prediction change in smoking status for self-changers, *Addictive Behaviors*, 10: 395–406.

Prochaska, J.O., Velicer, S., DiClemente, C.C., Guadagnoli, E. and Rossi, J.S. (1990) Patterns of change: dynamic typology applied to smoking cessation, *Multivariate Behavioral Research*, 25: 587–611.

Quintero, G. and Nichter, M. (1996) The semantics of addiction: moving beyond expert models to lay understandings, *Journal of Psychoactive Drugs*, 28: 219–28.

Rather, B.C. and Goldman, M.S. (1994) Drinking-related differences in the memory organization of alcohol expectancies, *Experimental and Clinical Psychopharmacology*, 2(2): 167–83.

Rather, B.C., Goldman, M.S., Roehrich, L. and Brannick, M. (1992) Empirical modeling of an alcohol expectancy memory network using multidimensional scaling, *Journal of Abnormal Psychology*, 101(1): 174–83.

Reich, T. (2000) The genetics of alcoholism. Presentation at the USC/Norris Comprehensive Cancer Center, Keck School of Medicine, University of Southern California Seminar Series, Los Angeles, March.

Resnik, H. and Wojcicki, M. (1991) Reaching and retaining high risk youth and their parents in prevention programs, in E.N. Goplerud (ed.) *Preventing Adolescent Drug Use: From Theory to Practice*, OSAP Prevention Monograph 8. Rockville, MD: Office for Substance Abuse Prevention (OSAP).

Richardson, J.L., Dwyer, K., McGuigan, K. *et al.* (1989) Substance use among eighth-grade students who take care of themselves after school, *Pediatrics*, 84: 556–66.

Roberts, L.J. and Marlatt, G.A. (1999) Harm reduction, in P.J. Ott, R.E. Tarter and R.T. Ammerman (eds) *Sourcebook on substance abuse, etiology, epidemiology, assessment, and treatment*. Boston, MA: Allyn and Bacon.

Rodgers, J.E. (1994) Addiction: a whole new view, *Psychology Today*, September–October: 32–8.

Roehrich, L. and Goldman, M.S. (1995) Implicit priming of alcohol expectancy memory processes and subsequent drinking behavior, *Experimental and Clinical Psychopharmacology*, 3(4): 402–10.

Rogers, E.M. (1983) *Diffusion of Innovations*, 3rd edn. New York: Free Press.

Rogers, R.W. (1975) A protection motivation theory of fear appeals and attitude change, *Journal of Psychology*, 91: 93–114.

Rohsenow, D.J., Monti, P.M., Martin, R.A., Michalec, E. and Abrams, D.B. (2000) Brief coping skills treatment for cocaine abuse: 12-month substance use outcomes, *Journal of Consulting and Clinical Psychology*, 68: 515–20.

Rokeach, M. (1973) *The Nature of Human Values*. New York: Free Press.

Rosch, E. (1978) *Cognition and Categorization*. New York: Erlbaum.

Rotter, J.B. (1954) *Social Learning and Clinical Psychology*. New York: Prentice Hall.

Rounsville, B.J., Kosten, T.R., Weissman, M.M. and Kleber, H.D. (1986) Prognostic significance of psychopathology in treated opiate addicts: a 2.5-year follow-up study, *Archives of General Psychiatry*, 43: 739–45.

Roy, A., Adinoff, B., Roehrich, L. *et al.* (1988) Pathological gambling: a psychobiological study, *Archives of General Psychiatry*, 45: 369–73.

Rychtarik, R.G., Koutsky, J.R. and Miller, W.R. (1998) Profiles of the alcohol use inventory: a large sample cluster analysis conducted with split-sample replication rules, *Psychological Assessment*, 10: 107–19.

Rychtarik, R.G., Koutsky, J.R. and Miller, W.R. (1999) Profiles of the alcohol use inventory: correction to Rychtarik, Koutsky, and Miller (1998), *Psychological Assessment*, 11: 396–402.

Rychtarik, R.G., Connors, G.J., Whitney, R.B., McGillicuddy, N.B. and Fitterling, J.M. (2000) Treatment settings for persons with alcoholism: evidence for matching clients to inpatient versus outpatient care, *Journal of Consulting and Clinical Psychology*, 68: 277–89.

Schaef, A.W. (1987) *When Society Becomes an Addict*. New York: HarperCollins.

Schlosser, S., Black, D.W., Repertinger, S. and Freet, D. (1994) Compulsive buying: demography, phenomenology, and comorbidity in 46 subjects, *General Hospital Psychiatry*, 16: 205–12.

Schneider, J.P. (1994) Sex addiction: controversy within mainstream addiction medicine, diagnosis based on the DSM-III-R, and physician case histories, *Sexual Addiction and Compulsivity*, 1: 19–44.

Schottenfeld, R.S. (1994) Assessment of the patient, in M. Galanter and H.D. Kleber (eds) *The American Psychiatric Press Textbook of Substance Abuse Treatment*. Washington, DC: American Psychiatric Press.

Schuckit, M.A. (1987) Biological vulnerability to alcoholism, *Journal of Consulting and Clinical Psychology*, 55: 301–9.

Schwartz, S.H. and Inbar-Saban, N. (1988) Value self-confrontation as a method to aid in weight loss, *Journal of Personality and Social Psychology*, 54: 396–404.

Selzer, M.L. (1971) The Michigan Alcoholism Screening Test: the quest for a new diagnostic instrument, *American Journal of Psychiatry*, 127: 1653–8.

Setlow, B. (1997) The nucleus accumbens and learning and memory, *Journal of Neuroscience Research*, 49: 515–21.

Shedler, J. and Block, J. (1990) Adolescent drug use and psychological health: a longitudinal inquiry, *American Psychologist*, 45: 612–30.

Sher, K.J. (1991) *Children of Alcoholics: A Critical Appraisal of Theory and Research*. Chicago: University of Chicago Press.

Sher, K.J. (1993) Children of alcoholics and the intergenerational transmission of alcoholism: a biopsychosocial perspective, in J.S. Baer, G.A. Marlatt and R.J. McMahon (eds) *Addictive Behaviors across the Life Span: Prevention, Treatment, and Policy Issues*. Newbury Park, CA: Sage.

Sher, K.J., Gershuny, B.S., Peterson, L. and Raskin, G. (1997) The role of childhood stressors in the intergenerational transmission of alcohol use disorders, *Journal of Studies on Alcohol*, 58: 414–27.

Single, E. (1995) Defining harm reduction, *Drug and Alcohol Review*, 14: 287–90.

Skogan, W.G. and Lurigio, A.J. (1992) The correlates of community antidrug activism, *Crime and Delinquency*, 38: 510–21.

Smith, C., Lizotte, A.J., Thornberry, T.P. and Krohn, M.D. (1995) Resilient youth: identifying factors that prevent high-risk youth from engaging in delinquency and drug use, in J. Hagan (ed.) *Delinquency and Disrepute in the Life Course*. Greenwich, CT: JAI Press.

Sommers, P.V. (1972) *The Biology of Behavior*. Sydney: John Wiley and Sons Australia.

Spence, J.T. and Robbins, A.S. (1992) Workaholism: definiation, measurement, and preliminary results, *Journal of Personality Assessment*, 58: 160–78.

Spiegel, E., and Mulder, E.A. (1986) The anonymous program and ego functioning, *Issues in Ego Psychology*, 19: 34–42.

Spitzer, R.L., Williams, J.B.W., Gibbon, M. and First, M.B. (1990) *Structured Clinical Interview for DSM-III-R-Patient Edition (SCID-P, Version 1.0)*. Washington, DC: American Psychiatric Association Press.

Spunt, B., Lesieur, H., Hunt, D. and Cahill, L. (1995) Gambling among methadone patients, *International Journal of the Addictions*, 30: 929–62.

Spunt, B., Dupont, I., Lesieur, H., Liberty, H.J. and Hunt, D. (1998) Pathological gambling and substance misuse: a review of the literature, *Substance Use and Misuse*, 33: 2535–60.

Stacy, A.W. (1995) Memory association and ambiguous cues in models of alcohol and marijuana use, *Experimental and Clinical Psychopharmacology*, 3(2): 183–94.

Stacy, A.W. (1997) Memory activation and expectancy as prospective predictors of alcohol and marijuana use, *Journal of Abnormal Psychology*, 106: 61–73.

Stacy, A.W. and Ames, S.L. (2001) Implicit cognition theory in drug use and driving under the influence interventions, in S. Sussman, *Handbook of Programme Development in Health Behavior Research and Practice*. Thousand Oaks, CA: Sage.

Stacy, A.W., Dent, C., Sussman, S. *et al.* (1990a) Expectancy accessibility and the influence of outcome expectancies on adolescent smokeless tobacco use, *Journal of Applied Social Psychology*, 20: 802–17.

Stacy, A.W., Widaman, K.F. and Marlatt, G.A. (1990b) Expectancy models of alcohol use, *Journal of Personality and Social Psychology*, 58: 918–28.

Stacy, A.W., Newcomb, M.D. and Bentler, P.M. (1991) Cognitive motivation and problem drug use: a 9-year longitudinal study, *Journal of Abnormal Psychology*, 100: 502–15.

Stacy, A.W., Newcomb, M.D. and Bentler, P.M. (1993) Cognitive motivations and sensation seeking as long-term predictors of drinking problems, *Journal of Social and Clinicial Psychology*, 12(1): 1–24.

Stacy, A.W., Leigh, B.C. and Weingardt, K.R. (1994) Memory accessibility and association of alcohol use and its positive outcomes, *Experimental and Clinical Psychopharmacology*, 2: 269–82.

Stacy, A.W., Ames, S.L., Sussman, S. and Dent, C.W. (1996) Implicit cognition in adolescent drug use, *Psychology of Addictive Behaviors*, 10(3): 190–203.

Stacy, A.W., Newcomb, M.D. and Ames, S.L. (2000) Implicit cognition and HIV risk behaviour, *Journal of Behavioral Medicine*, 23: 475–99.

Stevens, V.J., Glasgow, R.E., Hollis, J.F. and Mount, K. (2000) Implementation and effectiveness of a brief smoking-cessation intervention for hospital patients, *Medical Care*, 38: 451–9.

Stormack, K.M. and Hugdahl, K. (1997) Conditioned emotional cueing of spatial attentional shifts in a go/no go RT task, *International Journal of Psychophysiology*, 27(3): 241–8.

Stormack, K.M., Laberg, J.C., Nordby, H. and Hugdahl, K. (2000) Alcoholics' selective attention to alcohol stimuli automated processing? *Journal of Studies on Alcohol*, 61: 18–23.

Stroot, E.A. and Fromme, K. (1989) Comprehensive effects of alcohol: development of a new expectancy questionnaire. Paper presented at the Twenty-third Annual Meeting of the Association for Advancement of Behavior Therapy, Washington, DC, November.

Substance Abuse and Mental Health Services Administration (SAMHSA) (1998) *National Household Survey on Drug Abuse*. Washington, DC: US DHHS.

Sussman, S. (1996) Development of a school-based drug abuse prevention curriculum for high-risk youths, *Journal of Psychoactive Drugs*, 28: 169–82.

Sussman, S. (2001a) *Handbook of Program Development for Health Behavior Research and Practice*. Thousand Oaks, CA: Sage.

Sussman, S. (in press) Smoking cessation among persons in recovery, *Substance Use and Misuse*.

Sussman, S. and Dent, C.W. (1996) The correlates of addiction concern among adolescents at high risk for drug abuse, *Journal of Substance Abuse*, 8: 361–70.

Sussman, S., Rychtarik, R.G., Mueser, K., Glynn, S. and Prue, D.M. (1986) Ecological relevance of memory tests and the prediction of relapse in alcoholics, *Journal of Studies on Alcohol*, 47: 305–10.

Sussman, S., Charlin, V.L., Marks, G. *et al.* (1990a) Physical features, physical attractiveness and psychological adjustment among alcohol abuse inpatients, *International Journal of the Addictions*, 25: 927–42.

Sussman, S., Horn, J.L. and Gilewski, M. (1990b) Cue-exposure interventions for alcohol relapse prevention: need for a memory modification component, *International Journal of the Addictions*, 25: 917–26.

Sussman, S., Dent, C.W., Burton, D., Stacy, A.W. and Flay, B.R. (1995a) *Developing School-based Tobacco Use Prevention and Cessation Programs*. Thousand Oaks, CA: Sage.

Sussman, S., Dent, C.W., Stacy, A.W., Burton, D. and Flay, B.R. (1995b) Psychosocial predictors of health risk factors in adolescents, *Journal of Pediatric Psychology*, 18: 91–108.

Sussman, S., Parker, V.C., Lopes, C. *et al.* (1995c) Empirical development of brief tobacco use prevention videotapes which target African American adolescents, *International Journal of the Addictions*, 30: 1141–64.

Sussman, S., Dent, C.W. and Stacy, A.W. (1996a) The relations of pro-drug-use myths with self-reported drug use among youth at continuation high schools, *Journal of Applied Social Psychology*, 26: 2014–37.

Sussman, S., Petosa, R. and Clarke, P. (1996b) The use of empirical curriculum development to improve prevention research, *American Behavioral Scientist*, 39: 838–52.

Sussman, S., Stacy, A.W., Dent, C.W., Simon, T.R. and Johnson, C.A. (1996c) Marijuana use: current issues and new research directions, *Journal of Drug Issues*, 26: 695–733.

Sussman, S., Dent, C.W. and Galaif, E.R. (1997a) The correlates of substance abuse and dependence among adolescents at high risk for drug abuse, *Journal of Substance Abuse*, 9: 241–55.

Sussman, S., Nezami, E. and Mishra, S. (1997b) On operationalizing spiritual experience for health promotion research and practice, *Alternative Therapies in Clinical Practice*, 4: 120–5.

Sussman, S., Dent, C.W., Stacy, A. and Craig, S. (1998a) One-year outcomes of Project Towards No Drug Abuse, *Preventive Medicine*, 27: 632–42 (erratum: 27(5, pt 1): 766, 1998).

Sussman, S., Stacy, A.W., Ames, S.L. and Freedman, L.B. (1998b) Self-reported high-risk locations of adolescent drug use, *Addictive Behaviors*, 23: 405–11.

Sussman, S., Ames, S.L., Dent, C.W. and Stacy, A.W. (2000a) Self-reported high risk locations of drug use among drug offenders: ethnic differences, *Hispanic Journal of Behavioral Sciences*, 22: 237–53.

Sussman, S., Dent, C.W. and McCullar, W.J. (2000b) Group self-identification as a prospective predictor of drug use and violence in high-risk youth, *Psychology of Addictive Behaviors*, 14: 192–6.

Sussman, S., Dent, C.W. and Tsukamoto, H. (under review a) Alcoholic liver disease: a new domain for prevention, *Substance Use and Misuse*.

Sussman, S., Dent, C.W. and Stacy, A.W. (under review b) Project Towards No Drug Abuse: A review of the findings and future directions, *American Journal of Health Behavior*.

Sutton, S.R. and Eiser, J.R. (1984) The effect of fear-arousing communication on cigarette smoking: an expectancy-value approach, *Journal of Behavioral Medicine*, 7: 13–33.

Suzuki, K., Matsushita, S. and Ishii, T. (1997) Relationship between the flushing response and drinking behavior among Japanese high school students, *Alcoholism: Clinical and Experimental Research*, 21(9): 1726–9.

Svanum, S., Levitt, E. and McAdoo, W.G. (1982) Differentiating male and female alcoholics from psychiatric outpatients: the MacAndrew and Rosenberg alcoholism scales, *Journal of Personality Assessment*, 46: 81–4.

Swanson, J.W., Linskey, A.O., Quintero-Salinas, R., Pumariega, A.J. and Holzer, C.E. (1992) A binational school survey of depressive symptoms, drug use, and suicidal ideation, *Journal of the American Academy of Child and Adolescent Psychiatry*, 31: 669–78.

Szalay, L.B., Canino, G. and Vilov, S.K. (1993) Vulnerabilities and cultural change: drug use among Puerto Rican adolescents in the United States, *International Journal of the Addictions*, 28(4): 327–54.

Szalay, L.B., Inn, A. and Doherty, K.T. (1996) Social influences: effects of the social environment on the use of alcohol and other drugs, *Substance Use and Misuse*, 31(3): 343–73.

Tarter, R. (1990) Evaluation and treatment of adolescent substance abuse: a decision tree method, *American Journal of Drug and Alcohol Abuse*, 16: 1–46.

Teets, J.M. (1997) The incidence and experience of rape among chemically dependent women, *Journal of Psychoactive Drugs*, 29: 331–44.

Teichman, M., Barnea, Z. and Ravav, G. (1989) Personality and substance use among adolescents: a longitudinal study, *British Journal of the Addictions*, 84: 181–90.

Thaxton, L. (1982) Physiological and psychological effects of short-term exercise addiction on habitual runners, *Journal of Sport Psychology*, 4: 73–80.

Theus, K.T. (1994) Subliminal advertising and the psychology of processing unconscious stimuli: a review of research, *Psychology and Marketing*, 11: 271–90.

Tiffany, S.T. (1990) A cognitive model of drug urges and drug-use behavior: role of automatic and nonautomatic processes, *Psychological Review*, 97: 147–68.

Tiffany, S.T. and Carter, B.L. (1998) Is carving the source of compulsive drug use? *Journal of Psychopharmacology*, 12: 23–30.

Timmreck, T.C. (1998) *An Introduction to Epidemiology*. Boston, MA: Jones and Bartlett.

Tobler, N.S. (1986) Meta-analysis of 143 adolescent drug prevention programs: quantitative outcomes results of program participants compared to a control or comparison group, *Journal of Drug Issues*, 15: 535–67.

Tobler, N.S. and Stratton, H.H. (1997) Effectiveness of school-based drug prevention programs: a meta-analysis of the research, *Journal of Primary Prevention*, 18: 71–128.

Tobler, N.S., Roona, M.R., Ochshorn, P. *et al.* (2000) School-based adolescent drug prevention programs: 1998 meta-analysis, *The Journal of Primary Prevention*, 20: 275–36.

Trimpey, J. (1989) *The Small Book: A Revolutionary Alternative for Overcoming Alcohol and Drug Dependence*. New York: Delacorte Press.

Trimpey, J. (1996) *Rational Recovery: The New Cure for Substance Addiction*. New York: Pocket Books.

Tuyns, A.J. and Pequignot, G. (1984) Greater risk of ascitic cirrhosis in females in relation to alcohol consumption, *International Journal of Epidemiology*, 13(1): 53–7.

Uhlenhuth, E.H., Johanson, C.E., Kilgore, K. and Kosaba, S.C. (1981) Drug preferences and mood in humans: preference for d-amphetamine and subject characteristics, *Psychopharmacology*, 74: 191–4.

Upshaw, H.S. and Ostrom, T.M. (1984) Psychological perspective in attitude research, in J.R. Eiser (ed.) *Attitudinal Judgment*. New York: Springer-Verlag.

US Department of Health and Human Services (US DHHS) (1982) *The Health Consequences of Smoking: Cancer. A Report of the Surgeon General*, DHHS Publication no. [PHS] 82-50179. Washington, DC: Public Health Service.

US DHHS (1994) *Preventing Tobacco Use among Young People: A Report of the Surgeon General*, Publication no. S/N 017-001-00491-0. Washington, DC: Public Health Service.

US DHHS (1998) *International Epidemiology Work Group on Drug Abuse 1997 Proceedings*, Publication no. 98-4208B. Rockville, MD: NIH.

US Drug Enforcement Administration (US DEA) and National Guard (1996) *Drugs of Abuse*. Washington, DC: US Department of Justice.

US Drug Enforcement Administration and National Narcotics Intelligence Consumers Committee (US DEA-NNICC) (1997) *NNICC Report 1997*. Washington, DC: US Department of Justice.

US Office of Technology Assessment (US OTA) (1994) Individual risk and protective factors, in *Technologies for Understanding and Preventing Substance Abuse and Addiction*. Washington, DC: US OTA. (www.druglibrary.org/schaffer/library/studies/ota/ch6.htm)

Vaillant, G.E. (1983) *The Natural History of Alcoholism: Causes, Patterns, and Paths to Recovery*, Cambridge, MA: Harvard University Press.

Vaillant, G.E. (1990) We should retain the disease concept of alcoholism, *Harvard Medical School Mental Health Letter*, Harvard College, Boston, MA, August.

Van Furth, W.R. and van Ree, J. (1996) Sexual motivation: involvement of endogenous opioids in the ventral tegmental area, *Brain Research*, 729: 20–8.

Wadden, T.A. and Brownell, K.D. (1984) The development and modification of dietary practices in individuals, groups, and large populations, in J.D. Matarazzo, S.M. Weiss, J.A. Herd, N.E. Miller and S.M. Weiss (eds) *Behavioral Health: A Handbook of Health Enhancement and Disease Prevention*. New York: Wiley.

Wakefield, M.A., Chaloupka, F.J., Kaufman, N.J. *et al.* (2000) Effect of restrictions on smoking at home, school and in public places on teenage smoking: cross-sectional study, *British Medical Journal*, 321: 333–7.

Wall, T.L., Thomasson, H.R., Schuckit, M.A. and Ehlers, C.L. (1992) Subjective feelings of alcohol intoxication in Asians with genetic variations of ALDH2 alleles, *Alcoholism: Clinical and Experimental Research*, 16(5): 991–5.

Warner, L.A., Kessler, R.C., Hughes, M., Anthony, J.C. and Nelson, C.B. (1995) Prevalence and correlates of drug use and dependence in the United States: results from the National Comorbidity Survey, *Archives of General Psychiatry*, 52: 219–29.

Weiner, M.D., Sussman, S., McCuller, W.J. and Lichtman, K. (1999) Factors in marijuana cessation among high-risk youth, *Journal of Drug Education*, 29: 337–57.

Weingardt, K.R., Stacy, A.W. and Leigh, B.C. (1996) Automatic activation of alcohol concepts in response to positive outcomes of alcohol use, *Alcoholism: Clinical and Experimental Research*, 20(1): 25–9.

Weinstein, N.D. (1982) Unrealistic optimism about susceptibility to health problems, *Journal of Behavioral Medicine*, 10: 481–500.

White, T. (1999) *UN Office for Drug Control and Crime Prevention: Global Illicit Drug Trends*, Publication no. E.99.XI.16. New York: United Nations.

Williams, B.K. and Knight, S.M. (1994) Non-drug forms of dependence, Unit 5 (5.28–5.38), B.K. *Healthy for Life*. Pacific Grove, CA: Brooks/Cole.

Wills, T.A. (1986) Stress and coping in early adolescence: relationships to substance use in urban school samples, *Health Psychology*, 5: 503–29.

Wills, T.A., Pierce, J.P. and Evans, R.I. (1996) Large-scale environmental risk factors for substance use, *American Behavioral Scientist*, 39: 808–22.

Wilsnack, R.W., Wilsnack, S.C. and Klassen, A.D., Jr (1984) Women's drinking and drinking problems: patterns from a 1981 national survey, *American Journal of Public Health*, 74(11): 1231–8.

Wilsnack, S.C., Wilsnack, R.W. and Klassen, A.D. (1986) Epidemiological research on women's drinking, 1978–1984, in National Institute on Alcohol Abuse and Alcoholism, *Women and Alcohol: Health-Related Issues*. Research Monograph no 16 DHHS (ADM) 86-1139. Washington, DC: US Government Printing Office.

Winger, G., Hofmann, F.G. and Woods, J.H. (1992) *A Handbook on Drug and Alcohol Abuse: The Biomedical Aspects*. New York: Oxford University Press.

Winters, K. (1999) A new multiscale measure of adult substance abuse, *Journal of Substance Abuse Treatment*, 16: 237–46.

Winters, K. and Henly, G. (1989) *Personal Experiences Inventory (PEI): Test and Manual*. Los Angeles: Western Psychological Services.

Winters, K. and Henly, G. (1993) *Adolescent Diagnostic Interview (Manual)*. Los Angeles: Western Psychological Services.

Winters, K.C., Stinchfield, R.D. and Henly, G.A. (1993) Further validation of new scales measuring adolescent alcohol and other drug abuse, *Journal of Studies on Alcohol*, 54: 534–41.

Wise, R.A. (1988) The neurobiology of craving: implications for the understanding and treatment of addiction, *Journal of Abnormal Psychology*, 97: 118–32.

Wise, R. and Bozarth, M.A. (1984) Brain reward circuitry: four circuit elements 'wired' in apparent series, *Brain Research Bulletin*, 12: 203–8.

Wittgenstein, L. (1958) *Philosophical Investigations*. Oxford: Blackwell.

World Health Organization (1998) International Classification of Disease, Ninth revision (ICD-9). Geneva, Switzerland: World Health Organization (ICD-9-CM refers to Clinical Modification developed by the US National Center for Health Statistics, Hyattsville, MD: www.cdc.gov/nchs/icd9.htm)

Yoder, B. (1990) *The Resource Book*. New York: Simon & Schuster.

Young, P.T. (1936) *Motivation of Behavior.* New York: John Wiley.

Zajonc, R.B (1980) Feeling and thinking: preferences need no inferences, *American Psychologist*, 35(2): 151–75.

Zickler, P. (2000) Evidence accumulates that long-term marijuana users experience withdrawal, *NIDA Notes*, 15 (January): 6–7.

Zuckerman, M. (1987) Biological connection between sensation seeking and drug abuse, in J. Engel and L. Oreland (eds) *Brain Reward Systems and Abuse.* New York: Raven Press.

Zuckerman, M. (1993) Impulsive sensation seeking and its behavioral, psycho-physiological and biochemical correlates, *Neuropsychobiology*, 28(1–2): 30–6.

Zuckerman, M. (1994) *Behavioral Expressions and Biosocial Bases of Sensation Seeking.* New York: Cambridge University Press.

Zuckerman, M., Ball, S. and Black, J. (1990) Influences of sensation seeking, gender, risk appraisal, and situational motivation on smoking, *Addictive Behaviors*, 15: 209–20.

Zweben, J.E. (1993) Recovery oriented psychotherapy: a model for addiction treatment, *Psychotherapy*, 30: 259–68.

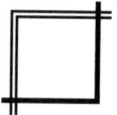

Index

HUMAN AGGRESSION
Second Edition

Russell G. Geen

- What sort of conditions provoke aggressive behaviour among humans?
- Why are some people more aggressive than others?
- How do normal human characteristics like thoughts and feelings enter into aggressive behaviour?

The fully revised and updated edition of this successful book offers a brief introduction to the psychology of human aggression. Aggression is defined as an act of intentional harm inflicted on another person in response to some provoking circumstance, through a process involving thought, feeling, judgement and motivation. Several theoretical schemes are discussed, according to which these psychological processes are shown to interact with each other to determine the likelihood and intensity of aggressive behaviour. The theoretical material is followed by chapters in which the psychological processes are used to analyse such practical problems as sexual and partner abuse, bullying, delinquency, and the effects of violence in the media, video games, and sporting events. The second edition includes new material on the difference between proactive versus reactive aggression, on social information-processing, and on the effects of violent games. It also pays increased attention to instrumental versus affective aggression, to age, sex and personality as moderators, and to the impact of aggression on everyday life. In all, the book provides an accessible text for students of psychology and others interested in obtaining a concise overview of research and theory on human aggression and violence.

Contents
Introduction to the study of aggression – The provocation of aggression – Intervening processes in aggression – Moderator variables in aggression – Aggression in life and society – Aggression in entertainment – Hostility, health and adjustment – Postscript – Glossary – References.

192pp   0 335 20471 6 (Paperback)   0 335 20472 4 (Hardback)

SOCIAL PSYCHOLOGY AND HEALTH
Second Edition

Wolfgang Stroebe

If you are a student of social or health psychology, or if you are working in one of the health professions, you are likely at some point to address questions such as the following:

- Which behaviour patterns are detrimental to health?
- Why do people engage in such behaviour, even if they know about its negative effects?
- How can people be influenced to change their behaviour?
- What do we mean by stressful life events and how can their impact on health be mediated?

In *Social Psychology and Health* you will find these major health topics discussed from a social psychological perspective. During recent decades there have been significant changes in conceptions of health and illness, with a move towards a broader conception of health to include physical, mental and social well-being. In line with these changes, health psychology has become a dominant force in the health sciences. This relatively new field of psychology is much influenced by social psychological theory and research, and the focus of the book reflects this.

Social Psychology and Health gives an up-to-date perspective on these key health psychology questions. The book argues for an integrative approach that combines psychological, economic and environmental interventions in order to reduce the potential risks to health arising from behaviour or stressful life events.

The second edition of this highly successful textbook has been extensively revised, expanded and updated. Much new material has been added based on research done in the past five years, in particular drawing on the author's own research into obesity and sexual risk behaviour. Many of the epidemiological examples and more than a third of the references have been updated. It is essentially a new book which will make an important contribution to the literature.

Contents
Changing conceptions of health and illness – Determinants of health behaviour: a social psychological analysis – Beyond persuasion: the modification of health behaviour – Behaviour and health: excessive appetites – Behaviour and health: self-protection – Stress and health – Moderators of the stress-health relationship – The role of social psychology in health promotion – Glossary – References – Author index – Subject index.

352pp   0 335 19921 6 (Paperback)   0 335 19922 4 (Hardback)

RELATING TO OTHERS – SECOND EDITION

Steve Duck

Reviews of the first edition:

Concise, readable, up-to-date, this volume is an excellent introduction to a new and expanding field.

Counseling Psychology Quarterly

. . . a wonderful book.

Newsletter of the American Association for Counseling and Development

. . . very exciting.

Counselling

- How do relationships get started successfully?
- How do relationships develop?
- What makes relationships decline and how can they be repaired?

As social psychologists become more aware of the ways in which relationships underpin almost everything in the social sciences, the need for an introductory book for students and scholars has further increased. This long-awaited second edition of a highly successful text summarizes the research on relationships, focusing not only on their growth and development but also on their negative aspects, breakdown and repair.

The author addresses the essential use of relationship issues within applied areas such as policing, health care, and the corporate world. He also emphasizes the importance of multidisciplinary studies and the integration of different frameworks and methods, by focusing less on static factors in relationships and more on the matter of process. Finally, he examines the need to contextualize relationship processes and take account of the daily issues of management by relational partners.

The second edition of *Relating to Others* is strongly grounded in a discussion of the contexts for relating, whether cultural, linguistic, or interpersonal. It focuses on a range of relationships, friendship, and types of marriage and is written in an engaging style for students of psychology and the wider social sciences by one of the top authorities in the scientific research on relationships.

Contents

The role of relationships in life – Contexts of relationships – Developing relationships and developing people – Developing a steady and exclusive partnership – Managing relationships – When relationships come apart – Putting relationships right – Overview – References – Index.

176pp   0 335 20163 6 (paperback)   0 335 20164 4 (hardback)